THE DIARY OF

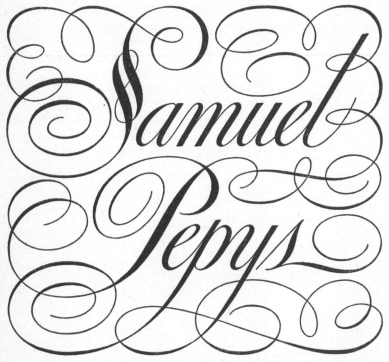

Samuel Pepys

FOR THE YEAR A. D. 1661

TRANSCRIBED BY THE REV. MYNORS BRIGHT
FROM THE SHORTHAND MANUSCRIPT IN THE
PEPYSIAN LIBRARY AT MAGDALENE COLLEGE
CAMBRIDGE AND EDITED WITH ADDITIONS
BY HENRY B. WHEATLEY, F. S. A.

THE LIMITED EDITIONS CLUB
New York, 1942

THE DIARY OF
SAMUEL PEPYS
1660-61

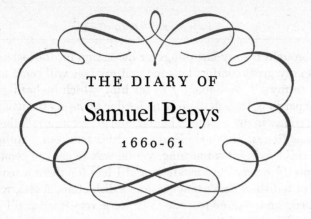

THE DIARY OF
Samuel Pepys
1660-61

AT THE END of the last and the beginning of this year, I do live in one of the houses belonging to the Navy Office, as one of the principal officers, and have done now about half a year. After much trouble with workmen I am now almost settled; my family being, myself, my wife, Jane, Will. Hewer, and Wayneman,[1] my girle's brother. Myself in constant good health, and in a most handsome and thriving condition. Blessed be Almighty God for it. I am now taking of my sister to come and live with me. As to things of State.—The King settled, and loved of all. The Duke of York matched to my Lord Chancellor's daughter, which do not please many. The Queen upon her return to France with the Princess Henrietta. The Princess of Orange[2] lately dead, and we into new mourning for her. We have been lately frighted with a great plot,[3] and many taken up on it, and the fright not quite over. The Parliament, which had done all this great good to the King, beginning to grow factious, the King did dissolve it December 29th last, and another likely to be chosen speedily. I take myself now to be worth £300 clear in money, and all my goods and all manner of debts paid, which are none at all.

[1660-61]. (January 1st). Called up this morning by Mr. Moore,

[1] Will Wayneman appears by this to have been forgiven for his theft (see *ante*, August 29th). He was dismissed on July 8th, 1663.

[2] Or Princess Royal.

[3] This was the rising of the Fifth Monarchy men under Thomas Venner. See *post*, January 7th, 1660-61.

who brought me my last things for me to sign for the last month, and to my great comfort tells me that my fees will come to £80 clear to myself, and about £25 for him, which he hath got out of the pardons, though there be no fee due to me at all out of them. Then comes in my brother Thomas, and after him my father, Dr. Thomas Pepys, my uncle Fenner and his two sons (Anthony's[1] only child dying this morning, yet he was so civil to come, and was pretty merry) to breakfast; and I had for them a barrel of oysters, a dish of neat's tongues, and a dish of anchovies, wine of all sorts, and Northdown ale. We were very merry till about eleven o'clock, and then they went away. At noon I carried my wife by coach to my cozen, Thomas Pepys, where we, with my father, Dr. Thomas, cozen Stradwick, Scott, and their wives, dined. Here I saw first his second wife, which is a very respectfull woman, but his dinner a sorry, poor dinner for a man of his estate, there being nothing but ordinary meat in it. To-day the King dined at a lord's, two doors from us. After dinner I took my wife to Whitehall, I sent her to Mrs. Pierce's (where we should have dined to-day), and I to the Privy Seal, where Mr. Moore took out all his money, and he and I went to Mr. Pierce's; in our way seeing the Duke of York bring his Lady this day to wait upon the Queen, the first time that ever she did since that great business; and the Queen is said to receive her now with much respect and love; and there he cast up the fees, and I told the money, by the same token one £100 bag, after I had told it, fell all about the room, and I fear I have lost some of it. That done I left my friends and went to my Lord's, but he being not come in I lodged the money with Mr. Shepley, and bade good night to Mr. Moore, and so returned to Mr. Pierce's, and there supped with them, and Mr. Pierce, the purser, and his wife and mine, where we had a calf's head carboned,[2] but it was raw, we could not eat it, and a good hen. But she is such a slut that I do not love her victualls. After supper I sent them home by coach, and I went to my Lord's and

---

[1] Anthony Joyce, who married Kate Fenner.

[2] Meat cut crosswise and broiled was said to be carboned. Falstaff says in "King Henry IV.," Part I., act v., sc. 3, "Well, if Percy be alive, I'll pierce him. If he do come in my way, so; if he do not, if I come in his willingly, let him make a carbonado of me."

there played till 12 at night at cards at Best with J. Goods and N. Osgood, and then to bed with Mr. Shepley.

[2d]. Up early, and being called up to my Lord he did give me many commands in his business. As about taking care to write to my uncle that Mr. Barnewell's[1] papers should be locked up, in case he should die, he being now suspected to be very ill. Also about consulting with Mr. W. Montagu for the settling of the £4,000 a-year that the King had promised my Lord. As also about getting of Mr. George Montagu to be chosen at Huntingdon this next Parliament, &c. That done he to White Hall stairs with much company, and I with him; where we took water for Lambeth, and there coach for Portsmouth. The Queen's things were all in White Hall Court ready to be sent away, and her Majesty ready to be gone an hour after to Hampton Court to-night, and so to be at Portsmouth on Saturday next. I by water to my office, and there all the morning, and so home to dinner, where I found Pall (my sister) was come; but I do not let her sit down at table with me, which I do at first that she may not expect it hereafter from me. After dinner I to Westminster by water, and there found my brother Spicer at the Leg with all the rest of the Exchequer men (most of whom I now do not know) at dinner. Here I staid and drank with them, and then to Mr. George Montagu about the business of election, and he did give me a piece in gold; so to my Lord's and got the chest of plate brought to the Exchequer, and my brother Spicer put it into his treasury. So to Will's with them to a pot of ale, and so parted. I took a turn in the Hall, and bought the King and Chancellor's speeches[2] at the dissolving the Parliament last Saturday. So to my Lord's, and took my money I brought thither last night and the silver candlesticks, and by coach left the latter at Alderman Backwell's, I having no use for them, and the former home. There stood a man at our door, when I carried it in, and saw me, which made me a little afeard. Up to my chamber and wrote letters to Huntingdon and

---

[1] Robert Barnwell died June, 1662. See June 4th.

[2] The King dissolved the Convention Parliament on December 24th, 1660. The King's and the Lord Chancellor's speeches are printed in Cobbett's "Parliamentary History," vol. iv., pp. 170-78.

did other business. This day I lent Sir W. Batten and Captn.
Rider my chine of beef for to serve at dinner to-morrow at Trinity House, the Duke of Albemarle being to be there and all the
rest of the Brethren, it being a great day for the reading over of
their new Charter, which the King hath newly given them.[1]

[3d]. Early in the morning to the Exchequer, where I told over
what money I had of my Lord's and my own there, which I found
to be £970. Thence to Will's, where Spicer and I eat our dinner
of a roasted leg of pork which Will did give us, and after that to
the Theatre, where was acted "Beggar's Bush,"[2] it being very
well done; and here the first time that ever I saw women[3] come
upon the stage. From thence to my father's, where I found my
mother gone by Bird, the carrier, to Brampton, upon my uncle's
great desire, my aunt being now in despair of life. So home.

[4th]. Office all the morning, my wife and Pall being gone to my
father's to dress dinner for Mr. Honiwood, my mother being
gone out of town. Dined at home, and Mr. Moore with me, with
whom I had been early this morning at White Hall, at the Jewell
Office,[4] to choose a piece of gilt plate for my Lord, in return of his
offering to the King (which it seems is usual at this time of year,
and an Earl gives twenty pieces in gold in a purse to the King). I
chose a gilt tankard, weighing 31 ounces and a half, and he is
allowed 30; so I paid 12s. for the ounce and half over what he is
to have; but strange it was for me to see what a company of small
fees I was called upon by a great many to pay there, which, I
perceive, is the manner that courtiers do get their estates. After

---

[1] The Trinity House was at Deptford. In 1671 the Corporation removed to
Water Lane, and in 1795 to the present house on Tower Hill.

[2] A comedy by Beaumont and Fletcher, acted at Whitehall in 1622, and published in 1647. It was revived in November, 1660.

[3] Downes does not give the cast of this play. After the Restoration the acting
of female characters by women became common. The first English profes-
sional actress was Mrs. Coleman, who acted Ianthe in Davenant's "Siege of
Rhodes," at Rutland House in 1656.

[4] Several of the Jewel Office rolls are in the British Museum. They recite all
the sums of money given to the King, and the particulars of all the plate distributed in his name, as well as gloves and sweetmeats. The Museum pos-
sesses these rolls for the 4th, 9th, 18th, 30th, and 31st Eliz.; for the 13th Charles
I.; and the 23rd, 24th, 26th, and 27th of Charles II.—B.

dinner Mr. Moore and I to the Theatre, where was "The Scornful Lady,"[1] acted very well, it being the first play that ever he saw. Thence with him to drink a cup of ale at Hercules Pillars, and so parted. I called to see my father, who told me by the way how Will and Mary Joyce[2] do live a strange life together, nothing but fighting, &c., so that sometimes her father has a mind to have them divorced. Thence home.

[5th]. Home all the morning. Several people came to me about business, among others the great Tom Fuller, who came to desire a kindness for a friend of his,[3] who hath a mind to go to Jamaica with these two ships that are going, which I promised to do. So to Whitehall to my Lady, whom I found at dinner and dined with her, and staid with her talking all the afternoon, and thence walked to Westminster Hall. So to Will's, and drank with Spicer, and thence by coach home, staying a little in Paul's Churchyard, to bespeak Ogilby's Æsop's Fables[4] and Tully's Officys[5] to be bound for me. So home and to bed.

[6th] (Lord's day). My wife and I to church this morning, and so home to dinner to a boiled leg of mutton all alone. To church again, where, before sermon, a long Psalm was set that lasted an hour, while the sexton gathered his year's contribucion through

[1] A comedy by Beaumont and Fletcher, first published in 1616.

[2] William Joyce, brother of Anthony, married Mary Fenner.

[3] Peter Beckford, who resided in Dr. Fuller's neighbourhood. Mr. Beckford, of Maidenhead, tailor, left two sons, one of whom, Thomas, a clothworker, became Sheriff of London, and was knighted on the 29th December, 1677. He is the slop-seller mentioned postea, February 21st, 1667-8. His brother, Peter Beckford, probably the person alluded to in January 1st, 1668-9, had a son of the same names, who rose to the rank of colonel in the army, having estates in Jamaica, and settling in that island. He became President of the Council there, in the latter part of Charles II.'s reign; was made Governor and Commander-in-Chief by William III., and died (1710) immensely rich. Governor Beckford had a son of the same names, who was father of the well-known Alderman Beckford, and grandfather of the author of "Vathek." There is a token of a Peter Beckford in Field Lane, "at the Guy of Worick," see "Boyne's Trade Tokens," ed. Williamson, vol. i., 1889, p. 598.

[4] "The Fables of Æsop paraphrased in verse by John Ogilby, London, 1665," a folio in vellum, is in the Pepysian Library.

[5] The edition of Tully's "Offices" in the Pepysian Library is dated 1699.

the whole church. After sermon home, and there I went to my chamber and wrote a letter to send to Mr. Coventry, with a piece of plate along with it, which I do preserve among my other letters. So to supper, and thence after prayers to bed.

[7th]. This morning, news was brought to me to my bedside, that there had been a great stir in the City this night by the Fanatiques,[1] who had been up and killed six or seven men, but all are fled. My Lord Mayor and the whole City had been in arms, above 40,000. To the office, and after that to dinner, where my brother Tom came and dined with me, and after dinner (leaving 12*d*. with the servants to buy a cake with at night, this day being kept as Twelfth day) Tom and I and my wife to the Theatre, and there saw "The Silent Woman."[2] The first time that ever I did see it, and it is an excellent play. Among other things here, Kinaston, the boy, had the good turn to appear in three shapes: first, as a poor woman in ordinary clothes, to please Morose; then in fine clothes, as a gallant, and in them was clearly the prettiest woman in the whole house, and lastly, as a man; and then likewise did appear the handsomest man in the house. From thence by link to my cozen Stradwick's, where my father and we and Dr. Pepys, Scott, and his wife, and one Mr. Ward and his; and

---

[1] "A great rising in the city of the Fifth-monarchy men, which did very much disturb the peace and liberty of the people, so that all the train-bands arose in arms, both in London and Westminster, as likewise all the king's guards; and most of the noblemen mounted, and put all their servants on coach horses, for the defence of his Majesty, and the peace of his kingdom."—Rugge's *Diurnal*.

The notorious Thomas Venner, the Fifth-monarchy man, a cooper and preacher to a conventicle in Swan Alley, Coleman Street, with a small following (about fifty in number) took arms on the 6th January for the avowed purpose of establishing the Millennium. He was a violent enthusiast, and persuaded his followers that they were invulnerable. After exciting much alarm in the City, and skirmishing with the Trained Bands, they marched to Caen Wood. They were driven out by a party of guards, but again entered the City, where they were overpowered by the Trained Bands. The men were brought to trial and condemned; four, however, were acquitted and two reprieved. The execution of some of these men is mentioned by Pepys under date January 19th and 21st. "A Relation of the Arraignment and Trial of those who made the late Rebellious Insurrections in London, 1661," is reprinted in "Somers Tracts," vol. vii. (1812), p. 469.

[2] Ben Jonson's comedy. Pepys mentions the play before under date June 6th, 1660.

after a good supper, we had an excellent cake, where the mark for the Queen was cut, and so there was two queens, my wife and Mrs. Ward; and the King being lost, they chose the Doctor to be King, so we made him send for some wine, and then home, and in our way home we were in many places strictly examined, more than in the worst of times, there being great fears of these Fanatiques rising again: for the present I do not hear that any of them are taken. Home, it being a clear moonshine and after 12 o'clock at night. Being come home we found that my people had been very merry, and my wife tells me afterwards that she had heard that they had got young Davis and some other neighbours with them to be merry, but no harm.

[8th]. My wife and I lay very long in bed to-day talking and pleasing one another in discourse. Being up, Mr. Warren came, and he and I agreed for the deals that my Lord is to have. Then Will and I to Westminster, where I dined with my Lady. After dinner I took my Lord Hinchinbroke and Mr. Sidney to the Theatre, and shewed them "The Widdow,"[1] an indifferent good play, but wronged by the women being to seek in their parts. That being done, my Lord's coach waited for us, and so back to my Lady's, where she made me drink of some Florence wine, and did give me two bottles for my wife. From thence walked to my cozen Stradwick's, and there chose a small banquet and some other things against our entertainment on Thursday next. Thence to Tom Pepys and bought a dozen of trenchers, and so home. Some talk to-day of a head of Fanatiques that do appear about Barnett, but I do not believe it. However, my Lord Mayor, Sir Richd. Browne, hath carried himself very honourably, and hath caused one of their meeting-houses in London to be pulled down.

[9th]. Waked in the morning about six o'clock, by people running up and down in Mr. Davis's house, talking that the Fanatiques were up in arms in the City. And so I rose and went forth; where in the street I found every body in arms at the doors. So I returned (though with no good courage at all, but that I might

---

[1] "The Widow," a comedy by Ben Jonson, Fletcher, and Middleton, published in 1652.

not seem to be afeared), and got my sword and pistol, which, however, I had no powder to charge; and went to the door, where I found Sir R. Ford, and with him I walked up and down as far as the Exchange, and there I left him. In our way, the streets full of Trainband; and great stories, what mischief these rogues have done; and I think near a dozen have been killed this morning

on both sides. Seeing the city in this condition, the shops shut, and all things in trouble, I went home and sat, it being office day, till noon. So home, and dined at home, my father with me, and after dinner he would needs have me go to my uncle Wight's (where I have been so long absent that I am ashamed to go). I found him at home and his wife, and I can see they have taken my absence ill, but all things are past and we good friends, and here I sat with my aunt till it was late, my uncle going forth about business. My aunt being very fearful to be alone. So home to my lute till late, and then to bed, there being strict guards all night in the City, though most of the enemies, they say, are killed or taken.[1] This morning my wife and Pall went forth early, and I staid within.

[10th]. There comes Mr. Hawley to me and brings me my money for the quarter of a year's salary of my place under Downing that I was at sea. So I did give him half, whereof he did in his nobleness give the odd 5s. to my Jane. So we both went forth (calling first to see how Sir W. Pen do, whom I found very ill), and at the Hoop by the bridge[2] we drank two pints of wormwood and sack. Talking of his wooing afresh of Mrs. Lane, and of his going to serve the Bishop of London. Thence by water to Whitehall, and found my wife at Mrs. Hunt's. Leaving her to dine there, I went and dined with my Lady, and staid to talk a while with her. After dinner Will. comes to tell me that he had presented my piece of plate to Mr. Coventry, who takes it very kindly, and sends me a very kind letter, and the plate back again; of which my heart is very glad. So to Mrs. Hunt, where I found a Frenchman, a lodger of her's, at dinner, and just as I came in was kissing my wife, which I did not like, though there could not be any hurt in it. Thence by coach to my Uncle Wight's with my wife, but they being out of doors we went home, where, after I had put some papers in order and entered some letters in my book which I have a mind to keep, I went with my wife to see Sir W. Pen, who we found ill still, but he do make very much of it. Here we sat a great while, at last comes in Mr. Davis and his lady (who takes it very ill that my wife never did go to see her), and so we fell to talk. Among other things Mr. Davis told us the particular examinations of these Fanatiques that are taken: and in short it is this, of all these Fanatiques that have done all this, viz., routed all the Train-bands that they met with, put the King's life-guards to the run, killed about twenty men, broke through the City gates twice; and all this in the day-time, when all the City was in arms;—are not in all about 31. Whereas we did believe them (because they were seen up and down in every place almost in the

---

[1] See *ante*, January 7th.

[2] The Hoop was in Thames Street, near London Bridge. It is registered in the list of taverns in London and Westminster in 1698 (Harl. MS. 4716).

City, and had been about Highgate[1] two or three days, and in several other places) to be at least 500. A thing that was never heard of, that so few men should dare and do so much mischief. Their word was, "The King Jesus, and the heads upon the gates." Few of them would receive any quarter, but such as were taken by force and kept alive; expecting Jesus to come here and reign in the world presently, and will not believe yet but their work will be carried on though they do die. The King this day came to town.

[11th]. Office day. This day comes news, by letters from Portsmouth, that the Princess Henrietta is fallen sick of the meazles on board the London, after the Queen and she was under sail. And so was forced to come back again into Portsmouth harbour; and in their way, by negligence of the pilot, run upon the Horse sand. The Queen and she continue aboard, and do not intend to come on shore till she sees what will become of the young Princess. This news do make people think something indeed, that three of the Royal Family should fall sick of the same disease, one after another. This morning likewise, we had order to see guards set in all the King's yards; and so we do appoint who and who should go to them. Sir Wm. Batten to Chatham, Colonel Slingsby and I to Deptford and Woolwich. Portsmouth being a garrison, needs none. Dined at home, discontented that my wife do not go neater now she has two maids. After dinner comes in Kate Sterpin (whom we had not seen a great while) and her husband to see us, with whom I staid a while, and then to the office, and left them with my wife. At night walked to Paul's Churchyard, and bespoke some books against next week, and from thence to the Coffee-house, where I met Captain Morrice, the upholster, who would fain have lent me a horse to-night to have rid with him upon the City-guards, with the Lord Mayor, there being some new expectations of these rogues; but I refused by reason of my going out of town to-morrow. So home to bed.

[12th]. With Colonel Slingsby and a friend of his, Major Waters

---

[1] Venner retreated with his followers to Caen Wood (there were about fifty). The extent of Caen Wood must not be estimated by the small portion now surrounding Lord Mansfield's mansion.

(a deaf and most amorous melancholy gentleman, who is under a despayr in love, as the Colonel told me, which makes him bad company, though a most good-natured man), by water to Redriffe, and so on foot to Deptford (our servants by water), where we fell to choosing four captains to command the guards, and choosing the places where to keep them, and other things in order thereunto. We dined at the Globe,[1] having our messenger with us to take care for us. Never till now did I see the great authority of my place, all the captains of the fleet coming cap in hand to us. Having staid very late there talking with the Colonel, I went home with Mr. Davis, storekeeper (whose wife is ill and so I could not see her), and was there most prince-like lodged, with so much respect and honour that I was at a loss how to behave myself.

[13th]. In the morning we all went to church, and sat in the pew belonging to us, where a cold sermon of a young man that never had preached before. Here Commissioner came with his wife and daughters, the eldest being his wife's daughter is a very comely black woman.[2] So to the Globe to dinner, and then with Commissioner Pett to his lodgings there (which he hath for the present while he is building the King's yacht, which will be a pretty thing, and much beyond the Dutchman's), and from thence with him and his wife and daughter-in-law by coach to Greenwich Church, where a good sermon, a fine church, and a great company of handsome women. After sermon to Deptford again; where, at the Commissioner's and the Globe, we staid long. And so I to Mr. Davis's to bed again. But no sooner in bed, but we had an alarm, and so we rose: and the Comptroller comes into the Yard to us; and seamen of all the ships present repair to us, and there we armed with every one a handspike, with which they were as fierce as could be. At last we hear that it was only five or six men that did ride through the guard in the town, without stopping to the guard that was there; and, some say, shot at them. But all being quiet there, we caused the seamen to go on board

---

[1] In the list of taverns in London and Westminster and ten miles round in 1698 (Harl. MS. 4716), the taverns at Deptford are given as the Castle, Angel, Swan, King's Head, and Red Lion. The Globe is not mentioned.

[2] The old expression for a brunette.

13

again. And so we all to bed (after I had sat awhile with Mr. Davis in his study, which is filled with good books and some very good song books) I likewise to bed.

[14th]. The arms being come this morning from the Tower, we caused them to be distributed. I spent much time walking with Lieutenant Lambert, walking up and down the yards, who did give me much light into things there, and so went along with me and dined with us. After dinner Mrs. Pett, her husband being gone this morning with Sir W. Batten to Chatham, lent us her coach, and carried us to Woolwich, where we did also dispose of the arms there and settle the guards. So to Mr. Pett's, the ship-wright, and there supped, where he did treat us very handsomely (and strange it is to see what neat houses all the officers of the King's yards have), his wife a proper woman, and has been hand-some, and yet has a very pretty hand. Thence I with Mr. Ack-worth to his house, where he has a very pretty house, and a very proper lovely woman to his wife, who both sat with me in my chamber, and they being gone, I went to bed, which was also most neat and fine.

[15th]. Up and down the yard all the morning and seeing the seamen exercise, which they do already very handsomely. Then to dinner at Mr. Ackworth's, where there also dined with us one Captain Bethell, a friend of the Comptroller's.[1] A good dinner and very handsome. After that and taking our leaves of the of-ficers of the yard, we walked to the waterside and in our way walked into the rope-yard, where I do look into the tar-houses and other places, and took great notice of all the several works be-longing to the making of a cable. So after a cup of burnt wine[2] at the tavern there, we took barge and went to Blackwall and viewed the dock and the new Wet dock, which is newly made there, and a brave new merchantman which is to be launched shortly, and they say to be called the Royal Oak. Hence we walked to Dick-

---

[1] And probably a relation, as Mary, daughter of Sir Henry Slingsby (cousin of the Comptroller) married Sir Walter Bethel, of Alne, Yorkshire.

[2] Burnt wine was somewhat similar to mulled wine, and a favourite drink. It is remembered by Bishop Corbet's witty message to Ben Jonson. Burnt wine is mentioned by Dickens in "Our Mutual Friend," book i., chap. xiii.

Shore,[1] and thence to the Towre and so home. Where I found my wife and Pall abroad, so I went to see Sir W. Pen, and there found Mr. Coventry come to see him, and now had an opportunity to thank him, and he did express much kindness to me. I sat a great while with Sir Wm. after he was gone, and had much talk with him. I perceive none of our officers care much for one another, but I do keep in with them all as much as I can. Sir W. Pen is still very ill as when I went. Home, where my wife not yet come home, so I went up to put my papers in order, and then was much troubled my wife was not come, it being 10 o'clock just now striking as I write this last line. This day I hear the Princess is recovered again. The King hath been this afternoon at Deptford, to see the yacht that Commissioner Pett[2] is building, which will be very pretty; as also that that his brother[3] at Woolwich is in making. By and by comes in my boy and tells me that his mistress do lie this night at Mrs. Hunt's, who is very ill, with which being something satisfied, I went to bed.

[16th]. This morning I went early to the Comptroller's and so with him by coach to Whitehall, to wait upon Mr. Coventry to give him an account of what we have done, which having done, I went away to wait upon my Lady; but coming to her lodgings I find that she is gone this morning to Chatham by coach, thinking

---

[1] Dick Shore, now Duck Shore, Limehouse, is a landing place or stairs at the narrow street end of Fore Street. It is not far from the great turn of the river southward, opposite to the Isle of Dogs. Dick's-Shore, Fore Street, Limehouse, and Dick's-Shore Alley by Dick's Shore, are both mentioned in Dodsley's "London and its Environs," vol. ii., p. 233, edit. 1761.

[2] Peter Pett. The great shipbuilding family of Pett was chiefly connected with the growth of the English navy from the reign of Henry VIII. to that of William III., but as the Christian names of Peter and Phineas appear to have been favourites in the family, it is very difficult to distinguish between some of them, and great confusion has been the result. Amongst the original Fellows of the Royal Society are mentioned Peter Pett, Esq., and Sir Peter Pett. The former of these two was the Commissioner (see *ante*, May 16th, 1660, note), and the latter was Advocate-General for Ireland, and Fellow of All Souls College, Oxford. Peter Pett, Esq., was the fifth son of Phineas Pett, "Master Shipwright to James I.," and was born in 1610. It is frequently stated that he was knighted, but this appears to be incorrect.

[3] Christopher Pett was the eleventh child of Phineas Pett, "Master Shipwright to James I.," and was born May 14th, 1620.

to meet me there, which did trouble me exceedingly, and I did not know what to do, being loth to follow her, and yet could not imagine what she would do when she found me not there. In this trouble, I went to take a walk in Westminster Hall and by chance met with Mr. Child, who went forth with my Lady to-day, but his horse being bad, he come back again, which then did trouble me more, so that I did resolve to go to her; and so by boat home and put on my boots, and so over to Southwarke to the posthouse, and there took horse and guide to Dartford and thence to Rochester (I having good horses and good way, come thither about half-an-hour after daylight, which was before 6 o'clock and I set forth after two), where I found my Lady and her daughter Jem., and Mrs. Browne[1] and five servants, all at a great loss, not finding me here, but at my coming she was overjoyed. The sport was how she had intended to have kept herself unknown, and how the Captain[2] (whom she had sent for) of the Charles had forsoothed[3] her, though he knew her well and she him. In fine we supped merry and so to bed, there coming several of the Charles's men to see me before I got to bed. The page lay with me.

[17th]. Up, and breakfast with my Lady. Then come Captains Cuttance and Blake to carry her in the barge on board, and so we went through Ham Creeke to the Soverayne[4] (a goodly sight all the way to see the brave ships that lie here) first, which is a most noble ship. I never saw her before. My Lady Sandwich, my Lady Jemimah, Mrs. Browne, Mrs. Grace, and Mary and the page, my lady's servants and myself, all went into the lanthorn together. From thence to the Charles, where my lady took great pleasure to see all the rooms, and to hear me tell her how things are when my Lord is there. After we had seen all, then the officers of the. ship had prepared a handsome breakfast for her, and while she

---

[1] Wife of Captain Arthur Browne, Sir William Batten's brother-in-law. See February 14th, 1660-61, and for his death, April 27th, 1663.

[2] Captain (afterwards Sir) Roger Cuttance. See February 15th, 1659-60 (note).

[3] To forsooth is to address in a polite and ceremonious manner. "Your city mannerly word *forsooth*, use it not too often in any case."—Ben Jonson's *Poetaster*, act iv., sc. i.

[4] The "Sovereign," a first-rate of one hundred guns, was built at Woolwich, in 1657, by Captain Phineas Pett, sen.

was pledging my Lord's health they give her five guns. That done, we went off, and then they give us thirteen guns more. I confess it was a great pleasure to myself to see the ship that I begun my good fortune in. From thence on board the Newcastle, to show my Lady the difference between a great and a small ship. Among these ships I did give away £7. So back again and went on shore at Chatham, where I had ordered the coach to wait for us. Here I heard that Sir William Batten and his lady (who I knew were here, and did endeavour to avoyd) were now gone this morning to London. So we took coach, and I went into the coach, and went through the town, without making stop at our inn, but left J. Goods to pay the reckoning. So I rode with my lady in the coach, and the page on the horse that I should have rid on—he desiring it. It begun to be dark before we could come to Dartford, and to rain hard, and the horses to fayle, which was our great care to prevent, for fear of my Lord's displeasure, so here we sat up for to-night, as also Captains Cuttance and Blake, who came along with us. We sat and talked till supper, and at supper my Lady and I entered into a great dispute concerning what were best for a man to do with his estate—whether to make his elder son heir, which my Lady is for, and I against, but rather to make all equall. This discourse took us much time, till it was time to go to bed; but we being merry, we bade my Lady good-night and intended to have gone to the Post-house to drink, and hear a pretty girl play of the cittern (and indeed we should have lain there, but by a mistake we did not), but it was late, and we could not hear her, and the guard came to examine what we were; so we returned to our Inn and to bed, the page and I in one bed, and the two captains in another, all in one chamber, where we had very good mirth with our most abominable lodging.

[18th]. The Captains went with me to the post-house about 9 o'clock, and after a morning draft I took horse and guide for London; and through some rain, and a great wind in my face, I got to London at eleven o'clock. At home found all well, but the monkey loose, which did anger me, and so I did strike her till she was almost dead, that they might make her fast again, which did still trouble me more. In the afternoon we met at the office and sat

17

till night, and then I to see my father who I found well, and took
him to Standing's[1] to drink a cup of ale. He told me my aunt at
Brampton is yet alive and my mother well there. In comes Will
Joyce to us drunk, and in a talking vapouring humour of his
state, and I know not what, which did vex me cruelly. After him
Mr. Hollier had learned at my father's that I was here (where I
had appointed to meet him) and so he did give me some things to
take for prevention. Will Joyce not letting us talk as I would I
left my father and him and took Mr. Hollier to the Greyhound,[2]
where he did advise me above all things, both as to the stone and
the decay of my memory (of which I now complain to him), to
avoid drinking often, which I am resolved, if I can, to leave off.
Hence home, and took home with me from the bookseller's Ogilby's Æsop, which he had bound for me, and indeed I am very
much pleased with the book. Home and to bed.

[19th]. To the Comptroller's, and with him by coach to White
Hall; in our way meeting Venner[3] and Pritchard upon a sledge,
who with two more Fifth Monarchy men were hanged to-day,
and the two first drawn and quartered. Where we walked up and
down, and at last found Sir G. Carteret, whom I had not seen a
great while, and did discourse with him about our assisting the
Commissioners in paying off the Fleet, which we think to decline.
Here the Treasurer did tell me that he did suspect Thos. Hater
to be an informer of them in this work, which we do take to be a
diminution of us, which do trouble me, and I do intend to find out
the truth. Hence to my Lady, who told me how Mr. Hetley is
dead of the small-pox going to Portsmouth with my Lord. My
Lady went forth to dinner to her father's, and so I went to the
Leg in King Street and had a rabbit for myself and my Will, and
after dinner I sent him home and myself went to the Theatre,

---

[1] Standing's was in Fleet Street.

[2] There was a Greyhound tavern in Tower Street, of which a token exists (see
"Boyne's Trade Tokens," ed. Williamson, vol. i., 1889, p. 777). Pepys may refer
to that, or more probably to the Greyhound in Fleet Street, see November
12th, 1662.

[3] Thomas Venner and Roger Hodgkins were executed in Coleman Street;
Giles Pritchard and William Oxman at the end of Wood Street. Others were
executed in various parts of London.

where I saw "The Lost Lady,"[1] which do not please me much. Here I was troubled to be seen by four of our office clerks, which sat in the half-crown box and I in the 1s. 6d. From thence by link, and bought two mouse traps of Thomas Pepys, the Turner, and so went and drank a cup of ale with him, and so home and wrote by post to Portsmouth to my Lord and so to bed.

[20th] (Lord's day). To Church in the morning. Dined at home. My wife and I to Church in the afternoon, and that being done we went to see my uncle and aunt Wight. There I left my wife and came back, and sat with Sir W. Pen, who is not yet well again. Thence back again to my wife and supped there, and were very merry and so home, and after prayers to write down my journall for the last five days, and so to bed.

[21st]. This morning Sir W. Batten, the Comptroller and I to Westminster, to the Commissioners for paying off the Army and Navy, where the Duke of Albemarle was; and we sat with our hats on, and did discourse about paying off the ships and do find that they do intend to undertake it without our help; and we are glad of it, for it is a work that will much displease the poor seamen, and so we are glad to have no hand in it. From thence to the Exchequer, and took £200 and carried it home, and so to the office till night, and then to see Sir W. Pen, whither came my Lady Batten and her daughter, and then I sent for my wife, and so we sat talking till it was late. So home to supper and then to bed, having eat no dinner to-day. It is strange what weather we have had all this winter; no cold at all; but the ways are dusty, and the flyes fly up and down, and the rose-bushes are full of leaves, such a time of the year as was never known in this world before here. This day many more of the Fifth Monarchy men were hanged.

[22nd]. To the Comptroller's house, where I read over his proposals to the Lord Admiral for the regulating of the officers of the Navy,[2] in which he hath taken much pains, only he do seem to

---

[1] A tragi-comedy, by Sir William Barclay, published in 1638.
[2] This document is in the British Museum, Add. MS. 11,602, and consists of twenty-two closely printed pages. It is entitled, "A Discourse touching the

have too good opinion of them himself. From thence in his coach to Mercer's Chappell,[1] and so up to the great hall, where we met with the King's Councell for Trade[2] upon some proposals of theirs for settling convoys for the whole English trade, and that by having 33 ships (four fourth-rates, nineteen fifths, ten sixths) settled by the King for that purpose, which indeed was argued very finely by many persons of honour and merchants that were there. It pleased me much now to come in this condition to this place, where I was once a petitioner for my exhibition in Paul's School; and also where Sir G. Downing (my late master) was chairman, and so but equally concerned with me. From thence home, and after a little dinner my wife and I by coach into London, and bought some glasses, and then to Whitehall to see Mrs. Fox, but she not within, my wife to my mother Bowyer, and I met with Dr. Thomas Fuller, and took him to the Dog, where he tells me of his last and great book that is coming out: that is, his History of all the Families in England;[3] and could tell me more of my own, than I knew myself. And also to what perfection he hath now brought the art of memory; that he did lately to four eminently great scholars dictate together in Latin, upon different subjects of their proposing, faster than they were able to write,

---

Past and Present State of the Navy, composed by that Ingenious Gentleman, Sir Robert Slingsby, Knt. and Baronet, Comptroller thereof."–B.

[1] Mercer's Hall and Chapel occupy the site of the ancient college or hospital of St. Thomas of Acon or Acres. These buildings were destroyed in the Great Fire, and rebuilt about 1672.

[2] Charles II. established a Council of Trade "for keeping a control and superintendence upon the whole commerce of the nation" on November 7th, 1660. On December 1st of the same year he created a Council of Foreign Plantations. The two were united in 1672. The present Board of Trade was constituted in 1786.

[3] The "Worthies of England" was published in 1662. During the Commonwealth period Fuller made a visit to the Committee of Sequestrations sitting at Waltham in Essex, when they talked about his remarkable memory, and he agreed to give them an example. "Gentlemen," said he, "I will give you an instance of my memory in the particular business in which you are employed. Your worships have thought fit to sequester an honest but poor cavalier parson, my neighbour, from his living, and committed him to prison. He has a large family of children, and his circumstances are but indifferent. If you will please to release him out of prison, and restore him to his living, I will never forget the kindness while I live."

till they were tired; and by the way in discourse tells me that the best way of beginning a sentence, if a man should be out and forget his last sentence (which he never was), that then his last refuge is to begin with an Utcunque.[1] From thence I to Mr. Bowyer's, and there sat a while, and so to Mr. Fox's, and sat with them a very little while, and then by coach home, and so to see Sir Wm. Pen, where we found Mrs. Martha Batten[2] and two handsome ladies more, and so we staid supper and were very merry, and so home to bed.

[23rd]. To the office all the morning. My wife and people at home busy to get things ready for to-morrow's dinner. At noon, without dinner, went into the City, and there meeting with Greatorex, we went and drank a pot of ale. He told me that he was upon a design to go to Teneriffe to try experiments there. With him to Gresham Colledge[3] (where I never was before), and saw the manner of the house, and found great company of persons of honour there; thence to my bookseller's, and for books, and to Stevens, the silversmith, to make clean some plate against to-morrow, and so home, by the way paying many little debts for wine and pictures, &c., which is my great pleasure. Home and found all things in a hurry of business, Slater, our messenger, being here as my cook till very late. I in my chamber all the evening looking over my Osborn's works[4] and new Emanuel Thesaurus Patriarchæ.[5] So late to bed, having ate nothing to-day but a piece of bread and cheese at the ale-house with Greatorex, and some bread and butter at home.

[1] Many years ago, but within my recollection, it was said that a former Public Orator of Cambridge, when in a similar difficulty, used to begin his sentence with "Verum enimvero."—M. B.

[2] Martha Batten was the daughter of Sir William Batten, and is frequently mentioned in the Diary. She married Mr. Castle.

[3] Gresham College occupied the house of Sir Thomas Gresham, in Bishopsgate Street, from 1596, when Lady Gresham, Sir Thomas's widow, died. The meeting which Pepys attended was an early one of the Royal Society, which was incorporated by royal charter in 1663.

[4] The seventh edition of Francis Osborn's works, 8vo., 1673, is in the Pepysian Library.

[5] "Patriarchæ, sive Christi Genealogia," by Emmanuele Tesauro, published at London in 1651 and frequently reprinted.

[24th]. At home all day. There dined with me Sir William Batten and his lady and daughter, Sir W. Pen, Mr. Fox (his lady being ill could not come), and Captain Cuttance; the first dinner I have made since I came hither. This cost me above £5, and merry we were—only my chimney smokes. In the afternoon Mr. Hater bringing me my last quarter's salary, which I received of him, and so I have now Mr. Barlow's money in my hands. The company all go away, and by and by Sir Wms. both and my Lady Batten and his daughter come again and supped with me and talked till late, and so to bed, being glad that the trouble is over.

[25th]. At the office all the morning. Dined at home and Mr. Hater with me, and so I did make even with him for the last quarter. After dinner he and I to look upon the instructions of my Lord Northumberland's,[1] but we were interrupted by Mr. Salisbury's coming in, who came to see me and to show me my Lord's picture in little, of his doing. And truly it is strange to what a perfection he is come in a year's time. From thence to Paul's Churchyard about books, and so back again home. This night comes two cages, which I bought this evening for my canary birds, which Captain Rooth[2] this day sent me. So to bed.

[26th]. Within all the morning. About noon comes one that had formerly known me and I him, but I know not his name, to borrow £5 of me, but I had the wit to deny him. There dined with me this day both the Pierces[3] and their wives, and Captain Cuttance, and Lieutenant Lambert, with whom we made ourselves very merry by taking away his ribbans and garters, having made him to confess that he is lately married.[4] The company being gone I went to my lute till night, and so to bed.

---

[1] Algernon Percy, Earl of Northumberland, held the office of Lord High Admiral from March, 1637, to June, 1642.

[2] Richard Rooth, who commanded the "Dartmouth"—one of the ships which attended Charles II. on his return to England from Scheveling. He was knighted March 9th, 1675.

[3] The surgeon and the purser.

[4] For a note on ribbons and garters at weddings, see January 24th, 1659-60.

[27th] (Lord's day). Before I rose, letters come to me from Portsmouth, telling me that the Princess is now well, and my Lord Sandwich set sail with the Queen and her yesterday from thence for France. To church, leaving my wife sick . . . at home, a poor dull sermon of a stranger. Home, and at dinner was very angry at my people's eating a fine pudding (made me by Slater, the cook, last Thursday) without my wife's leave. To church again, a good sermon of Mr. Mills, and after sermon Sir W. Pen and I an hour in the garden talking, and he did answer me to many things, I asked Mr. Coventry's opinion of me, and Sir W. Batten's of my Lord Sandwich, which do both please me. Then to Sir W. Batten's, where very merry, and here I met the Comptroller and his lady and daughter (the first time I ever saw them) and Mrs. Turner, who and her husband supped with us here (I having fetched my wife thither), and after supper we fell to oysters, and then Mr. Turner went and fetched some strong waters, and so being very merry we parted, and home to bed. This day the parson read a proclamation at church, for the keeping of Wednesday next, the 30th of January, a fast for the murther of the late King.[1]

[28th]. At the office all the morning; dine at home, and after dinner to Fleet Street, with my sword to Mr. Brigden (lately made Captain of the Auxiliaries) to be refreshed, and with him to an ale-house, where I met Mr. Davenport, and after some talk of Cromwell, Ireton and Bradshaw's bodies being taken out of their graves to-day,[2] I went to Mr. Crew's and thence to the Theatre, where I saw again "The Lost Lady," which do now please me better than before; and here I sitting behind in a dark

---

[1] "A Proclamation for the observation of the thirtieth of January as a day of Fast and Humiliation according to the late Act of Parliament for that purpose" is dated January 25th, 1660 [-1661].

[2] "The bodies of Oliver Cromwell, Henry Ireton, John Bradshaw, and Thomas Pride, were dug up out of their graves to be hanged at Tyburn, and buried under the gallows. Cromwell's vault having been opened, the people crowded very much to see him."—Rugge's *Diurnal*.

Henry Ireton (born 1610) married Bridget, eldest daughter of Oliver Cromwell, Jan. 15th, 1646-7. He was afterwards one of Charles I.'s judges, and one of the committee who superintended his execution. Lord Deputy of Ireland, 1650. He died at the siege of Limerick, November 26th, 1651.

23

place, a lady spit backward upon me by a mistake, not seeing me, but after seeing her to be a very pretty lady, I was not troubled at it at all. Thence to Mr. Crew's, and there met Mr. Moore, who came lately to me, and went with me to my father's, and with him to Standing's, whither came to us Dr. Fairbrother, who I

OLIVER CROMWELL

took and my father to the Bear and gave a pint of sack and a pint of claret. He do still continue his expressions of respect and love to me, and tells me my brother John will make a good scholar. Thence to see the Doctor at his lodging at Mr. Holden's, where I bought a hat, cost me 35s.[1] So home by moonshine, and by the

[1] Stubbes, speaking of the hats worn by the gentlemen of his day, says, "As the fashions be rare and strange, so are the things whereof their hats be made, diverse also; for some are of silk, some of velvet, some of taffety, some of sarcenet, some of wool, and which is more curious, some of a certain kind of fine hair, . . . these they call *bever* hats, of xx, xxx or xl shillings price, fetched from beyond the sea."—*The Anatomie of Abuses,* 1583.

way was overtaken by the Comptroller's coach, and so home to his house with him. So home and to bed. This noon I had my press set up in my chamber for papers to be put in.

[29th]. Mr. Moore making up accounts with me all this morning till Lieut. Lambert came, and so with them over the water to Southwark, and so over the fields to Lambeth, and there drank, it being a most glorious and warm day, even to amazement, for this time of the year. Thence to my Lord's, where we found my Lady gone with some company to see Hampton Court, so we three went to Blackfryers¹ (the first time I ever was there since plays begun), and there after great patience and little expectation, from so poor beginning, I saw three acts of "The Mayd in yᵉ Mill"² acted to my great content. But it being late, I left the play and them, and by water through bridge home, and so to Mr. Turner's house, where the Comptroller, Sir William Batten, and Mr. Davis and their ladies; and here we had a most neat little but costly and genteel supper, and after that a great deal of impertinent mirth by Mr. Davis, and some catches, and so broke up, and going away, Mr. Davis's eldest son took up my old Lady Slingsby³ in his arms, and carried her to the coach, and is said to be able to carry three of the biggest men that were in the company, which I wonder at. So home and to bed.

[30th] (Fast day). The first time that this day hath been yet observed: and Mr. Mills made a most excellent sermon, upon "Lord forgive us our former iniquities;" speaking excellently of the justice of God in punishing men for the sins of their ancestors. Home, and John Goods comes, and after dinner I did pay him £30 for my Lady, and after that Sir W. Pen and I into Moorfields and had a brave talk, it being a most pleasant day, and besides much discourse did please ourselves to see young Davis and Whitton,

---

¹ At Apothecaries' Hall, where Davenant produced the first and second parts of "The Siege of Rhodes." Downes says, in his "Roscius Anglicanus," that Davenant's company acted at "Pothecaries Hall" until the building in Lincoln's Inn Fields was ready.

² A comedy by Beaumont and Fletcher, first produced in 1623.

³ Margaret, daughter of Sir William Water, an alderman of York. She was mother of the Comptroller, and widow of Sir Guildford Slingsby.

two of our clerks, going by us in the field, who we observe to take much pleasure together, and I did most often see them at play together. Back to the Old James[1] in Bishopsgate Street, where Sir W. Batten and Sir Wm. Rider met him about business of the Trinity House. So I went home, and there understand that my mother is come home well from Brampton, and had a letter from my brother John, a very ingenious one, and he therein begs to have leave to come to town at the Coronacion. Then to my Lady Batten's; where my wife and she are lately come back again from being abroad, and seeing of Cromwell, Ireton,[2] and Bradshaw hanged and buried at Tyburn. Then I home.

[31st]. This morning with Mr. Coventry at Whitehall about getting a ship to carry my Lord's deals to Lynne,[3] and we have chosen the Gift. Thence at noon to my Lord's, where my Lady not well, so I eat a mouthfull of dinner there, and thence to the Theatre, and there sat in the pit among the company of fine ladys, &c.; and the house was exceeding full, to see Argalus and Parthenia,[4] the first time that it hath been acted: and indeed it is good, though wronged by my over great expectations, as all things else are. Thence to my father's to see my mother, who is pretty well after her journey from Brampton. She tells me my aunt is pretty well, yet cannot live long. My uncle pretty well too, and she believes would marry again were my aunt dead, which God forbid. So home.

---

[1] The Great James was in Bishopsgate Without. It is registered in the list of London taverns in 1698 (Harl. MS. 4716).

[2] "Jan. 30th was kept as a very solemn day of fasting and prayer. This morning the carcases of Cromwell, Ireton, and Bradshaw (which the day before had been brought from the Red Lion Inn, Holborn), were drawn upon a sledge to Tyburn, and then taken out of their coffins, and in their shrouds hanged by the neck, until the going down of the sun. They were then cut down, their heads cut off, and their bodies buried in a grave made under the gallows. The coffin in which was the body of Cromwell was a very rich thing, very full of gilded hinges and nails."—Rugge's *Diurnal*.

[3] The timber purchased from Warren (see *ante*, December 29th, 1660), sent to Lynn to be conveyed to Hinchinbroke as the barge was, mentioned June 20th, 1660.

[4] A tragi-comedy by Henry Glapthorne, founded on the story of the two lovers in Sydney's "Arcadia," and published in 1639.

[February 1st] (Friday). A full office all this morning, and busy about answering the Commissioners of Parliament to their letter, wherein they desire to borrow two clerks of ours, which we will not grant them. After dinner into London and bought some books, and a belt, and had my sword new furbished. To the ale-house with Mr. Brigden and W. Symons. At night home. So after a little music to bed, leaving my people up getting things ready against to-morrow's dinner.

[2nd]. Early to Mr. Moore, and with him to Sir Peter Ball,[1] who proffers my uncle Robert much civility in letting him continue in the grounds which he had hired of Hetley who is now dead. Thence home, where all things in a hurry for dinner, a strange cook being come in the room of Slater, who could not come. There dined here my uncle Wight and my aunt, my father and mother, and my brother Tom, Dr. Fairbrother and Mr. Mills, the parson, and his wife, who is a neighbour's daughter of my uncle Robert's, and knows my Aunt Wight and all her and my friends there; and so we had excellent company to-day. After dinner I was sent for to Sir G. Carteret's, where he was, and I found the Comptroller, who are upon writing a letter to the Commissioners of Parliament in some things a rougher stile than our last, because they seem to speak high to us. So the Comptroller and I thence to a tavern hard by, and there did agree upon drawing up some letters to be sent to all the pursers and Clerks of the Cheques to make up their accounts. Then home; where I found the parson and his wife gone. And by and by the rest of the company, very well pleased, and I too; it being the last dinner I intend to make a great while, it having now cost me almost £15 in three dinners within this fortnight. In the evening comes Sir W. Pen, pretty merry, to sit with me and talk, which we did for an hour or two, and so good night, and I to bed.

[3d] (Lord's day). This day I first begun to go forth in my coat and sword, as the manner now among gentlemen is. To Whitehall. In my way heard Mr. Thomas Fuller preach at the Savoy

---

[1] Sir Peter Ball, the Queen's Attorney-General, and possessor of Brampton manor.

upon our forgiving of other men's trespasses, shewing among other things that we are to go to law never to revenge, but only to repayre, which I think a good distinction. So to White Hall; where I staid to hear the trumpets and kettle-drums, and then the other drums, which are much cried up, though I think it dull, vulgar musique. So to Mr. Fox's, unbid; where I had a good dinner and special company. Among other discourse, I observed one story, how my Lord of Northwich,[1] at a public audience before the King of France, made the Duke of Anjou cry, by making ugly faces as he was stepping to the King, but undiscovered. And how Sir Phillip Warwick's[2] lady did wonder to have Mr. Darcy[3] send for several dozen bottles of Rhenish wine to her house, not knowing that the wine was his. Thence to my Lord's; where I am told how Sir Thomas Crew's Pedro, with two of his countrymen more, did last night kill one soldier of four that quarrelled with them in the street, about 10 o'clock. The other two are taken; but he is now hid at my Lord's till night, that he do intend to make his escape away. So up to my Lady, and sat and talked with her long, and so to Westminster Stairs, and there took boat to the bridge, and so home, where I met with letters to call us all up to-morrow morning to Whitehall about office business.

[1] This story relates to circumstances which had occurred many years previously. George, Lord Goring, was sent by Charles I. as Ambassador Extraordinary to France in 1644, to witness the oath of Louis XIV. to the observance of the treaties concluded with England by his father, Louis XIII., and his grandfather, Henry IV. Louis XIV. took this oath at Ruel, on July 3rd, 1644, when he was not yet six years of age, and when his brother Philippe, then called Duke of Anjou, was not four years old. Shortly after his return home, Lord Goring was created, in September, 1644, Earl of Norwich, the title by which he is here mentioned. Philippe, Duke of Anjou, who was frightened by the English nobleman's ugly faces, took the title of Duke of Orleans after the death of his uncle, Jean Baptiste Gaston, in 1660. He married his cousin, Henrietta of England, and (by his second wife) is the direct ancestor of the present Comte de Paris.—B.

[2] Sir Philip Warwick, born 1608, secretary to Charles I. when in the Isle of Wight, and Clerk of the Signet, to which place he was restored in 1660; knighted, and elected M.P. for Westminster. He was also Secretary to the Treasury under Lord Southampton till 1667. Died January 15th, 1682-3. He wrote "A Discourse on Government" and "Memoirs of Charles I." His second wife, here mentioned, was Joan, daughter to Sir Henry Fanshawe, and widow of Sir William Botteler, Bart.

[3] Marmaduke Darcy. See *ante*, May 23rd (note).

[4th]. Early up to Court with Sir W. Pen, where, at Mr. Coventry's chamber, we met with all our fellow officers, and there after a hot debate about the business of paying off the Fleet, and how far we should join with the Commissioners of Parliament, which is now the great business of this month more to determine, and about which there is a great deal of difference between us, and then how far we should be assistants to them therein. That being done, he and I back again home, where I met with my father and mother going to my cozen Snow's to Blackwall, and had promised to bring me and my wife along with them, which we could not do because we are to go to the Dolphin to-day to a dinner of Capt. Taylor's. So at last I let my wife go with them, and I to the tavern, where Sir William Pen and the Comptroller and several others were, men and women; and we had a very great and merry dinner; and after dinner the Comptroller begun some sports, among others the naming of people round and afterwards demanding questions of them that they are forced to answer their names to, which do make very good sport. And here I took pleasure to take the forfeits of the ladies who would not do their duty by kissing of them; among others a pretty lady, who I found afterwards to be wife to Sir W. Batten's son.[1] Home, and then with my wife to see Sir W. Batten, who could not be with us this day being ill, but we found him at cards, and here we sat late, talking with my Lady and others and Dr. Whistler,[2] who I found good company and a very ingenious man. So home and to bed.

[5th]. Washing-day. My wife and I by water to Westminster. She to her mother's and I to Westminster Hall, where I found a full term, and here I went to Will's, and there found Shaw and Ashwell and another Bragrave (who knew my mother washmaid to my Lady Veere), who by cursing and swearing made me

---

[1] Benjamin Batten.

[2] Daniel Whistler, M.D., Fellow of Merton College, whose inaugural dissertation on Rickets in 1645 contains the earliest printed account of that disease. He was Gresham Professor of Geometry, 1648-57, and held several offices at the College of Physicians, being elected President in 1683. He was one of the original Fellows of the Royal Society. Dr. Munk, in his "Roll of the Royal College of Physicians," speaks very unfavourably of Whistler, and says that he defrauded the college. He died May 11th, 1684.

weary of his company and so I went away. Into the Hall and there saw my Lord Treasurer[1] (who was sworn to-day at the Exchequer, with a great company of Lords and persons of honour to attend him) go up to the Treasury Offices, and take possession thereof; and also saw the heads of Cromwell, Bradshaw, and Ireton, set up upon the further end of the Hall. Then at Mrs. Michell's in the Hall met my wife and Shaw, and she and I and Captain Murford to the Dog, and there I gave them some wine, and after some mirth and talk (Mr. Langley coming in afterwards) I went by coach to the play-house at the Theatre, our coach in King Street breaking, and so took another. Here we saw Argalus and Parthenia, which I lately saw, but though pleasant for the dancing and singing, I do not find good for any wit or design therein. That done home by coach and to supper, being very hungry for want of dinner, and so to bed.

[6th]. Called up by my Cozen Snow, who sat by me while I was trimmed, and then I drank with him, he desiring a courtesy for a friend, which I have done for him. Then to the office, and there sat long, then to dinner, Captain Murford with me. I had a dish of fish and a good hare, which was sent me the other day by Goodenough the plasterer. So to the office again, where Sir W. Pen and I sat all alone, answering of petitions and nothing else, and so to Sir W. Batten's, where comes Mr. Jessop (one whom I could not formerly have looked upon, and now he comes cap in hand to us from the Commissioners of the Navy, though indeed he is a man of a great estate and of good report), about some business from them to us, which we answered by letter. Here I sat long with Sir W., who is not well, and then home and to my chamber, and some little music, and so to bed.

[7th]. With Sir W. Batten and Pen to Whitehall to Mr. Coventry's chamber, to debate upon the business we were upon the other day morning, and thence to Westminster Hall. And after a walk to my Lord's; where, while I and my Lady were in her

---

[1] Thomas Wriothesley, fourth and last Earl of Southampton, K.G., born 1607. He was one of the four who bore Charles I. to his burial. Burnet says, "he disdained to sell places." He died May 16th, 1667.

chamber in talk, in comes my Lord from sea, to our great wonder. He had dined at Havre de Grace on Monday last, and came to the Downs the next day, and lay at Canterbury that night; and so to Dartford, and thence this morning to White Hall. All my friends his servants well. Among others, Mr. Creed and Captain Ferrers tell me the stories of my Lord Duke of Buckingham's and my Lord's falling out at Havre de Grace, at cards; they two and my Lord St. Alban's playing. The Duke did, to my Lord's dishonour, often say that he did in his conscience know the contrary to what he then said, about the difference at cards; and so did take up the money that he should have lost to my Lord. Which my Lord resenting, said nothing then, but that he doubted not but there were ways enough to get his money of him. So they parted that night; and my Lord sent for Sir R. Stayner and sent him the next morning to the Duke, to know whether he did remember what he said last night, and whether he would own it with his sword and a second; which he said he would, and so both sides agreed. But my Lord St. Alban's, and the Queen and Ambassador Montagu, did waylay them at their lodgings till the difference was made up, to my Lord's honour; who hath got great reputation thereby. I dined with my Lord, and then with Mr. Shepley and Creed (who talked very high of France for a fine country) to the tavern, and then I home. To the office, where the two Sir Williams had staid for me, and then we drew up a letter to the Commissioners of Parliament again, and so to Sir W. Batten, where I staid late in talk, and so home, and after writing the letter fair then I went to bed.

[8th]. At the office all the morning. At noon to the Exchange to meet Mr. Warren the timber merchant, but could not meet with him. Here I met with many sea commanders, and among others Captain Cuttle,[1] and Curtis, and Mootham,[2] and I, went to the Fleece Tavern to drink; and there we spent till four o'clock, telling stories of Algiers, and the manner of the life of slaves there.[3]

---

[1] John Cuttle, captain of the "Hector."

[2] Peter Mootham, captain of the "Foresight;" afterwards slain in action.

[3] The Long Parliament imposed a tax on merchants' goods (called Algier Duty) for the redemption of captives in the Mediterranean.

And truly Captn. Mootham and Mr. Dawes[1] (who have been both slaves there) did make me fully acquainted with their condition there: as, how they eat nothing but bread and water. At their redemption they pay so much for the water they drink at the public fountaynes, during their being slaves. How they are beat upon the soles of their feet and bellies at the liberty of their padron. How they are all, at night, called into their master's Bagnard;[2] and there they lie. How the poorest men do use their slaves best. How some rogues do live well, if they do invent to bring their masters in so much a week by their industry or theft; and then they are put to no other work at all. And theft there is counted no great crime at all. Thence to Mr. Rawlinson's, having met my old friend Dick Scobell, and there I drank a great deal with him, and so home and to bed betimes, my head aching.

[9th]. To my Lord's with Mr. Creed (who has come to me this morning to get a bill of imprest signed), and my Lord being gone out, he and I to the Rhenish wine-house with Mr. Blackburne. To whom I did make known my fears of Will's[3] losing of his time, which he will take care to give him good advice about. Afterwards to my Lord's and Mr. Shepley, and I did make even his accounts and mine. And then with Mr. Creed and two friends of his (my late landlord Jones' son one of them), to an ordinary to dinner, and then Creed and I to Whitefriars[4] to the Play-house, and saw "The Mad Lover,"[5] the first time I ever saw it acted, which I like pretty well, and home.

[10th] (Lord's day). Took physique all day, and, God forgive me, did spend it in reading of some little French romances. At night my wife and I did please ourselves talking of our going into France, which I hope to effect this summer. At noon one came to ask for Mrs. Hunt that was here yesterday, and it seems is not come home yet, which makes us afraid of her. At night to bed.

---

[1] John Dawes, created a baronet in 1663, father of Sir William Dawes, Archbishop of York.

[2] Or prison.

[3] William Hewer.

[4] Salisbury Court Theatre, which was re-opened in 1660 by Rhodes's company.

[5] A tragi-comedy by Beaumont and Fletcher, printed in the folio of 1647.

[11th]. At the office all the morning. Dined at home, and then to the Exchequer, and took Mr. Warren with me to Mr. Kennard, the master joiner, at Whitehall, who was at a tavern, and there he and I to him, and agreed about getting some of my Lord's deals on board to-morrow. Then with young Mr. Reeve home to his house, who did there show me many pretty pleasures in perspectives,[1] that I have not seen before, and I did buy a little glass of him cost me 5s. And so to Mr. Crew's, and with Mr. Moore to see how my father and mother did, and so with him to Mr. Adam Chard's[2] (the first time I ever was at his house since he was married) to drink, then we parted, and I home to my study, and set some papers and money in order, and so to bed.

[12th]. To my Lord's, and there with him all the morning, and then (he going out to dinner) I and Mr. Pickering, Creed, and Captain Ferrers to the Leg in the Palace to dinner, where strange Pickering's impertinences. Thence the two others and I after a great dispute whither to go, we went by water to Salsbury Court[3] play-house, where not liking to sit, we went out again, and by coach to the Theatre, and there saw "The Scornfull Lady,"[4] now done by a woman,[5] which makes the play appear much better than ever it did to me. Then Creed and I (the other being lost in the crowd) to drink a cup of ale at Temple Bar, and there we parted, and I (seeing my father and mother by the way) went home.

[13th]. At the office all the morning; dined at home, and poor Mr. Wood with me, who after dinner would have borrowed

---

[1] " 'Telescope' and 'microscope' are both as old as Milton, but for a long while 'perspective' (glass being sometimes understood and sometimes expressed) did the work of these. It is sometimes written 'prospective.' Our present use of 'perspective' does not, I suppose, date farther back than Dryden."—Trench's *Select Glossary.*—M. B.

[2] Adam Chard is mentioned previously in the Diary. See March 7th, 1659-60.

[3] See *ante*, on the 9th of this month, where it is called Whitefriars.

[4] Beaumont and Fletcher's comedy. See January 4th, 1660-1 (note).

[5] According to Downes's "Roscius Anglicanus" the characters were taken as follows:—Elder Lovelace: Burt; Young Lovelace: Kynaston; Welford: Hart; Sir Roger: Lacy; The Lady: Mrs. Marshall; Martha: Mrs. Rutter; Abigil: Mrs. Corey.

money of me, but I would lend none. Then to Whitehall by coach with Sir W. Pen, where we did very little business, and so back to Mr. Rawlinson's, where I took him and gave him a cup of wine, he having formerly known Mr. Rawlinson, and here I met my uncle Wight, and he drank with us, and with him to Sir W. Batten's, whither I sent for my wife, and we chose Valentines[1] against to-morrow. My wife chose me, which did much please me; my Lady Batten Sir W. Pen, &c. Here we sat late, and so home to bed, having got my Lady Batten to give me a spoonful of honey for my cold.

[14th] (Valentine's day). Up early and to Sir W. Batten's, but would not go in till I asked whether they that opened the door was a man or a woman, and Mingo, who was there, answered a woman, which, with his tone, made me laugh; so up I went and took Mrs. Martha[2] for my Valentine (which I do only for complacency), and Sir W. Batten he go in the same manner to my wife, and so we were very merry. About 10 o'clock we, with a great deal of company, went down by our barge to Deptford, and there only went to see how forward Mr. Pett's yacht is; and so all into the barge again, and so to Woolwich, on board the Rose-bush, Captain Brown's[3] ship, that is brother-in-law to Sir W. Batten, where we had a very fine dinner, dressed on shore, and great mirth and all things successfull; the first time I ever carried my wife a-ship-board, as also my boy Wayneman, who hath all this day been called young Pepys, as Sir W. Pen's boy young Pen. So home by barge again; good weather, but pretty cold. I to my study, and began to make up my accounts for my Lord, which I intend to end to-morrow. To bed. The talk of the town now is, who the King is like to have for his Queen: and whether Lent

---

[1] The observation of St. Valentine's day is very ancient in this country. Shakespeare makes Ophelia sing—

"To-morrow is Saint Valentine's day,
All in the morning betime,
And I a maid at your window
To be your Valentine."

Hamlet, act iv. sc. 5.—M. B.

[2] Mrs. Martha Batten, Sir W. Batten's daughter.

[3] Captain Arthur Browne. See January 16th, 1660-61 (note).

shall be kept with the strictness of the King's proclamation;[1] which it is thought cannot be, because of the poor, who cannot buy fish. And also the great preparation for the King's crowning is now much thought upon and talked of.

[15th]. At the office all the morning, and in the afternoon at making up my accounts for my Lord to-morrow; and that being done I found myself to be clear (as I think) £350 in the world, besides my goods in my house and all things paid for.

[16th]. To my Lord in the morning, who looked over my accounts and agreed to them. I did also get him to sign a bill (which do make my heart merry) for £60 to me, in consideration of my work extraordinary at sea this last voyage, which I hope to get paid. I dined with my Lord and then to the Theatre, where I saw "The Virgin Martyr,"[2] a good but too sober a play for the company. Then home.

[17th] (Lord's day). A most tedious, unreasonable, and impertinent sermon, by an Irish Doctor. His text was "Scatter them, O Lord, that delight in war." Sir Wm. Batten and I very much angry with the parson. And so I to Westminster as soon as I came home to my Lord's, where I dined with Shepley and Howe. After dinner (without speaking to my Lord), Mr. Shepley and I into the city, and so I home and took my wife to my uncle Wight's, and there did sup with them, and so home again and to bed.

[18th]. At the office all the morning, dined at home with a very good dinner, only my wife and I, which is not yet very usual. In the afternoon my wife and I and Mrs. Martha Batten, my Valentine, to the Exchange, and there upon a payre of embroydered and six payre of plain white gloves I laid out 40s. upon her. Then we went to a mercer's at the end of Lombard Street, and there she bought a suit of Lutestring[3] for herself, and so home. And at

---

[1] "A Proclamation for restraint of killing, dressing, and eating of Flesh in Lent or on fish-dayes appointed by the law to be observed," was dated 29th January, 1660 [-61].

[2] A tragedy by Massinger and Decker, printed in 1622.

[3] More properly called "lustring"; a fine glossy silk.

night I got the whole company and Sir Wm. Pen home to my house, and there I did give them Rhenish wine and sugar, and continued together till it was late, and so to bed. It is much talked that the King is already married to the niece of the Prince de Ligne,[1] and that he hath two sons already by her: which I am sorry to hear; but yet am gladder that it should be so, than that the Duke of York and his family should come to the crown, he being a professed friend to the Catholiques.

[19th]. By coach to Whitehall with Colonel Slingsby (carrying Mrs. Turner with us) and there he and I up into the house, where we met with Sir G. Carteret: who afterwards, with the Duke of York, my Lord Sandwich, and others, went into a private room to consult: and we were a little troubled that we were not called in with the rest. But I do believe it was upon something very private. We staid walking in the gallery; where we met with Mr. Slingsby,[2] that was formerly a great friend of Mons. Blondeau, who showed me the stamps of the King's new coyne; which is strange to see, how good they are in the stamp and bad in the money, for lack of skill to make them. But he says Blondeau[3] will shortly come over, and then we shall have it better, and the best in the world. The Comptroller and I to the Commissioners of Parliament, and after some talk away again and to drink a cup of ale. He tells me, he is sure that the King is not yet married, as it is said; nor that it is known who he will have. To my Lord's and found him dined, and so I lost my dinner, but I staid and played with him and Mr. Child, &c., some things of four parts, and so it raining hard and bitter cold (the first winter day we have yet had this winter), I took coach home and spent the evening in read-

---

[1] The Prince de Ligne had no niece, and probably Pepys has made some mistake in the name. Charles at one time made an offer of marriage to Mazarin's niece, Hortense Mancini.

[2] Henry Slingsby, Master of the Mint of Kilpax, near Leeds, member of the first Council of the Royal Society, named in Charles II.'s charter dated April 22nd, 1663, but expelled from the Society January 24th, 1675.

[3] Peter Blondeau, medallist, was invited to London from Paris in 1649, and appointed by the Council of State to coin their money; but the moneyers succeeded in driving him out of the country. Soon after the Restoration he returned, and was appointed engineer to the mint.

ing of a Latin play, the "Naufragium Joculare."[1] And so to bed.

[20th]. All the morning at the office, dined at home and my brother Tom with me, who brought me a pair of fine slippers which he gave me. By and by comes little Luellin and friend to see me, and then my coz Stradwick, who was never here before. With them I drank a bottle of wine or two, and to the office again,

and there staid about business late, and then all of us to Sir W. Pen's, where we had, and my Lady Batten, Mrs. Martha, and my wife, and other company, a good supper, and sat playing at cards and talking till 12 at night, and so all to our lodgings.

[21st]. To Westminster by coach with Sir W. Pen, and in our way saw the city begin to build scaffolds against the Coronacion. To my Lord, and there found him out of doors. So to the Hall and called for some caps that I have a making there, and here met

---

[1] A comedy by Abraham Cowley, published in 1638. The scene was laid at Dunkirk.

with Mr. Hawley, and with him to Will's and drank, and then by coach with Mr. Langley our old friend into the city. I set him down by the way, and I home and there staid all day within, having found Mr. Moore, who staid with me till late at night talking and reading some good books. Then he went away, and I to bed.

[22nd]. All the morning at the office. At noon with my wife and Pall to my father's to dinner, where Dr. Thos. Pepys and my coz Snow and Joyce Norton. After dinner came The. Turner, and so I home with her to her mother, good woman, whom I had not seen through my great neglect this half year, but she would not be angry with me. Here I staid all the afternoon talking of the King's being married, which is now the town talk, but I believe false. In the evening Mrs. The. and Joyce took us all into the coach home, calling in Bishopsgate Street, thinking to have seen a new Harpsicon[1] that she had a making there, but it was not done, and so we did not see it. Then to my home, where I made very much of her, and then she went home. Then my wife to Sir W. Batten's, and there sat awhile; he having yesterday sent my wife half-a-dozen pairs of gloves, and a pair of silk stockings and garters, for her Valentine's gift. Then home and to bed.

[23rd]. This is my birthday, 28 years. This morning Sir W. Batten, Pen, and I did some business, and then I by water to Whitehall, having met Mr. Hartlibb[2] by the way at Alderman Backwell's. So he did give me a glass of Rhenish wine at the Steeleyard,[3] and so to Whitehall by water. He continues of the same

---

[1] The harpsichord is an instrument larger than a spinet, with two or three strings to a note.

[2] Samuel Hartlib, son of a Polish merchant, and author of several ingenious works on agriculture, for which he received a pension from Cromwell. Milton's "Tractate of Education" is addressed to him. Evelyn describes him in his Diary, November 27th, 1655, as "honest and learned," and calls him "a public-spirited and ingenious person who had propagated many useful things and arts." He lived in Axe Yard about 1661, and had a son named Samuel and a daughter, Nan, who married John Roder or Roth, afterwards knighted. Evelyn says that Claudius, referred to before (see July 10th, 1660, of this Diary), was Hartlib's son-in-law. If so, Hartlib must have had another daughter. He seems to have been in some poverty at the end of his life.

[3] The Steelyard was situated where Cannon Street Station now stands. The Rhenish wine-house occupied the ground floors of the front in Thames Street.

bold impertinent humour that he was always of and will ever be. He told me how my Lord Chancellor had lately got the Duke of York and Duchess, and her woman, my Lord Ossory,[1] and a Doctor, to make oath before most of the Judges of the kingdom, concerning all the circumstances of their marriage. And in fine, it is confessed that they were not fully married till about a month or two before she was brought to bed; but that they were contracted long before, and time enough for the child to be legitimate.[2] But I do not hear that it was put to the Judges to determine whether it was so or no. To my Lord and there spoke to him about his opinion of the Light, the sea-mark that Captain Murford is about, and do offer me an eighth part to concern myself with it, and my Lord do give me some encouragement in it, and I shall go on. I dined here with Mr. Shepley and Howe. After dinner to Whitehall Chappell with Mr. Child, and there did hear Captain Cooke and his boy make a trial of an Anthem against to-morrow, which was brave musique. Then by water to Whitefriars to the Playhouse, and there saw "The Changeling,"[3] the first time it hath been acted these twenty years, and it takes exceedingly. Besides, I see the gallants do begin to be tyred with the vanity and pride of the theatre actors who are indeed grown very proud and rich. Then by link home, and there to my book awhile and to bed. I met to-day with Mr. Townsend, who tells me that the old man is yet alive in whose place in the Wardrobe he hopes to get my father, which I do resolve to put for. I also met with the Comptroller, who told me how it was easy for us all, the principall officers, and proper for us, to labour to get into the next Parliament; and would have me to ask the Duke's letter,[4] but I shall not endeavour it because it will spend much money, though I am sure I could well obtain it. This is now 28 years that I am born. And

---

[1] Thomas, Earl of Ossory, K.G., the accomplished son of the Duke of Ormond. Died 1680, aged forty-six.

[2] The Duke of York's marriage took place September 3rd, 1660. Anne Hyde was contracted to the Duke at Breda, November 24th, 1659.

[3] A tragedy, by Thomas Middleton, acted before the court at Whitehall, January 4th, 1623-4. The plot is taken from a story in Reynolds's "God's Revenge against Murder," book i., hist. iv.

[4] Perhaps a letter of recommendation to some constituency.

blessed be God, in a state of full content, and great hopes to be a happy man in all respects, both to myself and friends.

[24th] (Sunday). Mr. Mills made as excellent a sermon in the morning against drunkenness as ever I heard in my life. I dined at home; another good one of his in the afternoon. My Valentine had her fine gloves on at church to-day that I did give her. After sermon my wife and I unto Sir Wm. Batten and sat awhile. Then home, I to read, then to supper and to bed.

[25th]. Sir Wm. Pen and I to my Lord Sandwich's by coach in the morning to see him, but he takes physic to-day and so we could not see him. So he went away, and I with Luellin to Mr. Mount's chamber at the Cockpit, where he did lie of old, and there we drank, and from thence to W. Symons where we found him abroad, but she, like a good lady, within, and there we did eat some nettle porrige, which was made on purpose to-day for some of their coming, and was very good. With her we sat a good while, merry in discourse, and so away, Luellin and I to my Lord's, and there dined. He told me one of the prettiest stories, how Mr. Blurton, his friend that was with him at my house three or four days ago, did go with him the same day from my house to the Fleece tavern by Guildhall, and there (by some pretence) got the mistress of the house into their company, and by and by Luellin calling him Doctor she thought that he really was so, and did privately discover her disease to him, which was only some ordinary infirmity belonging to women, and he proffering her physic, she desired him to come some day and bring it, which he did. After dinner by water to the office, and there Sir W. Pen and I met and did business all the afternoon, and then I got him to my house and eat a lobster together, and so to bed.

[26th] (Shrove Tuesday). I left my wife in bed, being indisposed. . . . I to Mrs. Turner's, who I found busy with The. and Joyce making things ready for fritters, so to Mr. Crew's and there delivered Cotgrave's Dictionary[1] to my Lady Jemimah, and then with Mr. Moore to my coz Tom Pepys, but he being out of town

---

[1] Randle Cotgrave's valuable "French and English Dictionary" was first published in 1611, and several editions were subsequently issued.

I spoke with his lady, though not of the business I went about, which was to borrow £1,000 for my Lord. Back to Mrs. Turner's, where several friends, all strangers to me but Mr. Armiger, dined. Very merry and the best fritters that ever I eat in my life. After that looked out at window; saw the flinging at cocks.[1] Then Mrs. The. and I, and a gentleman that dined there and his daughter, a perfect handsome young and very tall lady that lately came out of the country, and Mr. Thatcher the Virginall Maister to Bishopsgate Street, and there saw the new Harpsicon made for Mrs. The. We offered £12, they demanded £14. The Master not being at home, we could make no bargain, so parted for to-night. So all by coach to my house, where I found my Valentine with my wife, and here they drank, and then went away. Then I sat and talked with my Valentine and my wife a good while, and then saw her home, and went to Sir W. Batten to the Dolphin, where Mr. Newborne, &c., were, and there after a quart or two of wine, we home, and I to bed. . . .

[27th]. At the office all the morning, that done I walked in the garden with little Captain Murford, where he and I had some discourse concerning the Light-House again, and I think I shall appear in the business, he promising me that if I can bring it about, it will be worth £100 per annum. Then came into the garden to me young Mr. Powell and Mr. Hooke that I once knew at Cambridge, and I took them in and gave them a bottle of wine, and so parted. Then I called for a dish of fish, which we had for dinner, this being the first day of Lent; and I do intend to try whether I can keep it or no. My father dined with me and did show me a letter from my brother John, wherein he tells us that he is chosen Schollar of the house,[2] which do please me much, because I do perceive now it must chiefly come from his merit and not the power of his Tutor, Dr. Widdrington, who is now quite out of interest there and hath put over his pupils to Mr. Pepper, a young Fellow of the College. With my father to Mr. Rawlinson's, where we met my uncle Wight, and after a pint or two away. I walked

---

[1] The cruel custom of throwing at cocks on Shrove Tuesday is of considerable antiquity. It is shown in the first print of Hogarth's "Four Stages of Cruelty."
[2] Christ's College, Cambridge.

with my father (who gave me an account of the great falling out between my uncle Fenner and his son Will)[1] as far as Paul's Churchyard, and so left him, and I home. This day the Commissioners of Parliament begin to pay off the Fleet, beginning with the Hampshire,[2] and do it at Guildhall, for fear of going out of town into the power of the seamen, who are highly incensed against them.

[28th]. Early to wait on my Lord, and after a little talk with him I took boat at Whitehall for Redriffe, but in my way overtook Captain Cuttance and Teddiman in a boat and so ashore with them at Queenhithe, and so to a tavern with them to a barrel of oysters, and so away. Capt. Cuttance and I walked from Redriffe to Deptford, where I found both Sir Williams and Sir G. Carteret at Mr. Uthwayt's, and there we dined, and notwithstanding my resolution, yet for want of other victualls, I did eat flesh this Lent, but am resolved to eat as little as I can. After dinner we went to Captain Bodilaw's, and there made sale of many old stores by the candle, and good sport it was to see how from a small matter bid at first they would come to double and treble the price of things. After that Sir W. Pen and I and my Lady Batten and her daughter by land to Redriffe, staying a little at halfway house, and when we came to take boat, found Sir George, &c., to have staid with the barge a great while for us, which troubled us. Home and to bed. This month ends with two great secrets under dispute but yet known to very few: first, Who the King will marry; and What the meaning of this fleet is which we are now sheathing to set out for the southward. Most think against Algier against the Turk, or to the East Indys against the Dutch who, we hear, are setting out a great fleet thither.

[March 1st]. All the morning at the office. Dined at home only upon fish, and Mr. Shepley and Tom Hater with me. After dinner Mr. Shepley and I in private talking about my Lord's intentions to go speedily into the country, but to what end we know not.

---

[1] His son-in-law William Joyce.

[2] The "Hampshire" was a fourth-rate of thirty-eight guns, built at Deptford in 1653 by Phineas Pett.

We fear he is to go to sea with this fleet now preparing. But we wish that he could get his £4,000 per annum settled before he do go. Then he and I walked into London, he to the Wardrobe and I to Whitefryars, and saw "The Bondman"[1] acted; an excellent play and well done. But above all that ever I saw, Betterton[2] do the Bondman the best. Then to my father's and found my mother ill. After staying a while with them, I went home and sat up late, spending my thoughts how to get money to bear me out in my great expense at the Coronacion, against which all provide, and scaffolds setting up in every street. I had many designs in my head to get some, but know not which will take. To bed.

[2d]. Early with Mr. Moore about Sir Paul Neale's[3] business with my uncle and other things all the morning. Dined with him at Mr. Crew's, and after dinner I went to the Theatre, where I found so few people (which is strange, and the reason I did not know) that I went out again, and so to Salsbury Court, where the house as full as could be; and it seems it was a new play, "The Queen's Maske,"[4] wherein there are some good humours: among others, a good jeer to the old story of the Siege of Troy, making

---

[1] Massinger's play, which was first published in 1624.

[2] Thomas Betterton, younger but eldest surviving son of Matthew Betterton of Westminster, said to be under-cook to Charles I., but who (writes Colonel Chester) described himself in his will as a "gentleman." Thomas was baptized at St. Margaret's, Westminster, August 11th, 1635. He joined the company of actors formed by Rhodes, bookseller (and formerly wardrobe keeper to the Blackfriars Company), which commenced to act at the Cockpit, in Drury Lane, in 1659. When, after the Restoration, Davenant took over Rhodes's company, Betterton became his principal actor. Betterton died April 28th, 1710, and was buried in the East Cloister of Westminster Abbey on May 2nd.

[3] Sir Paul Neile, of White Waltham, Berks, son of Richard Neile, Archbishop of York (1632-40). A member of the first council of the Royal Society, and a constant attendant at the meetings. He was frequently the bearer of messages from Charles II. We learn from Birch's "History of the Royal Society," that on July 17th, 1661, "Sir Paul Neile having mentioned that the king had within four days past desired to have a reason assigned why the sensitive plants stir and contract themselves upon being touched, it was resolved that Dr. Wilkins, Dr. Clarke, Mr. Boyle, Mr. Evelyn, and Dr. Goddard be curators for examining the fact relating to these plants."

[4] "Love's Mistress, or The Queen's Masque," by Thomas Heywood, published in 1636. The plot is borrowed from the "Golden Ass" of Apuleius.

it to be a common country tale. But above all it was strange to see so little a boy as that was to act Cupid, which is one of the greatest parts in it. Then home and to bed.

[3rd] (Lord's day). Mr. Woodcocke[1] preached at our church a very good sermon upon the imaginacions of the thoughts of man's heart being only evil. So home, where being told that my Lord had sent for me I went, and got there to dine with my Lord, who is to go into the country to-morrow. I did give up the mortgage made to me by Sir R. Parkhurst for £2,000. In the Abby all the afternoon. Then at Mr. Pierce's the surgeon, where Shepley and I supped. So to my Lord's, who comes in late and tells us how news is come to-day of Mazarin's[2] being dead, which is very great news and of great consequence. I lay to-night with Mr. Shepley here, because of my Lord's going to-morrow.

[4th]. My Lord went this morning on his journey to Hinching-broke, Mr. Parker with him; the chief business being to look over and determine how, and in what manner, his great work of building shall be done. Before his going he did give me some jewells to keep for him, viz., that that the King of Sweden did give him, with the King's own picture in it,[3] most excellently done; and a brave George, all of diamonds, and this with the greatest expressions of love and confidence that I could imagine or hope for, which is a very great joy to me. To the office all the forenoon. Then to dinner and so to Whitehall to Mr. Coventry about several businesses, and then with Mr. Moore, who went with me to drink a cup of ale, and after some good discourse then home and sat late talking with Sir W. Batten. So home and to bed.

[5th]. With Mr. Pierce, purser, to Westminster Hall, and there met with Captain Cuttance, Lieut. Lambert, and Pierce, surgeon, thinking to have met with the Commissioners of Parliament, but they not sitting, we went to the Swan, where I did give them a barrel of oysters; and so I to my Lady's and there dined, and had

---

[1] Thomas Woodcock, afterwards ejected from St. Andrew's Undershaft.

[2] This report of the death of Cardinal Mazarin appears to have been premature, for he did not die until the 9th of March, 1661.

[3] Charles XI., son of Charles (X.) Gustavus. He succeeded his father in 1660.

very much talk and pleasant discourse with my Lady, my esteem growing every day higher and higher in her and my Lord. So to my father Bowyer's where my wife was, and to the Commissioners of Parliament, and there did take some course about having my Lord's salary paid to-morrow when the Charles is paid off, but I was troubled to see how high they carry themselves, when in good truth nobody cares for them. So home by coach and my wife. I then to the office, where Sir Williams both and I set about making an estimate of all the officers' salaries in ordinary in the Navy till 10 o'clock at night. So home, and I with my head full of thoughts how to get a little present money, I eat a bit of bread and cheese, and so to bed.

[6th]. At the office all the morning. At dinner Sir W. Batten came and took me and my wife to his house to dinner, my Lady being in the country, where we had a good Lenten dinner. Then to Whitehall with Captn. Cuttle, and there I did some business with Mr. Coventry, and after that home, thinking to have had Sir W. Batten, &c., to have eat a wigg[1] at my house at night. But my Lady being come home out of the country ill by reason of much rain that has fallen lately, and the waters being very high, we could not, and so I home and to bed.

[7th]. This morning Sir Williams both went to Woolwich to sell some old provisions there. I to Whitehall, and up and down about many businesses. Dined at my Lord's, then to Mr. Crew to Mr. Moore, and he and I to London to Guildhall to see the seamen paid off, but could not without trouble, and so I took him to the Fleece tavern, where the pretty woman that Luellin lately told me the story of dwells, but I could not see her. Then towards home and met Spicer, D. Vines, Ruddiard, and a company more of my old acquaintance, and went into a place to drink some ale, and there we staid playing the fool till late, and so I home. At home met with ill news that my hopes of getting some money for the Charles were spoiled through Mr. Waith's perverseness, which did so vex me that I could not sleep at night. But I wrote a

---

[1] Wigg, a kind of north country bun or tea-cake, still so called, to my knowledge, in Staffordshire.—M. B.

letter to him to send to-morrow morning for him to take my money for me, and so with good words I thought to coy with him. To bed.

[8th]. All the morning at the office. At noon Sir W. Batten, Col. Slingsby and I by coach to the Tower, to Sir John Robinson's, to dinner; where great good cheer. High company; among others the Duchess of Albemarle, who is ever a plain homely dowdy. After dinner, to drink all the afternoon. Towards night the Duchess and ladies went away. Then we set to it again till it was very late. And at last came in Sir William Wale,[1] almost fuddled; and

because I was set between him and another, only to keep them from talking and spoiling the company (as we did to others), he fell out with the Lieutenant of the Tower; but with much ado we made him understand his error, and then all quiet. And so he carried Sir William Batten and I home again in his coach, and so I almost overcome with drink went to bed. I was much contented

[1] Alderman and Colonel of the red regiment of Trainbands. He was one of the Commissioners sent to Breda to desire Charles II. to return to England immediately.

to ride in such state into the Tower, and be received among such
high company, while Mr. Mount, my Lady Duchess's gentleman
usher, stood waiting at table, whom I ever thought a man so much
above me in all respects; also to hear the discourse of so many
high Cavaliers of things past. It was a great content and joy to me.

[9th]. To Whitehall, and there with Mr. Creed took a most pleasant walk for two hours in the park, which is now a very fair place.
Here we had a long and candid discourse one to another of one
another's condition, and he giving me an occasion I told him of
my intention to get £60 paid me by him for a gratuity for my

labour extraordinary at sea. Which he did not seem unwilling to,
and therefore I am very glad it is out. To my Lord's, where we
found him lately come from Hinchingbroke, where he left my
uncle very well, but my aunt not likely to live. I staid and dined
with him. He took me aside, and asked me what the world spoke
of the King's marriage. Which I answering as one that knew
nothing, he enquired no further of me. But I do perceive by it that
there is something in it that is ready to come out that the world
knows not of yet. After dinner into London to Mrs. Turner's and

my father's, made visits and then home, where I sat late making of my Journal for four days past, and so to bed.

[10th] (Lord's day). Heard Mr. Mills in the morning, a good sermon. Dined at home on a poor Lenten dinner of coleworts and bacon. In the afternoon again to church, and there heard one Castle, whom I knew of my year at Cambridge. He made a dull sermon. After sermon came my uncle and aunt Wight to see us, and we sat together a great while. Then to reading and at night to bed.

[11th]. At the office all the morning, dined at home and my father and Dr. Thos. Pepys with him upon a poor dinner, my wife being abroad. After dinner I went to the theatre, and saw "Love's Mistress"[1] done by them, which I do not like in some things as well as their acting in Salsbury Court. At night home and found my wife come home, and among other things she hath got her teeth new done by La Roche, and are indeed now pretty handsome, and I was much pleased with it. So to bed.

[12th]. At the office about business all the morning, so to the Exchange, and there met with Nick Osborne lately married, and with him to the Fleece, where we drank a glass of wine. So home, where I found Mrs. Hunt in great trouble about her husband's losing of his place in the Excise. From thence to Guildhall, and there set my hand to the book before Colonel King for my sea pay, and blessed be God! they have cast me at midshipman's pay, which do make my heart very glad. So home, and there had Sir W. Batten and my Lady and all their company and Capt. Browne and his wife to a collation at my house till it was late, and then to bed.

[13th]. Early up in the morning to read "The Seaman's Grammar and Dictionary" I lately have got, which do please me exceeding well. At the office all the morning, dined at home, and Mrs. Turner, The., Joyce, and Mr. Armiger, and my father and mother with me, where they staid till I was weary of their com-

---

[1] When Pepys saw this play on March 1st he called it by its second title "The Queen's Masque."

pany and so away. Then up to my chamber, and there set papers
and things in order, and so to bed.

[14th]. With Sir W. Batten and Pen to Mr. Coventry's, and
there had a dispute about my claim to the place of Purveyor of
Petty-provisions, and at last to my content did conclude to have
my hand to all the bills for these provisions and Mr. Turner to
purvey them, because I would not have him to lose the place.
Then to my Lord's, and so with Mr. Creed to an alehouse, where
he told me a long story of his amours at Portsmouth to one of
Mrs. Boat's daughters, which was very pleasant. Dined with my
Lord and Lady, and so with Mr. Creed to the Theatre, and there
saw "King and no King,"[1] well acted. Thence with him to the
Cock alehouse at Temple Bar, where he did ask my advice about
his amours, and I did give him it, which was to enquire into the
condition of his competitor, who is a son of Mr. Gauden's, and
that I promise to do for him, and he to make [what] use he can
of it to his advantage. Home and to bed.

[15th]. At the office all the morning. At noon Sir Williams both
and I at a great fish dinner at the Dolphin, given us by two tax
merchants, and very merry we were till night, and so home. This
day my wife and Pall went to see my Lady Kingston, her brother's[2] lady.

[16th]. Early at Sir Wm. Pen's, and there before Mr. Turner did
reconcile the business of the purveyance between us two. Then to
Whitehall to my Lord's, and dined with him, and so to Whitefriars and saw "The Spanish Curate,"[3] in which I had no great
content. So home, and was very much troubled that Will. staid
out late, and went to bed early, intending not to let him come in,
but by and by he comes and I did let him in, and he did tell me
that he was at Guildhall helping to pay off the seamen, and cast
the books late. Which since I found to be true. So to sleep, being
in bed when he came.

---

[1] A comedy by Beaumont and Fletcher, acted before the court in 1611 by the
King's Players.
[2] Although Balthasar St. Michel, Mrs. Pepys's brother, is frequently mentioned, there is no further notice of this lady in the Diary.
[3] A comedy by Beaumont and Fletcher, acted before the court in 1622.

[17th] (Lord's day). At church in the morning, a stranger preached a good honest and painfull sermon. My wife and I dined upon a chine of beef at Sir W. Batten's, so to church again. Then home, and put some papers in order. Then to supper at Sir W. Batten's again, where my wife by chance fell down and hurt her knees exceedingly. So home and to bed.

[18th]. This morning early Sir W. Batten went to Rochester, where he expects to be chosen Parliament¹ man. At the office all the morning, dined at home and with my wife to Westminster, where I had business with the Commissioner for paying the seamen about my Lord's pay, and my wife at Mrs. Hunt's. I called her home, and made inquiry at Greatorex's and in other places to hear of Mr. Barlow (thinking to hear that he is dead), but I cannot find it so, but the contrary. Home and called at my Lady Batten's, and supped there, and so home. This day an ambassador from Florence was brought into the town in state. Good hopes given me to-day that Mrs. Davis is going away from us, her husband going shortly to Ireland. Yesterday it was said was to be the day that the Princess Henrietta was to marry the Duke d'Anjou² in France. This day I found in the newes-booke that Roger Pepys is chosen at Cambridge for the town, the first place that we hear of to have made their choice yet. To bed with my head and mind full of business, which do a little put me out of order, and I do find myself to become more and more thoughtful about getting of money than ever heretofore.

[19th]. We met at the office this morning about some particular business, and then I to Whitehall, and there dined with my Lord, and after dinner Mr. Creed and I to White-Fryars, where we saw "The Bondman" acted most excellently, and though I have seen it often, yet I am every time more and more pleased with Betterton's action. From thence with him and young Mr. Jones to Pen-

---

¹ Sir William Batten was elected M. P. for Rochester March 21st, 1660-61, and held the seat till his death, when he was succeeded by Richard Head, Alderman of Rochester, who was elected November 2nd, 1667.

² The Duke of Anjou became Duke of Orleans on the death of his uncle Gaston in 1660.

ell's in Fleet Street, and there we drank and talked a good while, and so I home and to bed.

[20th]. At the office all the morning, dined at home and Mr. Creed and Mr. Shepley with me, and after dinner we did a good deal of business in my study about my Lord's accounts to be made up and presented to our office. That done to White Hall to Mr. Coventry, where I did some business with him, and so with Sir W. Pen (who I found with Mr. Coventry teaching of him upon the map to understand Jamaica).[1] By water in the dark home, and so to my Lady Batten's where my wife was, and there we sat and eat and drank till very late, and so home to bed. The great talk of the town is the strange election that the City of London made yesterday for Parliament-men; viz. Fowke, Love, Jones, and . . . . ,[2] men that are so far from being episcopall that they are thought to be Anabaptists; and chosen with a great deal of zeal, in spite of the other party that thought themselves very strong, calling out in the Hall, "No Bishops! no Lord Bishops!" It do make people to fear it may come to worse, by being an example to the country to do the same. And indeed the Bishops are so high, that very few do love them.

[21st]. Up very early, and to work and study in my chamber, and then to Whitehall to my Lord, and there did stay with him a good while discoursing upon his accounts. Here I staid with Mr. Creed all the morning, and at noon dined with my Lord, who was very merry, and after dinner we sang and fiddled a great while. Then I by water (Mr. Shepley, Pinkney, and others going part of the way) home, and then hard at work setting my papers in order, and writing letters till night, and so to bed. This day I saw the Florence Ambassador go to his audience, the weather very foul, and yet he and his company very gallant. After I was a-bed Sir W. Pen sent to desire me to go with him to-morrow morning to meet Sir W. Batten coming from Rochester.

---

[1] Sir William Penn was well fitted to give this information, as it was he who took the island from the Spaniards in 1655.

[2] The four members elected for London were Alderman John Fowke, Alderman William Love, John Jones, and Alderman Sir William Thompson.

[22nd]. This morning I rose early, and my Lady Batten knocked at her door that comes into one of my chambers, and called me to know whether I and my wife were ready to go. So my wife got her ready, and about eight o'clock I got a horseback, and my Lady and her two daughters, and Sir W. Pen into coach, and so over London Bridge, and thence to Dartford. The day very pleasant, though the way bad. Here we met with Sir W. Batten, and some company along with him, who had assisted him in his election at Rochester; and so we dined and were very merry. At 5 o'clock we set out again in a coach home, and were very merry all the way. At Deptford we met with Mr. Newborne, and some other friends and their wives in a coach to meet us, and so they went home with us, and at Sir W. Batten's we supped, and thence to bed, my head akeing mightily through the wine that I drank to-day.

[23d]. All the morning at home putting papers in order, dined at home, and then out to the Red Bull[1] (where I had not been since plays come up again), but coming too soon I went out again and walked all up and down the Charterhouse yard and Aldersgate street. At last came back again and went in, where I was led by a seaman that knew me, but is here as a servant, up to the tireing-room, where strange the confusion and disorder that there is among them in fitting themselves, especially here, where the clothes are very poor, and the actors but common fellows. At last into the pitt, where I think there was not above ten more than myself, and not one hundred in the whole house. And the play, which is called "All's lost by Lust,"[2] poorly done; and with so much disorder, among others, that in the musique-room the boy that was to sing a song, not singing it right, his master fell about his ears and beat him so, that it put the whole house in an uprore. Thence homewards, and at the Mitre met my uncle Wight, and with him Lieut-Col. Baron,[3] who told us how Crofton,[4] the great

---

[1] The Red Bull was situated in St. John's Street, Clerkenwell.

[2] A tragedy, by W. Rowley.

[3] Probably Argal Baron, of Croydon, Lieutenant-Governor of Windsor Castle, and said to have been a distinguished Royalist.—B.

[4] Zachary Croften, born in Ireland. His first living was at Wrenbury, Cheshire, from which he was expelled in 1648 for refusing to take the Engage-

Presbyterian minister that had lately preached so highly against
Bishops, is clapped up this day into the Tower. Which do please
some, and displease others exceedingly. Home and to bed.

[24th] (Lord's day). My wife and I to church, and then home
with Sir W. Batten and my Lady to dinner, where very merry,
and then to church again, where Mr. Mills made a good sermon.
Home again, and after a walk in the garden Sir W. Batten's two
daughters came and sat with us a while, and I then up to my
chamber to read.

[25th] (Lady day). This morning came workmen to begin the
making of me a new pair of stairs up out of my parler, which,
with other work that I have to do, I doubt will keep me this two
months and so long I shall be all in dirt; but the work do please
me very well. To the office, and there all the morning, dined at
home, and after dinner comes Mr. Salisbury to see me, and
shewed me a face or two of his paynting, and indeed I perceive
that he will be a great master. I took him to Whitehall with me
by water, but he would not by any means be moved to go through
bridge, and so we were fain to go round by the Old Swan. To my
Lord's and there I shewed him the King's picture, which he intends to copy out in little. After that I and Captain Ferrers to
Salisbury Court by water, and saw part of the "Queene's Maske."
Then I to Mrs. Turner, and there staid talking late, The. Turner
being in a great chafe, about being disappointed of a room to
stand in at the Coronacion. Then to my father's, and there staid
talking with my mother and him late about my dinner to-
morrow. So homewards and took up a boy that had a lanthorn,
that was picking up of rags, and got him to light me home, and
had great discourse with him how he could get sometimes three
or four bushells of rags in a day, and got 3*d*. a bushell for them,
and many other discourses, what and how many ways there

---

ment. When he came to London he was for some time minister of St. James's,
Garlickhithe, and then obtained the cure of St. Botolph, Aldgate, which he
held till he was ejected for Nonconformity. He was said to be zealous for the
Restoration, but he was committed to the Tower for defending the Solemn
League and Covenant. In 1667 he opened a school near Aldgate. He was the
author of several works, and died in 1672.

are for poor children to get their livings honestly. So home and I
to bed at 12 o'clock at night, being pleased well with the work
that my workmen have begun to-day.

[26th]. Up early to do business in my study. This is my great
day that three years ago I was cut of the stone, and, blessed be
God, I do yet find myself very free from pain again. All this
morning I staid at home looking after my workmen to my great
content about my stairs, and at noon by coach to my father's,
where Mrs. Turner, The., Joyce, Mr. Morrice, Mr. Armiger, Mr.
Pierce, the surgeon, and his wife, my father and mother, and myself and my wife. Very merry at dinner; among other things,
because Mrs. Turner and her company eat no flesh at all this
Lent, and I had a great deal of good flesh which made their
mouths water. After dinner Mrs. Pierce and her husband and I
and my wife to Salisbury Court, where coming late he and she
light of Col. Boone that made room for them, and I and my wife
sat in the pit, and there met with Mr. Lewes and Tom Whitton,
and saw "The Bondman" done to admiration. So home by coach,
and after a view of what the workmen had done to-day I went
to bed.

[27th]. Up early to see my workmen at work. My brother Tom
comes to me, and among other things I looked over my old clothes
and did give him a suit of black stuff clothes and a hat and some
shoes. At the office all the morning, where Sir G. Carteret comes,
and there I did get him to promise me some money upon a bill
of exchange, whereby I shall secure myself of £60 which otherwise I should not know how to get. At noon I found my stairs
quite broke down, that I could not get up but by a ladder; and
my wife not being well she kept her chamber all this day. To the
Dolphin to a dinner of Mr. Harris's, where Sir Williams both and
my Lady Batten, and her two daughters, and other company,
where a great deal of mirth, and there staid till 11 o'clock at
night; and in our mirth I sang and sometimes fiddled (there being a noise[1] of fiddlers there), and at last we fell to dancing, the
first time that ever I did in my life, which I did wonder to see

---

[1] Noise, see *ante*, May 7th, 1660.

myself to do. At last we made Mingo, Sir W. Batten's black, and
Jack, Sir W. Pen's, dance, and it was strange how the first did
dance with a great deal of seeming skill. Home, where I found
my wife all day in her chamber. So to bed.

[28th]. Up early among my workmen, then Mr. Creed coming
to see me I went along with him to Sir Robert Slingsby (he being
newly maister of that title by being made a Baronett) to discourse about Mr. Creed's accounts to be made up, and from
thence by coach to my cozen Thomas Pepys, to borrow £1,000
for my Lord, which I am to expect an answer to to-morrow. So to
my Lord's, and there staid and dined, and after dinner did get
my Lord to view Mr. Shepley's accounts as I had examined them,
and also to sign me a bond for my £500. Then with Mr. Shepley
to the Theatre and saw "Rollo"[1] ill acted. That done to drink a

---

[1] "Rollo, Duke of Normandy," a tragedy by John Fletcher, published in 1640.
It was previously published in 1639 as "The Bloody Brother."

cup of ale and so by coach to London, and having set him down in Cheapside I went home, where I found a great deal of work done to-day, and also £70 paid me by the Treasurer upon the bill of exchange that I have had hopes of so long, so that, my heart in great content, I went to bed.

[29th]. Up among my workmen with great pleasure. Then to the office, where I found Sir W. Pen sent down yesterday to Chatham to get two great ships in readiness presently to go to the East Indies upon some design against the Dutch, we think, at Goa,[1] but it is a great secret yet. Dined at home, came Mr. Shepley and Moore, and did business with both of them. After that to Sir W. Batten's, where great store of company at dinner. Among others my schoolfellow, Mr. Christmas, where very merry, and hither came letters from above for the fitting of two other ships for the East Indies in all haste, and so we got orders presently for the Hampshire and Nonsuch. Then home and there put some papers in order, and not knowing what to do, the house being so dirty, I went to bed.

[30th]. At the office we and Sir W. Rider to advise what sort of provisions to get ready for these ships going to the Indies. Then the Comptroller and I by water to Mr. Coventry, and there discoursed upon the same thing. So to my coz. Tho. Pepys, and got him to promise me £1,000 to lend my Lord upon his and my uncle Robert's and my security. So to my Lord's, and there got him to sign a bond to him, which I also signed too, and he did sign counter security to us both. Then into London up and down and drank a pint of wine with Mr. Creed, and so home and sent a letter and the bonds to my uncle to sign for my Lord. This day I spoke with Dr. Castle about making up the dividend for the last quarter, and agreed to meet about it on Monday.

[31st] (Sunday). At church, where a stranger preached like a fool. From thence home and dined with my wife, she staying at home, being unwilling to dress herself, the house being all dirty. To church again, and after sermon I walked to my father's, and to Mrs. Turner's, where I could not woo The. to give me a lesson

---

[1] A Portuguese city on the Malabar or western coast of Hindostan.

upon the harpsicon and was angry at it. So home and finding Will abroad at Sir W. Batten's talking with the people there (Sir W. and my Lady being in the country), I took occasion to be angry with him, and so to prayers and to bed.

[April 1st]. This day my waiting at the Privy Seal comes in again. Up early among my workmen. So to the office, and went home to dinner with Sir W. Batten, and after that to the Goat tavern by Charing Cross to meet Dr. Castle, where he and I drank a pint of wine and talked about Privy Seal business. Then to the Privy Seal Office and there found Mr. Moore, but no business yet. Then to Whitefryars, and there saw part of "Rule a wife and have a wife,"[1] which I never saw before, but do not like it. So to my father, and there finding a discontent between my father and mother about the maid (which my father likes and my mother dislikes), I staid till 10 at night, persuading my mother to understand herself, and that in some high words, which I was sorry for, but she is grown, poor woman, very froward. So leaving them in the same discontent I went away home, it being a brave moonshine, and to bed.

[2d]. Among my workmen early and then along with my wife and Pall to my Father's by coach there to have them lie a while till my house be done. I found my mother alone weeping upon my last night's quarrel and so left her, and took my wife to Charing Cross and there left her to see her mother who is not well. So I into St. James's Park, where I saw the Duke of York playing at Pelemele,[2] the first time that ever I saw the sport. Then to my Lord's, where I dined with my Lady, and after we had dined in comes my Lord and Ned Pickering hungry, and there was not a bit of meat left in the house, the servants having eat up all, at which my Lord was very angry, and at last got something dressed. Then to the Privy Seal, and signed some things, and so

---

[1] A comedy by John Fletcher, licensed October, 1624.

[2] The game was originally played in the road now styled Pall Mall, near St. James's Square, but at the Restoration when sports came in fashion again the street was so much built over, that it became necessary to find another ground. The Mall in St. James's Park was then laid out for the purpose.

to White-fryars and saw "The Little Thiefe,"[1] which is a very merry and pretty play, and the little boy do very well. Then to my Father's, where I found my mother and my wife in a very good mood, and so left them and went home. Then to the Dolphin to Sir W. Batten, and Pen, and other company; among others Mr. Delabar; where strange how these men, who at other times are all wise men, do now, in their drink, betwitt and reproach one another with their former conditions, and their actions as in public concernments, till I was ashamed to see it. But parted all friends at 12 at night after drinking a great deal of wine. So home and alone to bed.

[3rd]. Up among my workmen, my head akeing all day from last night's debauch. To the office all the morning, and at noon dined with Sir W. Batten and Pen, who would needs have me drink two drafts of sack to-day to cure me of last night's disease, which I thought strange but I think find it true.[2] Then home with my workmen all the afternoon, at night into the garden to play on my flageolette, it being moonshine, where I staid a good while, and so home and to bed. This day I hear that the Dutch have sent the King a great present of money, which we think will stop the match with Portugal; and judge this to be the reason that our so great haste in sending the two ships to the East Indys is also stayed.

[4th]. To my workmen, then to my Lord's, and there dined with Mr. Shepley. After dinner I went in to my Lord and there we had a great deal of musique, and then came my cozen Tom Pepys and there did accept of the security which we gave him for his £1,000 that we borrow of him, and so the money to be paid next week. Then to the Privy Seal, and so with Mr. Moore to my father's, where some friends did sup there and we with them and late went home, leaving my wife still there. So to bed.

---

[1] "The Night Walker, or the Little Thief," a comedy by John Fletcher, acted at court in 1633.

[2] The proverb, "A hair of the dog that bit you," which probably had originally a literal meaning, has long been used to inculcate the advice of the two Sir Williams.

[5th]. Up among my workmen and so to the office, and then to Sir W. Pen's with the other Sir William and Sir John Lawson to dinner, and after that, with them to Mr. Lucy's, a merchant, where much good company, and there drank a great deal of wine, and in discourse fell to talk of the weight of people, which did occasion some wagers, and where, among others, I won half a piece to be spent. Then home, and at night to Sir W. Batten's, and there very merry with a good barrell of oysters, and this is the present life I lead. Home and to bed.

[6th]. Up among my workmen, then to Whitehall, and there at Privy Seal and elsewhere did business, and among other things met with Mr. Townsend, who told of his mistake the other day, to put both his legs through one of his knees of his breeches, and went so all day. Then with Mr. Creed and Moore to the Leg in the Palace to dinner which I gave them, and after dinner I saw the girl of the house, being very pretty, go into a chamber, and I went in after her and kissed her. Then by water, Creed and I, to Salisbury Court and there saw "Love's Quarrell"[1] acted the first time, but I do not like the design or words. So calling at my father's, where they and my wife well, and so home and to bed.

[7th] (Lord's day). All the morning at home making up my accounts (God forgive me!) to give up to my Lord this afternoon. Then about 11 o'clock out of doors towards Westminster and put in at Paul's, where I saw our minister, Mr. Mills, preaching before my Lord Mayor. So to White Hall, and there I met with Dr. Fuller of Twickenham, newly come from Ireland; and took him to my Lord's, where he and I dined; and he did give my Lord and me a good account of the condition of Ireland, and how it come to pass, through the joyning of the Fanatiques and the Presbyterians, that the latter and the former are in their declaration put together under the names of Fanatiques. After dinner, my Lord and I and Mr. Shepley did look over our accounts and settle matters of money between us; and my Lord did tell me much of his mind about getting money and other things of his family, &c. Then to my father's, where I found Mr. Hunt and his wife at

---

[1] The play is not known otherwise than by this notice.

supper with my father and mother and my wife, where after supper I left them and so home, and then I went to Sir W. Batten's and resolved of a journey to-morrow to Chatham, and so home and to bed.

[8th]. Up early, my Lady Batten knocking at her door that comes into one of my chambers. I did give directions to my people and workmen, and so about 8 o'clock we took barge at the Tower, Sir William Batten and his lady, Mrs. Turner, Mr. Fowler and I. A very pleasant passage and so to Gravesend, where we dined, and from thence a coach took them and me, and Mr. Fowler with some others came from Rochester to meet us, on horseback. At Rochester, where alight at Mr. Alcock's and there drank and had good sport, with his bringing out so many sorts of cheese. Then to the Hill-house at Chatham,[1] where I never was before, and I found a pretty pleasant house and am pleased with the arms that hang up there. Here we supped very merry, and late to bed; Sir William telling me that old Edgeborrow,[2] his predecessor, did die and walk in my chamber, did make me somewhat afeard, but not so much as for mirth's sake I did seem. So to bed in the treasurer's chamber.

[9th]. And lay and slept well till 3 in the morning, and then waking, and by the light of the moon I saw my pillow (which overnight I flung from me) stand upright, but not bethinking myself what it might be, I was a little afeard, but sleep overcame all and so lay till high morning, at which time I had a candle brought me and a good fire made, and in general it was a great pleasure all the time I staid here to see how I am respected and honoured by all people; and I find that I begin to know now how to receive so much reverence, which at the beginning I could not

---

[1] A plan, with front and side elevations, of the Hill-house as it was in 1698, is in King's MS. 43. The ground on which it stood is now included in the Marine Barracks. In the "Memoirs of English Affairs, chiefly Naval, from the year 1660 to 1673, written by James, Duke of York," there is a letter from James to the principal officers of the Navy (dated May 10th, 1661), in which he recommends that the lease of the Hill-house should be bought by them if it can be obtained at a reasonable rate, as the said house "is very convenient for the service of his Majesty's Navy."

[2] Kenrick Edisbury, Surveyor of the Navy, 1632-38.

tell how to do. Sir William and I by coach to the dock and there viewed all the storehouses and the old goods that are this day to be sold, which was great pleasure to me, and so back again by coach home, where we had a good dinner, and among other strangers that come, there was Mr. Hempson and his wife, a pretty woman, and speaks Latin; Mr. Allen and two daughters of his, both very tall and the youngest very handsome,[1] so much as I could not forbear to love her exceedingly, having, among other things, the best hand that ever I saw. After dinner, we went to fit books and things (Tom Hater being this morning come to us) for the sale, by an inch of candle, and very good sport we and the ladies that stood by had, to see the people bid. Among other things sold there was all the State's arms,[2] which Sir W. Batten bought; intending to set up some of the images in his garden, and the rest to burn on the Coronacion night. The sale being done, the ladies and I and Captain Pett[3] and Mr. Castle took barge and down we went to see the Sovereign, which we did, taking great pleasure therein, singing all the way, and, among other pleasures, I put my Lady, Mrs. Turner, Mrs. Hempson, and the two Mrs. Allens into the lanthorn and I went in and kissed them, demanding it as a fee due to a principall officer, with all which we were exceeding merry, and drunk some bottles of wine and neat's tongue, &c. Then back again home and so supped, and after much mirth to bed.

[10th]. In the morning to see the Dockhouses. First, Mr. Pett's, the builder, and there was very kindly received, and among other things he did offer my Lady Batten a parrot, the best I ever saw, that knew Mingo[4] so soon as it saw him, having been bred formerly in the house with them; but for talking and singing I never heard the like. My Lady did accept of it. Then to see Commis-

---

[1] Rebecca, who afterwards married Lieutenant Jowles. See Diary, April 1st, 1667. Her father, formerly Clerk of the Rope Yard at Chatham, is sometimes referred to as Mr. and sometimes as Captain Allen. Under the latter title he may be confused with Captain (afterwards Sir Thomas) Allen.

[2] *i.e.*, coats of arms.

[3] Captain Phineas Pett, when in command of the "Tiger" frigate, was killed in action with a Zealand privateer. This may be the same man.

[4] Sir William Batten's black servant.

sioner Pett's house, he and his family being absent, and here I
wondered how my Lady Batten walked up and down with
envious looks to see how neat and rich everything is (and indeed
both the house and garden is most handsome), saying that she
would get it, for it belonged formerly to the Surveyor of the
Navy. Then on board the Prince,[1] now in the dock, and indeed it
has one and no more rich cabins for carved work, but no gold in
her. After that back home, and there eat a little dinner. Then to
Rochester, and there saw the Cathedrall, which is now fitting for
use, and the organ then a-tuning. Then away thence, observing
the great doors of the church, which, they say, was covered with
the skins of the Danes,[2] and also had much mirth at a tomb, on
which was "Come sweet Jesu," and I read "Come sweet Mall,"
&c., at which Captain Pett and I had good laughter. So to the
Salutacion tavern, where Mr. Alcock and many of the town came
and entertained us with wine and oysters and other things, and
hither come Sir John Minnes[3] to us, who is come to-day to see

---

[1] The "Prince" (originally the "Resolution") was a first-rate of eighty guns,
built at Woolwich in 1641 by Capt. Phineas Pett, sen. It ran aground on the
Galloper Sands, and was burnt by the Dutch, 1666. See *post*, June 7th, 1666.

[2] Traditions similar to that at Rochester, here alluded to, are to be found in
other places in England. Sir Harry Englefield, in a communication made to
the Society of Antiquaries, July 2nd, 1789, called attention to the curious
popular tale preserved in the village of Hadstock, Essex, that the door of the
church had been covered with the skin of a Danish pirate, who had plundered
the church. At Worcester, likewise, it was asserted that the north doors of the
cathedral had been covered with the skin of a person who had sacrilegiously
robbed the high altar. The date of these doors appears to be the latter part of
the fourteenth century, the north porch having been built about 1385. Dart,
in his "History of the Abbey Church of St. Peter's, Westminster," 1723 (vol.
i., book ii., p. 64), relates a like tradition then preserved in reference to a door,
one of three which closed off a chamber from the south transept—namely, a
certain building once known as the Chapel of Henry VIII., and used as a
"Revestry." This chamber, he states, "is inclosed with three doors, the inner
cancellated, the middle, which is very thick, lined with skins like parchment,
and driven full of nails. These skins, they by tradition tell us, were some skins
of the Danes, tann'd and given here as a memorial of our delivery from them."
Portions of this supposed human skin were examined under the microscope
by the late Mr. John Quekett of the Hunterian Museum, who ascertained, beyond question, that in each of the cases the skin was human.—*From a communication by the late Mr. Albert Way, F.S.A., to the late Lord Braybrooke.*

[3] John Minnes (Mennes or Mennis), son of Andrew Minnes of Sandwich, born
in that town March 1st, 1598, and educated at Corpus Christi College, Oxford,

"the Henery," in which he intends to ride as Vice-Admiral in the narrow seas all this summer. Here much mirth, but I was a little troubled to stay too long, because of going to Hempson's, which afterwards we did, and found it in all things a most pretty house, and rarely furnished, only it had a most ill access on all sides to

it, which is a greatest fault that I think can be in a house. Here we had, for my sake, two fiddles, the one a base viall, on which he that played, played well some lyra lessons, but both together made the worst musique that ever I heard. We had a fine col-

became afterwards a great traveller and noted seaman. He was knighted by Charles I. at Dover in 1641, and in 1642 he was captain of the "Rainbow." When the Earl of Warwick was nominated by the Parliament Lord High Admiral he refused to act under him. After the Restoration he was appointed Governor of Dover Castle, and his warrant from the Duke of York to act as Vice-Admiral and Commander-in-Chief in the Narrow Seas was dated May 18th, 1661. He was Comptroller of the Navy from 1661 till his death in 1671. He is buried in the Church of St. Olave, Hart Street, where, in the south aisle, part of a monument to his memory is still to be seen. Wood describes him as an honest and stout man, generous and religious, well skilled in physic and chemistry. He was part-author of "Musarum Deliciæ."

lacion, but I took little pleasure in that, for the illness of the musique and for the intentness of my mind upon Mrs. Rebecca Allen. After we had done eating, the ladies went to dance, and among the men we had, I was forced to dance too; and did make an ugly shift. Mrs. R. Allen danced very well, and seems the best humoured woman that ever I saw. About 9 o'clock Sir William and my Lady went home, and we continued dancing an hour or two, and so broke up very pleasant and merry, and so walked home, I leading Mrs. Rebecca, who seemed, I know not why, in that and other things, to be desirous of my favours and would in all things show me respects. Going home, she would needs have me sing, and I did pretty well and was highly esteemed by them. So to Captain Allen's (where we were last night, and heard him play on the harpsicon, and I find him to be a perfect good musician), and there, having no mind to leave Mrs. Rebecca, what with talk and singing (her father and I), Mrs. Turner and I staid there till 2 o'clock in the morning and was most exceeding merry, and I had the opportunity of kissing Mrs. Rebecca very often. Among other things Captain Pett was saying that he thought that he had got his wife with child since I came thither. Which I took hold of and was merrily asking him what he would take to have it said for my honour that it was of my getting? He merrily answered that he would if I would promise to be godfather to it if it did come within the time just, and I said that I would. So that I must remember to compute it when the time comes.

[11th]. At 2 o'clock, with very great mirth, we went to our lodging and to bed, and lay till 7, and then called up by Sir W. Batten, so I arose and we did some business, and then came Captn. Allen, and he and I withdrew and sang a song or two, and among others took pleasure in "Goe and bee hanged, that's good-bye." The young ladies come too, and so I did again please myself with Mrs. Rebecca, and about 9 o'clock, after we had breakfasted, we sett forth for London, and indeed I was a little troubled to part with Mrs. Rebecca, for which God forgive me. Thus we went away through Rochester, calling and taking leave of Mr. Alcock at the door, Captn. Cuttance going with us. We baited at Dartford, and thence to London, but of all the journeys that ever I made this

was the merriest, and I was in a strange mood for mirth. Among other things, I got my Lady to let her maid, Mrs. Anne, to ride all the way on horseback, and she rides exceeding well; and so I called her my clerk, that she went to wait upon me. I met two little schoolboys going with pitchers of ale to their schoolmaster to break up against Easter, and I did drink of some of one of them and give him two pence. By and by we come to two little girls keeping cows, and I saw one of them very pretty, so I had a mind to make her ask my blessing, and telling her that I was her godfather, she asked me innocently whether I was not Ned Wooding, and I said that I was, so she kneeled down and very simply called, "Pray, godfather, pray to God to bless me," which made us very merry, and I gave her twopence. In several places, I asked women whether they would sell me their children, but they denied me all, but said they would give me one to keep for them, if I would. Mrs. Anne and I rode under the man that hangs upon Shooter's Hill,[1] and a filthy sight it was to see how his flesh is shrunk to his bones. So home and I found all well, and a deal of work done since I went. I sent to see how my wife do, who is well, and my brother John come from Cambridge. To Sir W. Batten's and there supped, and very merry with the young ladies. So to bed very sleepy for last nights' work, concluding that it is the pleasantest journey in all respects that ever I had in my life.

[12th]. Up among my workmen, and about 7 o'clock comes my wife to see me and my brother John with her, who I am glad to see, but I sent them away because of going to the office, and there dined with Sir W. Batten, all fish dinner, it being Good Friday. Then home and looking over my workmen, and then into the City and saw in what forwardness all things are for the Coronacion, which will be very magnificent. Then back again home and to my chamber, to set down in my diary all my late journey, which I do with great pleasure; and while I am now writing comes one with a tickett, to invite me to Captain Robert Blake's buriall, for whose death I am very sorry, and do much wonder

---

[1] Shooter's Hill, Kent, between the eighth and ninth milestones on the Dover road. It was long a notorious haunt of highwaymen. The custom was to leave the bodies of criminals hanging until the bones fell to the ground.

at it, he being a little while since a very likely man to live as any I knew. Since my going out of town, there is one Alexander Rosse taken and sent to the Counter by Sir Thomas Allen, for counterfeiting my hand to a ticket, and we this day at the office have given order to Mr. Smith to prosecute him. To bed.

[13th]. To Whitehall by water from Towre-wharf, where we could not pass the ordinary way, because they were mending of the great stone steps against the Coronacion. With Sir W. Pen, then to my Lord's, and thence with Capt. Cuttance and Capt. Clark to drink our morning draught together, and before we could get back again my Lord was gone out. So to Whitehall again and met with my Lord above with the Duke; and after a little talk with him, I went to the Banquet-house, and there saw the King heal, the first time that ever I saw him do it; which he did with great gravity, and it seemed to me to be an ugly office and a simple one. That done to my Lord's and dined there, and so by water with parson Turner[1] towards London, and upon my telling of him of Mr. Moore to be a fit man to do his business with Bishop Wren,[2] about which he was going, he went back out of my boat into another to Whitehall, and so I forwards home and there by and by took coach with Sir W. Pen and Captain Terne and went to the buriall of Captain Robert Blake, at Wapping, and there had each of us a ring, but it being dirty, we would not go to church with them, but with our coach we returned home, and there staid a little, and then he and I alone to the Dolphin (Sir W. Batten being this day gone with his wife to Walthamstow to keep Easter), and there had a supper by ourselves, we both being very hungry, and staying there late drinking I became very sleepy, and so we went home and I to bed.

[14th] (Easter. Lord's day). In the morning towards my father's, and by the way heard Mr. Jacomb,[3] at Ludgate, upon these words,

---

[1] Rev. John Turner, rector of Eynesbury.

[2] Matthew Wren, Bishop of Hereford, 1634-35; Bishop of Norwich, 1635-38; Bishop of Ely, 1638-67. He died April 24th, 1667, aged eighty-one.

[3] Thomas Jacomb, of Burton Lazers, Leicestershire, entered at Magdalen Hall, Oxford, in 1640; but removing to Cambridge on the breaking out of the Rebellion, he obtained a Fellowship at Trinity College, in the place of a royal-

"Christ loved you and therefore let us love one another," and
made a lazy sermon, like a Presbyterian. Then to my father's
and dined there, and Dr. Fairbrother (lately come to town) with
us. After dinner I went to the Temple and there heard Dr. Griffith,[1] a good sermon for the day; so with Mr. Moore (whom I met
there) to my Lord's, and there he shewed me a copy of my Lord
Chancellor's patent for Earl, and I read the preamble, which is
very short, modest, and good. Here my Lord saw us and spoke to
me about getting Mr. Moore to come and govern his house while
he goes to sea, which I promised him to do and did afterwards
speak to Mr. Moore, and he is willing. Then hearing that Mr.
Barnwell[2] was come, with some of my Lord's little children, yesterday to town, to see the Coronacion, I went and found them at
the Goat, at Charing Cross, and there I went and drank with
them a good while, whom I found in very good health and very
merry. Then to my father's, and after supper seemed willing to
go home, and my wife seeming to be so too I went away in a discontent, but she, poor wretch, followed me as far in the rain and
the dark as Fleet Bridge to fetch me back again, and so I did, and
lay with her to-night, which I have not done these eight or ten
days before.

[15th]. From my father's, it being a very foul morning for the
King and Lords to go to Windsor, I went to the office and there
met Mr. Coventry and Sir Robt. Slingsby, but did no business,
but only appoint to go to Deptford together to-morrow. Mr. Coventry being gone, and I having at home laid up £200 which I
had brought this morning home from Alderman Blackwell's, I
went home by coach with Sir R. Slingsby and dined with him,

---

ist ejected, and had the degree of M.A. conferred on him. He afterwards became rector of St. Martin's-infra-Ludgate, in London; and was put out for
nonconformity in 1662, being then D.D. He subsequently followed the trade
of conventicling, which brought him into trouble; and he died March 27th,
1687, in the house of the Countess of Exeter, to whom he was domestic chap-
lain. Abridged from Kennett's "Register."—B.

[1] Matthew Griffith, D.D., rector of St. Mary Magdalene, Old Fish Street, and
preacher at the Temple. He was an Episcopalian, and author of several printed
sermons. He died in 1665.—B.

[2] Robert Barnwell, who died in June, 1662.

and had a very good dinner. His lady[1] seems a good woman and very desirous they were to hear this noon by the post how the election has gone at Newcastle,[2] wherein he is concerned, but the letters are not come yet. To my uncle Wight's, and after a little stay with them he and I to Mr. Rawlinson's, and there staid all the afternoon, it being very foul, and had a little talk with him what good I might make of these ships that go to Portugal by venturing some money by them, and he will give me an answer to it shortly. So home and sent for the Barber, and after that to bed.

[16th]. So soon as word was brought me that Mr. Coventry was come with the barge to the Towre, I went to him, and found him reading of the Psalms in short hand (which he is now busy about), and had good sport about the long marks that are made there for sentences in divinity, which he is never like to make use of. Here he and I sat till the Comptroller came and then we put off for Deptford, where we went on board the King's pleasure boat that Commissioner Pett is making, and indeed it will be a most pretty thing. From thence to Commr. Pett's lodging, and there had a good breakfast, and in came the two Sir Wms. from Walthamstow, and so we sat down and did a great deal of public business about the fitting of the fleet that is now going out. That done we went to the Globe and there had a good dinner, and by and by took barge again and so home. By the way they would have me sing, which I did to Mr. Coventry, who went up to Sir William Batten's, and there we staid and talked a good while, and then broke up and I home, and then to my father's and there lay with my wife.

[17th]. By land and saw the arches,[3] which are now almost done

---

[1] Elizabeth, daughter of Sir Edward Radclyffe, of Dilston, Northumberland, and widow of Sir William Fenwick, Bart., of Meldon. Sir R. Slingsby's first wife was Elizabeth, daughter and heir of Robert Brooke, of Newcells.—B.

[2] Sir Francis Anderson and Sir John Morley were elected for Newcastle-on-Tyne, April 10th, 1661.

[3] Four triumphal arches were raised in the City in honour of the Coronation. The first was at the Lime Street end of Leadenhall Street, where Rebellion and Monarchy were personated. The second near the Royal Exchange, where one representing the River Thames made an address. The third, representing

and are very fine, and I saw the picture of the ships and other
things this morning, set up before the East Indy House,[1] which
are well done. So to the office, and that being done I went to dinner with Sir W. Batten, and then home to my workmen, and saw
them go on with great content to me. Then comes Mr. Allen of
Chatham, and I took him to the Mitre and there did drink with
him, and did get of him the song that pleased me so well there the
other day, "Of Shitten come Shites the beginning of love." His
daughters are to come to town to-morrow, but I know not whether
I shall see them or no. That done I went to the Dolphin by appointment and there I met Sir Wms. both and Mr. Castle, and
did eat a barrel of oysters and two lobsters, which I did give them,
and were very merry. Here we had great talk of Mr. Warren's
being knighted by the King, and Sir W. B. seemed to be very
much incensed against him. So home.

[18th]. Up with my workmen and then about 9 o'clock took
horse with both the Sir Williams for Walthamstow, and there we
found my Lady and her daughters all; and a pleasant day it was,
and all things else, but that my Lady was in a bad mood, which
we were troubled at, and had she been noble she would not have
been so with her servants, when we came thither, and this Sir W.
Pen took notice of, as well as I. After dinner we all went to the
Church stile,[2] and there eat and drank, and I was as merry as I
could counterfeit myself to be. Then, it raining hard, we left Sir
W. Batten, and we two returned and called at Mr. ——, and
drank some brave wine there, and then homewards again and in
our way met with two country fellows upon one horse, which I
did, without much ado, give the way to, but Sir W. Pen would

the Temple of Concord, was placed on the side of Cheapside Cross. The fourth
arch, representing Plenty, stood in Fleet Street, near Whitefriars.

[1] The old East India House in Leadenhall Street, which existed from 1648 to
1726, had figures of ships and dolphins on the upper part of the front.

[2] "Church stile" is in long hand, and not in cipher. In an old book of accounts
belonging to Warrington Parish, the following minute occurs: "Nov. 5, 1688.
Payd for drink at the *Church-Steele*, 13s."; and in 1732, "it is ordered that
hereafter no money be spent on yᵉ 5th of November, or any other *state* day,
on the parish account, either at the *Church-Stile*, or at any other place."—*Gent.
Mag.*, November, 1852, p. 442.—B.

not, but struck them and they him, and so passed away, but they giving him some high words, he went back again and struck them off their horse, in a simple fury, and without much honour, in my mind, and so came away. Home, and I sat with him a good while talking, and then home and to bed.

[19th]. Among my workmen and then to the office, and after that dined with Sir W. Batten, and then home, where Sir W. Warren came, and I took him and Mr. Shepley and Moore with me to the Mitre, and there I cleared with Warren for the deals I bought lately for my Lord of him, and he went away, and we staid afterwards a good while and talked, and so parted, it being so foul that I could not go to Whitehall to see the Knights of the Bath[1] made to-day, which do trouble me mightily. So home, and having staid awhile till Will came in (with whom I was vexed for staying abroad), he comes and then I went by water to my father's, and then after supper to bed with my wife.

[20th]. Here comes my boy to tell me that the Duke of York had sent for all the principall officers, &c., to come to him to-day. So I went by water to Mr. Coventry's, and there staid and talked a good while with him till all the rest come. We went up and saw the Duke dress himself, and in his night habitt he is a very plain man. Then he sent us to his closett, where we saw among other things two very fine chests, covered with gold and Indian varnish, given him by the East Indy Company of Holland. The Duke comes; and after he had told us that the fleet was designed for Algier (which was kept from us till now), we did advise about many things as to the fitting of the fleet, and so went away. And from thence to the Privy Seal, where little to do, and after that took Mr. Creed and Moore and gave them their morning draught, and after that to my Lord's, where Sir W. Pen came to me, and dined with my Lord. After dinner he and others that dined there went away, and then my Lord looked upon his pages' and foot-men's liverys, which are come home to-day, and will be hand-some, though not gaudy. Then with my Lady and my Lady Wright to White Hall; and in the Banqueting-house saw the King

---

[1] A large number of Knights of the Bath were made at the Coronation. A list is given in Haydn's "Book of Dignities," by Ockerby, 1890, p. 763.

create my Lord Chancellor and several others, Earls,[1] and Mr. Crew and several others, Barons:[2] the first being led up by Heralds and five old Earls to the King, and there the patent is read, and the King puts on his vest, and sword, and coronet, and gives him the patent. And then he kisseth the King's hand, and rises and stands covered before the king. And the same for the Barons, only he is led up but by three of the old Barons, and are girt with swords before they go to the King. That being done (which was very pleasant to see their habits), I carried my Lady back, and I found my Lord angry, for that his page had let my Lord's new beaver be changed for an old hat; then I went away, and with Mr. Creed to the Exchange and bought some things, as gloves and bandstrings, &c. So back to the Cockpitt,[3] and there, by the favour of one Mr. Bowman, he and I got in, and there saw the King and Duke of York and his Duchess (which is a plain woman, and like her mother, my Lady Chancellor). And so saw "The Humersome Lieutenant"[4] acted before the King, but not very well done. But my pleasure was great to see the manner of it, and so many great beauties, but above all Mrs. Palmer, with whom the King do discover a great deal of familiarity. So Mr. Creed and I (the play being done) went to Mrs. Harper's, and there sat and drank, it being about twelve at night. The ways being now so dirty, and stopped up with the rayles which are this day set up in the streets, I would not go home, but went with him to his lodging at Mr. Ware's, and there lay all night.

---

[1] Edward Hyde (Lord Hyde), Viscount Cornbury, and Earl of Clarendon; Arthur (Lord Capel), Viscount Malden, and Earl of Essex; Thomas (Lord Brudenell), Earl of Cardigan; Charles Howard, Lord Dacre, Viscount Howard of Morpeth, and Earl of Carlisle; Sir Arthur Annesley (Viscount Valentia), Lord Annesley, and Earl of Anglesea; Sir John Granville, Viscount Granville of Lansdowne, and Earl of Bath.

[2] John Crew, Baron Crew of Stene; Denzil Holles, Baron Holles of Ifield; Sir Frederic Cornwallis, Bart., Baron Cornwallis of Eye; Sir Horace Townshend, Bart., Baron Townshend of King's Lynn (merged in the Marquisate); Sir Anthony Ashley Cooper, Bart., Baron Ashley of Wimborne St. Giles (merged in the Earldom of Shaftesbury); Sir George Booth, Bart., Baron Delamere of Dunham Massey.

[3] The Cockpit at Whitehall, the residence of the Duke of Albemarle.

[4] "The Humorous Lieutenant," a tragi-comedy, by Beaumont and Fletcher. Published in the folio of 1647.

[21st] (Lord's day). In the morning we were troubled to hear it rain as it did, because of the great show to-morrow. After I was ready I walked to my father's and there found the late maid to be gone and another come by my mother's choice, which my father do not like, and so great difference there will be between my father and mother about it. Here dined Doctor Thos. Pepys and Dr. Fayrebrother; and all our talk about to-morrow's show, and our trouble that it is like to be a wet day. After dinner comes in my coz. Snow and his wife, and I think stay there till the show be over. Then I went home, and all the way is so thronged with people to see the triumphal arches, that I could hardly pass for them. So home, people being at church, and I got home unseen, and so up to my chamber and saw done these last five or six days' diarys. My mind a little troubled about my workmen, which, being foreigners,[1] are like to be troubled by a couple of lazy rogues that worked with me the other day, that are citizens, and so my work will be hindered, but I must prevent it if I can.

22d. KING'S GOING FROM Y TOWER TO WHITE HALL.[2]

Up early and made myself as fine as I could, and put on my velvet coat, the first day that I put it on, though made half a year ago. And being ready, Sir W. Batten, my Lady, and his two daughters and his son and wife, and Sir W. Pen and his son and I, went to Mr. Young's, the flag-maker, in Corne-hill;[3] and there we had a good room to ourselves, with wine and good cake, and saw the show very well. In which it is impossible to relate the glory of this day, expressed in the clothes of them that rid, and their horses and horses-clothes, among others, my Lord Sandwich's. Embroidery and diamonds were ordinary among them. The Knights of the Bath was a brave sight of itself; and their

---

[1] Foreigners were workmen dwelling outside the city.

[2] The king in the early morning of the 22nd went from Whitehall to the Tower by water, so that he might proceed from thence through the City to Westminster Abbey, there to be crowned.

[3] The members of the Navy Office appear to have chosen Mr. Young's house on account of its nearness to the second triumphal arch, situated near the Royal Exchange, which was dedicated to the Navy.

Esquires, among which Mr. Armiger was an Esquire to one of the Knights. Remarquable were the two men that represent the two Dukes of Normandy and Aquitane.[1] The Bishops come next after Barons, which is the higher place; which makes me think that the next Parliament they will be called to the House of Lords. My Lord Monk rode bare after the King, and led in his hand a spare horse, as being Master of the Horse. The King, in a most rich embroidered suit and cloak, looked most noble. Wadlow,[2] the vintner, at the Devil,[3] in Fleet-street, did lead a fine company of soldiers, all young comely men, in white doublets. There followed the Vice-Chamberlain, Sir G. Carteret, a company of men all like Turks;[4] but I know not yet what they are for. The streets all gravelled, and the houses hung with carpets before them, made brave show, and the ladies out of the windows, one of which over against us I took much notice of, and spoke of her, which made good sport among us. So glorious was the show

---

[1] John Carie and Sir Francis Lawley, two gentlemen of the Privy Chamber, represented the Dukes of Normandy and Aquitaine.

[2] Simon Wadlow was the original of "old Sir Simon the king," the favourite air of Squire Western in "Tom Jones."

> "Hang up all the poor hop-drinkers,
> Cries old Sim, the king of skinkers."
> Ben Jonson, *Verses over the door into the Apollo.*

The Simon Wadlow alluded to by Ben Jonson died March 30th, 1627. The Ashmolean Museum Catalogue mentions "Eight verses upon Simon Wadloe, Vintner, dwelling att ye sign of ye Devill and St. Dunstan," commencing "Apollo et cohors musarum." The Wadlow of Pepys was John, apparently the son of Simon. (See "Boyne's Trade Tokens," ed. Williamson, vol. 1., 1889, p. 766.)

[3] We do not see any reason for discrediting the statement that the whole of the Devil Tavern was pulled down in 1787, and of its having been purchased by Messrs. Child and Co. for the sum of £2,800, and in the year following the row of houses now known as Child's Place was built upon the site. It may be worth recording that excellent cellars also run beneath the open space in front of those houses, as they were in all probability the cellars in which Simon Wadlow (the landlord at the sign of "St. Dunstan pulling the Devil by the nose," commonly known as the "Old Devil") kept his celebrated wines. The great room was called the Apollo. Here Jonson lorded it with greater authority than Dryden did afterwards at Will's, or Addison at Button's. Taken from Price's ye *Marigold.*—M. B.

[4] This company is represented in the curious contemporary picture by Stoop, at Goodrich Court, Herefordshire.—B.

with gold and silver, that we were not able to look at it, our eyes at last being so much overcome with it. Both the King and the Duke of York took notice of us, as he saw us at the window. The show being ended, Mr. Young did give us a dinner, at which we were very merry, and pleased above imagination at what we have seen. Sir W. Batten going home, he and I called and drunk some mum[1] and laid our wager about my Lady Faulconbridge's name,[2] which he says not to be Mary, and so I won above 20s. So home, where Will and the boy staid and saw the show upon Towre Hill, and Jane at T. Pepys's, The. Turner, and my wife at Charles Glassecocke's, in Fleet Street. In the evening by water to White Hall to my Lord's, and there I spoke with my Lord. He talked with me about his suit, which was made in France, and cost him £200, and very rich it is with embroidery. I lay with Mr. Shepley, and

CORONACION DAY.

[23d]. About 4 I rose and got to the Abbey, where I followed Sir J. Denham,[3] the Surveyor, with some company that he was leading in. And with much ado, by the favour of Mr. Cooper, his man, did get up into a great scaffold across the North end of the Abbey, where with a great deal of patience I sat from past 4 till 11 before the King came in. And a great pleasure it was to see the Abbey raised in the middle, all covered with red, and a throne

---

[1] Mum. Ale brewed with wheat at Brunswick.

> "Sedulous and stout
> With bowls of fattening *mum*."
> J. Phillips, *Cyder*, vol. ii. p. 231.

As soon as the beer begins to work, they put into it the inner rind of fir, tops of fir and birch, betony, marjory, pennyroyal, wild thyme, &c. Our English brewers use cardamum, ginger, and sassafras, instead of the inner rind of fir, and add also walnut rinds, madder, red sanders, and elecampane.—M. B.

[2] Mary, third daughter of Oliver Cromwell, and second wife of Thomas Bellasis, second Viscount Fauconberg, created Earl of Fauconberg, April 9th, 1689.

[3] Born at Dublin in 1615, created K.B. at the Coronation, and appointed Surveyor-General of all the King's buildings; better known as the author of "Cooper's Hill." Died March, 1668-69, and was buried in Westminster Abbey.

(that is a chair)[1] and footstool on the top of it; and all the officers of all kinds, so much as the very fidlers, in red vests. At last comes in the Dean[2] and Prebends of Westminster, with the Bishops (many of them in cloth of gold copes), and after them the Nobility, all in their Parliament robes, which was a most magnificent sight. Then the Duke, and the King with a scepter[3] (carried by my Lord Sandwich) and sword and mond[4] before him, and the crown too. The King in his robes, bare-headed, which was very fine. And after all had placed themselves, there was a sermon and the service; and then in the Quire at the high altar, the King passed through all the ceremonies of the Coronacion, which to my great grief I and most in the Abbey could not see. The crown being put upon his head, a great shout begun, and he came forth to the throne, and there passed more ceremonies: as taking the oath, and having things read to him by the Bishop;[5] and his lords (who put on their caps as soon as the King put on his crown[6]) and bishops come, and kneeled before him. And three times the King at Arms[7] went to the three open places on the scaffold,[8] and proclaimed, that if any one could show any reason why Charles Stewart should not be King of England, that now he should come and speak. And a Generall Pardon also was read by the Lord Chancellor, and meddalls flung up and down by my

---

[1] The Coronation chair in Westminster Abbey is an object of the greatest interest. Beneath the seat is the "Stone of Destiny," carried off from Scone by Edward I. in 1296.

[2] John Earle, D.D., see *ante*, May 24th, 1660.

[3] A long sceptre or staff of gold, with a cross at the top, and a pike at the foot of steel, called St. Edward's staff. There were two other sceptres.

[4] Mond or orb of gold, with a cross set with precious stones, carried by the Duke of Buckingham.

[5] Gilbert Sheldon, Bishop of London, acting for Juxon, Archbishop of Canterbury, whose age and infirmities prevented him from performing the whole of the service. Sheldon succeeded Juxon in the archbishopric when the latter died in 1663.

[6] As yet barons had no coronet. A grant of that outward mark of dignity was made to them by Charles soon after his coronation. Queen Elizabeth had assigned coronets to viscounts.—B.

[7] Sir Edward Walker, Garter King of Arms, who wrote an account of the Coronation, which was published from his MS. in 1820.

[8] The south, west, and north sides.—B.

Lord Cornwallis,[1] of silver, but I could not come by any. But so
great a noise that I could make but little of the musique; and indeed, it was lost to every body. But I had so great a lust to . . .
that I went out a little while before the King had done all his
ceremonies, and went round the Abbey to Westminster Hall, all
the way within rayles, and 10,000 people, with the ground covered with blue cloth; and scaffolds all the way. Into the Hall I
got, where it was very fine with hangings and scaffolds one upon
another full of brave ladies; and my wife in one little one, on the
right hand. Here I staid walking up and down, and at last upon
one of the side stalls I stood and saw the King come in with all the
persons (but the soldiers) that were yesterday in the cavalcade;
and a most pleasant sight it was to see them in their several robes.
And the King came in with his crown on, and his sceptre in his
hand, under a canopy borne up by six silver staves, carried by
Barons of the Cinque Ports,[2] and little bells at every end. And
after a long time, he got up to the farther end, and all set themselves down at their several tables; and that was also a brave
sight: and the King's first course carried up by the Knights of
the Bath. And many fine ceremonies there was of the Heralds
leading up people before him, and bowing; and my Lord of
Albemarle's going to the kitchin and eat a bit of the first dish
that was to go to the King's table. But, above all, was these
three Lords, Northumberland[3] and Suffolk,[4] and the Duke of Or-

---

[1] Sir Frederick Cornwallis, Baronet, had been created a baron three days before the coronation. He was Treasurer of His Majesty's Household, and a
Privy Councillor. He had married Elizabeth, daughter of John Ashburnham.
His wife, therefore, and her brother John Ashburnham, were first cousins to
Villiers, Duke of Buckingham. Rugge states in July, 1660, that "the King
supped with Sir Frederick Cornwallis at Durham Yard, in the Strand." He
died in January, 1661-62, and was buried with his ancestors at Brome, on the
18th. See *post*, January 16th, 1661-62. Collins and other writers erroneously
state his death to have occurred on the 31st. The medals which he received as
his fee (nearly one hundred in number) were carefully preserved in the family, and have been arranged, so as to form the setting of a large silver cup, at
Audley End.—B.

[2] Pepys was himself one of the Barons of the Cinque Ports at the Coronation
of James II.

[3] Algernon Percy, tenth Earl of Northumberland, acting as Lord High Con-
stable of England on this occasion.—B.

[4] James Howard, third Earl of Suffolk, acting as Earl Marshal of England.—B.

mond,[1] coming before the courses on horseback, and staying so all dinner-time, and at last to bring up [Dymock][2] the King's Champion, all in armour on horseback, with his spear and targett carried before him. And a Herald[3] proclaims "That if any dare deny Charles Stewart to be lawful King of England, here was a Champion that would fight with him;"[4] and with these words, the Champion flings down his gauntlet, and all this he do three times in his going towards the King's table. At last when he is come, the King drinks to him, and then sends him the cup which is of gold, and he drinks it off, and then rides back again with the cup in his hand. I went from table to table to see the Bishops and all others at their dinner, and was infinitely pleased with it. And at the Lords' table, I met with William Howe, and he spoke to my Lord for me, and he did give me four rabbits and a pullet, and so I got it and Mr. Creed and I got Mr. Michell to give us some bread, and so we at a stall eat it, as every body else did what they could get. I took a great deal of pleasure to go up and down, and look upon the ladies, and to hear the musique of all sorts, but above all, the 24 violins.[5] About six at night they had dined, and I went up to my wife, and there met with a pretty lady (Mrs. Frankleyn, a

[1] James Butler, first Duke of Ormonde, Lord High Steward of England and bearer of the crown.

[2] Sir Edward Dymock, as Lord of the Manor of Scrivelsby, co. Lincoln. This service was last performed by one of that family at the coronation of George IV., and with the coronation dinner has since been dispensed with.—B.

[3] York Herald, George Owen, who, it will be seen, rescued the canopy from the *valetaille*.—B.

[4] The terms of the Champion's challenge were as follows: "If any person of what degree soever, high or low, shall deny or gainsay our Soveraigne Lord King Charles the Second, King of England, Scotland, France and Ireland, defender of the faith, Sonne and next heire to our Soveraigne Lord Charles the First, the last King deceased, to be right heire to the Imperiall Crowne of this Realme of England, or that hee ought not to enjoy the same; here is his champion, who sayth that he lyeth and is a false Traytor, being ready in person to combate with him, and in this quarrell will venture his life against him, on what day soever hee shall be appointed."

[5] See some congratulatory lines, "On the Thunder happening after the Solemnity of the Coronation of Charles II.," by Henry Bold, of New College, Oxford, in the "Somers Tracts," ed. 1817, vol. vii. p. 514. They commence thus:—

"Heavens! we thank you that you thundered so!
As we did here, you cannonado'd too."

Doctor's wife, a friend of Mr. Bowyer's), and kissed them both, and by and by took them down to Mr. Bowyer's. And strange it is to think, that these two days have held up fair till now that all is done, and the King gone out of the Hall; and then it fell a-raining and thundering and lightening as I have not seen it do for some years:[1] which people did take great notice of; God's blessing of the work of these two days, which is a foolery to take too much notice of such things. I observed little disorder in all this, but only the King's footmen had got hold of the canopy, and would keep it from the Barons of the Cinque Ports,[2] which they endeavoured to force from them again, but could not do it till my Lord Duke of Albemarle caused it to be put into Sir R. Pye's[3] hand till

---

[1] Baxter, in his "Life," mentions this storm. "On April 23, was His Majesty's coronation-day, the day being very serene and fair, till suddenly in the afternoon, as they were returning from Westminster Hall, there was very terrible thunders when none expected it, which made me remember his father's coronation, on which, being a boy at school, and having leave to play for the solemnity, an earthquake, about two o'clock in the afternoon did affright the boys, and all the neighbourhood. I intend no commentary on these, but only to relate the matter of fact."—B.

[2] Bishop Kennett gives a somewhat fuller account of this unseemly broil: "No sooner had the aforesaid Barons brought up the King to the foot of the stairs in Westminster Hall, ascending to his throne, and turned on the left hand (towards their own table) out of the way, but the King's footmen most insolently and violently seized upon the canopy, which the Barons endeavouring to keep and defend, were by their number and strength dragged down to the lower end of the Hall, nevertheless still keeping their hold; and had not Mr. Owen, York Herald, being accidentally near the Hall door, and seeing the contest, caused the same to be shut, the footmen had certainly carried it away by force. But in the interim also (speedy notice hereof having been given the King) one of the Querries were sent from him, with command to imprison the footmen, and dismiss them out of his service, which put an end to the present disturbance. These footmen were also commanded to make their submission to the Court of Claims, which was accordingly done by them the 30th April following, and the canopy then delivered back to the said Barons." Whilst this disturbance happened, the upper end of the first table, which had been appointed for the Barons of the Cinque Ports, was taken up by the Bishops, Judges, &c., probably nothing loth to take precedence of them; and the poor Barons, naturally unwilling to lose their dinner, were necessitated to eat it at the bottom of the second table, below the Masters of Chancery and others of the long robe.—B.

[3] Sir Robert Pye, Bart., of Faringdon House, Berks; married Anne, daughter of the celebrated John Hampden. They lived together sixty years, and died in 1701, within a few weeks of each other.

to-morrow to be decided. At Mr. Bowyer's; a great deal of company, some I knew, others I did not. Here we staid upon the leads and below till it was late, expecting to see the fire-works, but they were not performed to-night: only the City had a light like a glory round about it with bonfires. At last I went to King-street, and there sent Crockford to my father's and my house, to tell them I could not come home to-night, because of the dirt, and a coach could not be had. And so after drinking a pot of ale alone· at Mrs. Harper's I returned to Mr. Bowyer's, and after a little stay more I took my wife and Mrs. Frankleyn (who I proffered the civility of lying with my wife at Mrs. Hunt's to-night) to Axe-yard, in which at the further end there were three great bonfires, and a great many great gallants, men and women; and they laid hold of us, and would have us drink the King's health upon our knees, kneeling upon a faggot, which we all did, they drinking to us one after another. Which we thought a strange frolique; but these gallants continued thus a great while, and I wondered to see how the ladies did tipple. At last I sent my wife and her bedfellow to bed, and Mr. Hunt and I went in with Mr. Thornbury (who did give the company all their wine, he being yeoman of the wine-cellar to the King) to his house; and there, with his wife and two of his sisters, and some gallant sparks that were there, we drank the King's health, and nothing else, till one of the gentlemen fell down stark drunk, and there lay spewing; and I went to my Lord's pretty well. But no sooner a-bed with Mr. Shepley but my head began to hum, and I to vomit, and if ever I was foxed it was now, which I cannot say yet, because I fell asleep and slept till morning. Only when I waked I found myself wet with my spewing. Thus did the day end with joy every where; and blessed be God, I have not heard of any mischance to any body through it all, but only to Serj^t. Glynne,[1] whose horse fell upon him yesterday, and is like to kill him, which people do please themselves to see how just God is to punish the rogue at

---

[1] John Glynne (born 1602) had been Recorder of London (1643); and during the Protectorate, Chief Justice of the Upper Bench (1655); nevertheless, he acted with considerable adroitness at the time of the Restoration, and was in consequence knighted and appointed King's Serjeant, and his son created a baronet. He died November 15th, 1666.

such a time as this; he being now one of the King's Serjeants, and rode in the cavalcade with Maynard,[1] to whom people wish the same fortune. There was also this night in King-street, [a woman] had her eye put out by a boy's flinging a firebrand into the coach. Now, after all this, I can say that, besides the pleasure of the sight of these glorious things, I may now shut my eyes against any other objects, nor for the future trouble myself to see things of state and show, as being sure never to see the like again in this world.

[24th]. Waked in the morning with my head in a sad taking through the last night's drink, which I am very sorry for; so rose and went out with Mr. Creed to drink our morning draft, which he did give me in chocolate[2] to settle my stomach. And after that I to my wife, who lay with Mrs. Frankelyn at the next door to Mrs. Hunt's, and they were ready, and so I took them up in a coach, and carried the ladies to Paul's, and there set her down, and so my wife and I home, and I to the office. That being done my wife and I went to dinner to Sir W. Batten, and all our talk about the happy conclusion of these last solemnities. After dinner home, and advised with my wife about ordering things in my house, and then she went away to my father's to lie, and I staid with my workmen, who do please me very well with their work.

[1] John Maynard, the eminent lawyer; M.P. for Totnes, 1640; made Serjeant to Cromwell in 1653, and afterwards King's Serjeant by Charles II., who knighted him. In 1661 he was chosen burgess for Berealston, and sat in every Parliament till the Revolution, for that borough, or Plymouth. It was he who made one of the most famous of legal jokes. William III., in allusion to his age, having said that he must have outlived most of the judges and lawyers of his own standing, Maynard answered, "And I had like to have outlived the law itself if your Highness had not come over." In March, 1689, he was appointed one of the Commissioners of the Great Seal; and, soon resigning from infirmity, died October 9th, 1690, aged eighty-eight. The popular feeling respecting Glynne and Maynard was echoed by Butler, who wrote:—

"Did not the learned Glynne and Maynard
To make good subjects traitors strain hard?"

[2] Chocolate was introduced into England about the year 1652. In the "Publick Advertiser" of Tuesday, June 16-22, 1657, we find the following: "In Bishopsgate Street in Queen's Head Alley, at a Frenchman's house, is an excellent West India drink called *chocolate*, to be sold, where you may have it ready at any time, and also unmade at reasonable rates."—M. B.

At night, set myself to write down these three days' diary, and while I am about it, I hear the noise of the chambers,[1] and other things of the fire-works, which are now playing upon the Thames before the King; and I wish myself with them, being sorry not to see them. So to bed.

[25th]. All the morning with my workmen with great pleasure to see them near coming to an end. At noon Mr. Moore and I went to an Ordinary at the King's Head in Towre Street,[2] and there had a dirty dinner. Afterwards home and having done some business with him, in comes Mr. Sheply and Pierce the surgeon, and they and I to the Mitre and there staid a while and drank, and so home and after a little reading to bed.

[26th]. At the office all the morning, and at noon dined by myself at home on a piece of meat from the cook's, and so at home all the afternoon with my workmen, and at night to bed, having some thoughts to order my business so as to go to Portsmouth the next week with Sir Robert Slingsby.

[27th]. In the morning to my Lord's, and there dined with my Lady, and after dinner with Mr. Creed and Captain Ferrers to the Theatre to see "The Chances,"[3] and after that to the Cock alehouse,[4] where we had a harp and viallin played to us, and so home by coach to Sir W. Batten's, who seems so inquisitive when my house will be made an end of that I am troubled to go thither. So home with some trouble in my mind about it.

[28th] (Lord's day). In the morning to my father's, where I dined, and in the afternoon to their church, where come Mrs. Turner and Mrs. Edward Pepys,[5] and several other ladies, and so

---

[1] A chamber is a small piece of ordnance.

[2] There are several tokens of the King's Head in Tower Street. One of these of Thomas Mills, is dated 1666, see "Boyne's Trade Tokens," ed. Williamson, vol. i., 1889, p. 778.

[3] "The Chances," a comedy by Beaumont and Fletcher, published in the folio of 1647. Revived at this time.

[4] At Temple Bar. See *ante*, March 7th, 1659-60 (note).

[5] Elizabeth Walpole of Broomsthorpe, married to Edward Pepys, who died December 22nd, 1663. She died in 1669.

I went out of the pew into another. And after sermon home with them, and there staid a while and talked with them and was sent for to my father's, where my cozen Angier and his wife, of Cambridge, to whom I went, and was glad to see them, and sent for wine for them, and they supped with my father. After supper my father told me of an odd passage the other night in bed between my mother and him, and she would not let him come to bed to her out of jealousy of him and an ugly wench that lived there lately, the most ill-favoured slut that ever I saw in my life, which I was ashamed to hear that my mother should be become such a fool, and my father bid me to take notice of it to my mother, and to make peace between him and her. All which do trouble me very much. So to bed to my wife.

[29th]. Up and with my father towards my house, and by the way met with Lieut. Lambert, and with him to the Dolphin in Tower Street and drank our morning draught, he being much troubled about his being offered a fourth rate ship to be Lieutenant of her now he has been two years Lieutenant in a first rate. So to the office, where it is determined that I should go to-morrow to Portsmouth. So I went out of the office to Whitehall presently, and there spoke with Sir W. Pen and Sir George Carteret and had their advice as to my going, and so back again home, where I directed Mr. Hater what to do in order to our going to-morrow, and so back again by coach to Whitehall and there eat something in the buttery at my Lord's with John Goods and Ned Osgood. And so home again, and gave order to my workmen what to do in my absence. At night to Sir W. Batten's, and by his and Sir W. Pen's persuasion I sent for my wife from my father's, who came to us to Mrs. Turner's, where we were all at a collacion to-night till twelve o'clock, there being a gentlewoman there that did play well and sang well to the Harpsicon, and very merry we were. So home and to bed, where my wife had not lain a great while.

[30th]. This morning, after order given to my workmen, my wife and I and Mr. Creed took coach, and in Fish-street took up Mr. Hater and his wife, who through her mask seemed at first to be an old woman, but afterwards I found her to be a very pretty

modest black woman. We got a small bait at Leatherhead, and so
to Godlyman,[1] where we lay all night, and were very merry, having this day no other extraordinary rencontre, but my hat falling
off my head at Newington into the water, by which it was spoiled,
and I ashamed of it. I am sorry that I am not at London, to be
at Hide-parke to-morrow, among the great gallants and ladies,
which will be very fine.[2]

[May 1st]. Up early, and bated at Petersfield, in the room which
the King lay in lately at his being there. Here very merry, and
played us and our wives at bowls. Then we set forth again, and
so to Portsmouth, seeming to me to be a very pleasant and strong
place; and we lay at the Red Lyon, where Haselrigge and Scott
and Walton did hold their councill, when they were here, against
Lambert and the Committee of Safety. Several officers of the
Yard came to see us to-night, and merry we were, but troubled to
have no better lodgings.

[2nd].Up, and Mr. Creed and I to walk round the town upon the
walls. Then to our inn, and there all the officers of the Yard to see
me with great respect, and I walked with them to the Dock and
saw all the stores, and much pleased with the sight of the place.
Back and brought them all to dinner with me, and treated them
handsomely; and so after dinner by water to the Yard, and there
we made the sale of the old provisions. Then we and our wives
all to see the Montagu,[3] which is a fine ship, and so to the town
again by water, and then to see the room where the Duke of
Buckingham[4] was killed by Felton. So to our lodging, and to sup-

---

[1] Godalming, Surrey. It has been supposed that Godliman Street in London
obtained its name from the sale of leather prepared at Godalming.

[2] It was an established custom for all classes to go a-maying in Hyde Park.
The practice was for a time discontinued during the Commonwealth, but
about 1654 it was revived, to the disgust of the Puritans.

[3] The "Montagu" (formerly the "Lime") was a third-rate of fifty-two guns,
built at Portsmouth in 1654 by Mr. Tippetts.

[4] The house wherein the murder was committed in August, 1628, is situated
at the upper end of the High Street, at Portsmouth, and a portion still remains. A representation of the front of the house is given in Brayley's "Graph-
ic Illustrator," p. 240.—B.

84

per and to bed. To-night came Mr. Stevens to town to help us to pay off the Fox.

[3rd]. Early to walk with Mr. Creed up and down the town, and it was in his and some others' thoughts to have got me made free of the town, but the Mayor, it seems, unwilling, and so they could not do it. Then to the payhouse, and there paid off the ship, and so to a short dinner, and then took coach, leaving Mrs. Hater there to stay with her husband's friends, and we to Petersfield, having nothing more of trouble in all my journey, but the exceeding unmannerly and most epicure-like palate of Mr. Creed. Here my wife and I lay in the room the Queen lately lay at her going into France.

[4th]. Up in the morning and took coach, and so to Gilford, where we lay at the Red Lyon, the best Inn,[1] and lay in the room the King lately lay in, where we had time to see the Hospital, built by Archbishop Abbott, and the free school,[2] and were civilly treated by the Mayster. So to supper, and to bed, being very merry about our discourse with the Drawers concerning the minister of the Town, with a red face and a girdle. So to bed, where we lay and sleep well.

[5th] (Lord's day). Mr. Creed and I went to the red-faced Parson's church, and heard a good sermon of him, better than I looked for. Then home, and had a good dinner, and after dinner fell in some talk in Divinity with Mr. Stevens that kept us till it was past Church time. Anon we walked into the garden, and there played the fool a great while, trying who of Mr. Creed or I could go best over the edge of an old fountain well, and I won a quart of sack of him. Then to supper in the banquet house, and there my wife and I did talk high, she against and I for Mrs. Pierce (that she was a beauty), till we were both angry. Then to walk in the fields, and so to our quarters, and to bed.

---

[1] A Red Lion still exists in High Street, at the corner of Market Street, but it is no longer the best inn in the town.

[2] Archbishop Abbot's Hospital, on the north side of the High Street, Guildford, was founded in 1619. The Grammar School, at the upper end of High Street, dates from the reign of Henry VIII.

[6th]. Up by four o'clock and took coach. Mr. Creed rode, and left us that we know not whither he went. We went on, thinking to be at home before the officers rose, but finding we could not we staid by the way and eat some cakes, and so home, where I was much troubled to see no more work done in my absence than there was, but it could not be helped. I sent my wife to my father's, and I went and sat till late with my Lady Batten, both the Sir Williams being gone this day to pay off some ships at Deptford. So home and to bed without seeing of them. I hear to-night that the Duke of York's son[1] is this day dead, which I believe will please every body; and I hear that the Duke and his Lady themselves are not much troubled at it.

[7th]. In the morning to Mr. Coventry, Sir G. Carteret, and my Lord's to give them an account of my return. My Lady, I find, is, since my going, gone to the Wardrobe. Then with Mr. Creed into London, to several places about his and my business, being much stopped in our way by the City trayne-bands, who go in much solemnity and pomp this day to muster before the King and the Duke, and shops in the City are shut up every where all this day. He carried me to an ordinary by the Old Exchange, where we come a little too late, but we had very good cheer for our 18d. a-piece, and an excellent droll too, my host, and his wife so fine a woman, and sung and played so well that I staid a great while and drunk a great deal of wine. Then home and staid among my workmen all day, and took order for things for the finishing of their work, and so at night to Sir W. Batten's, and there supped and so home and to bed, having sent my Lord a letter to-night to excuse myself for not going with him to-morrow to the Hope, whither he is to go to see in what condition the fleet is in.

[8th]. This morning came my brother John to take his leave of me, he being to return to Cambridge to-morrow, and after I had chid him for going with my Will the other day to Deptford with the principal officers, I did give him some good counsell and 20s. in money, and so he went away. All this day I staid at home with my workmen without eating anything, and took much pleasure

---

[1] Charles Stuart, Duke of Cambridge, born October 22nd, 1660, died May 5th, 1661. He was the first of eight children by Anne Hyde.—B.

to see my work go forward. At night comes my wife not well from my father's, having had a fore-tooth drawn out to-day, which do trouble me, and the more because I am now in the greatest of all my dirt. My Will also returned to-night pretty well, he being gone yesterday not very well to his father's. To-day I received a letter from my uncle, to beg an old fiddle of me for my Cozen Perkin,[1] the miller, whose mill the wind hath lately broke down, and now he hath nothing to live by but fiddling, and he must needs have it against Whitsuntide to play to the country girls; but it vexed me to see how my uncle writes to me, as if he were not able to buy him one. But I intend to-morrow to send him one. At night I set down my journal of my late journey to this time, and so to bed. My wife not being well and I very angry with her for her coming hither in that condition.

[9th]. With my workmen all the morning, my wife being ill and in great pain with her old pain, which troubled me much because that my house is in this condition of dirt. In the afternoon I went to Whitehall and there spoke with my Lord at his lodgings, and there being with him my Lord Chamberlain, I spoke for my old waterman Payne, to get into White's place, who was waterman to my Lord Chamberlain, and is now to go master of the barge to my Lord to sea, and my Lord Chamberlain[2] did promise that Payne should be entertained in White's place with him. From thence to Sir G. Carteret, and there did get his promise for the payment of the remainder of the bill of Mr. Creed's, wherein of late I have been so much concerned, which did so much rejoice me that I meeting with Mr. Childe took him to the Swan Tavern in King Street,[3] and there did give him a tankard of white wine and sugar,[4] and so I went by water home and set myself to get

---

[1] Frank Perkin. Jane, youngest sister of Pepys's father, married J. Perkin.

[2] Edward, second Earl of Manchester, appointed to this office on June 1st, 1660.

[3]
      "Whatever the Swans may have done in the City,
        The Swan here in King Street has sung her last Ditty,"
from "The Search after Claret, or a Visitation of the Vintners," a poem in two cantos, printed for E. Hawkins, London, February 24th, 1691.

[4] The popular taste was formerly for sweet wines, and sugar was frequently mixed with the wine.

my Lord's accounts made up, which was till nine at night before I could finish, and then I walked to the Wardrobe, being the first time I was there since my Lady came thither, who I found all alone, and so she shewed me all the lodgings as they are now fitted, and they seem pretty pleasant. By and by comes in my Lord, and so, after looking over my accounts, I returned home, being a dirty and dark walk. So to bed.

[10th]. At the office all the morning, and the afternoon among my workmen with great pleasure, because being near an end of their work. This afternoon came Mr. Blackburn and Creed to see me, and I took them to the Dolphin, and there drank a great deal of Rhenish wine with them and so home, having some talk with Mr. Blackburn about his kinsman my Will, and he did give me good satisfaction in that it is his desire that his kinsman should do me all service, and that he would give him the best counsel he could to make him good. Which I begin of late to fear that he will not because of the bad company that I find that he do begin to take. This afternoon Mr. Hater received for me the £225 due upon Mr. Creed's bill in which I am concerned so much, which do make me very glad. At night to Sir W. Batten and sat a while. So to bed.

[11th]. This morning I went by water with Payne (Mr. Moore being with me) to my Lord Chamberlain at Whitehall, and there spoke with my Lord, and he did accept of Payne for his water-man, as I had lately endeavoured to get him to be. After that Mr. Cooling did give Payne an order to be entertained, and so I left him and Mr. Moore, and I went to Graye's Inne, and there to a barber's, where I was trimmed, and had my haire cut, in which I am lately become a little curious, finding that the length of it do become me very much. So, calling at my father's, I went home, and there staid and saw my workmen follow their work, which this night is brought to a very good condition. This afternoon Mr. Shepley, Moore, and Creed came to me all about their several ac-counts with me, and we did something with them all, and so they went away. This evening Mr. Hater brought my last quarter's salary, of which I was very glad, because I have lost my first bill

for it, and so this morning was forced to get another signed by three of my fellow officers for it. All this evening till late setting my accounts and papers in order, and so to bed.

[12th]. My wife had a very troublesome night this night and in great pain, but about the morning her swelling broke, and she was in great ease presently as she useth to be. So I put in a vent (which Dr. Williams sent me yesterday) into the hole to keep it open till all the matter be come out, and so I question not that she will soon be well again. I staid at home all this morning, being the Lord's day, making up my private accounts and setting papers in order. At noon went with my Lady Montagu at the Wardrobe, but I found it so late that I came back again, and so dined with my wife in her chamber. After dinner I went awhile to my chamber to set my papers right. Then I walked forth towards Westminster and at the Savoy heard Dr. Fuller preach upon David's words, "I will wait with patience all the days of my appointed time until my change comes;"[1] but methought it was a poor dry sermon. And I am afeard my former high esteem of his preaching was more out of opinion than judgment. From thence homewards, but met with Mr. Creed, with whom I went and walked in Grayes-Inn-walks, and from thence to Islington, and there eat and drank at the house my father and we were wont of old to go to;[2] and after that walked homeward, and parted in Smithfield: and so I home, much wondering to see how things are altered with Mr. Creed, who, twelve months ago, might have been got to hang himself almost as soon as go to a drinking-house on a Sunday.

[13th]. All the morning at home among my workmen. At noon Mr. Creed and I went to the ordinary behind the Exchange, where we lately were, but I do not like it so well as I did. So home with him and to the office, where we sat late, and he did deliver his accounts to us. The office being done I went home and took pleasure to see my work draw to an end.

---

[1] The text meant is Job xiv. 14, "All the days of my appointed time will I wait till my change come."—B.

[2] The King's Head, see March 27th, 1664.—B.

[14th]. Up early and by water to Whitehall to my Lord, and there had much talk with him about getting some money for him. He told me of his intention to get the Muster Master's place for Mr. Pierce, the purser, who he has a mind to carry to sea with him, and spoke very slightingly of Mr. Creed, as that he had no opinion at all of him, but only he was forced to make use of him because of his present accounts. Thence to drink with Mr. Shepley and Mr. Pinkny, and so home and among my workmen all day. In the evening Mr. Shepley came to me for some money, and so he and I to the Mitre, and there we had good wine and a gammon of bacon. My uncle Wight, Mr. Talbot, and others were with us, and we were pretty merry. So at night home and to bed. Finding my head grow weak now-a-days if I come to drink wine, and therefore hope that I shall leave it off of myself, which I pray God I could do.

[15th]. With my workmen all day till the afternoon, and then to the office, where Mr. Creed's accounts were passed. Home and found all my joyner's work now done, but only a small job or two, which please me very well. This afternoon there came two men with an order from a Committee of Lords to demand some books of me out of the office, in order to the examining of Mr. Hutchinson's accounts,[1] but I give them a surly answer, and they went away to complain, which put me into some trouble with myself, but I resolve to go to-morrow myself to these Lords and answer them. To bed, being in great fear because of the shavings which lay all up and down the house and cellar, for fear of fire.

[16th]. Up early to see whether the work of my house be quite done, and I found it to my mind. Staid at home all the morning, and about 2 o'clock went in my velvet coat by water to the Savoy, and there, having staid a good while, I was called into the Lords, and there, quite contrary to my expectations, they did treat me very civilly, telling me that what they had done was out of zeal to the King's service, and that they would joyne with the governors of the chest with all their hearts, since they knew that

---

[1] Richard Hutchinson, Treasurer for the Navy from 1651. He was succeeded by Sir George Carteret in 1660.

there was any, which they did not before. I give them very respectful answer and so went away to the Theatre, and there saw the latter end of "The Mayd's Tragedy,"[1] which I never saw before, and methinks it is too sad and melancholy. Thence homewards, and meeting Mr. Creed I took him by water to the Wardrobe with me, and there we found my Lord newly gone away with the Duke of Ormond and some others, whom he had had to the collacion; and so we, with the rest of the servants in the hall, sat down and eat of the best cold meats that ever I eat on in all my life. From thence I went home (Mr. Moore with me to the waterside, telling me how kindly he is used by my Lord and my Lady since his coming hither as a servant), and to bed.

[17th]. All the morning at home. At noon Lieutenant Lambert came to me, and he and I to the Exchange, and thence to an ordinary over against it, where to our dinner we had a fellow play well upon the bagpipes and whistle like a bird exceeding well, and I had a fancy to learn to whistle as he do, and did promise to come some other day and give him an angell to teach me. To the office, and sat there all the afternoon till 9 at night. So home to my musique, and my wife and I sat singing in my chamber a good while together, and then to bed.

[18th]. Towards Westminster, from the Towre, by water, and was fain to stand upon one of the piers about the bridge,[2] before the men could drag their boat through the lock, and which they could not do till another was called to help them. Being through bridge I found the Thames full of boats and gallys, and upon inquiry found that there was a wager to be run this morning. So spying of Payne in a gally, I went into him, and there staid, thinking to have gone to Chelsy with them. But upon the start, the wager boats fell foul one of another, till at last one of them gives over, pretending foul play, and so the other row away alone, and all our sport lost. So I went ashore at Westminster; and to the Hall I went, where it was very pleasant to see the Hall in the

---

[1] By Beaumont and Fletcher. Acted at court in 1613. After the Restoration, Mohun played Melantius; Hart, Amintor; and Mrs. Marshall, Evadne.

[2] The dangers of shooting the bridge were so great that a popular proverb has it—"London bridge was made for wise men to go over and fools to go under."

condition it is now, with the Judges on the benches at the further end of it,[1] which I had not seen all this term till now. Thence with Mr. Spicer, Creed, and some others to drink. And so away homewards by water with Mr. Creed, whom I left in London going

THE TOWER OF LONDON

about business, and I home, where I staid all the afternoon, and in the garden reading "Faber Fortunæ" with great pleasure. So home to bed.

[19th] (Lord's day). I walked in the morning towards Westminster, and, seeing many people at York House,[2] I went down

---

[1] The Courts of Chancery and King's Bench were long held at the upper end of the hall. It is related that Sir Thomas More every day, before presiding in his own Court of Chancery, knelt for the blessing of his aged father, who was a judge of the King's Bench.

[2] York House belonged to the See of York, but appears to have been let to the Lord Keepers of the Great Seal, and Chancellors Egerton and Bacon resided there. It was obtained by James I. in 1624, after which it was granted to Villiers, Duke of Buckingham. The second duke obtained the house again by his marriage to the daughter of Lord Fairfax. He sold it in 1672, when it was pulled down, and streets built on the site which still bear his names.

and found them at mass, it being the Spanish ambassadors;[1] and so I got into one of the gallerys, and there heard two masses done, I think, not in so much state as I have seen them heretofore. After that into the garden, and walked a turn or two, but found it not so fine a place as I always took it for by the outside. Thence to my Lord's and there spake with him about business, and then he went to Whitehall to dinner, and Capt. Ferrers and Mr. Howe and myself to Mr. Wilkinson's at the Crown,[2] and though he had no meat of his own, yet we happened to find our cook Mr. Robinson there, who had a dinner for himself and some friends, and so he did give us a very fine dinner. Then to my Lord's, where we went and sat talking and laughing in the drawing-room a great while. All our talk about their going to sea this voyage, which Capt. Ferrers is in some doubt whether he shall go or no, but swears that he would go, if he were sure never to come back again; and I, giving him some hopes, he grew so mad with joy that he fell a-dancing and leaping like a madman. Now it fell out so that the balcone windows were open, and he went to the rayle and made an offer to leap over, and asked what if he should leap over there. I told him I would give him £40 if he did not go to sea. With that thought I shut the doors, and W. Howe hindered him all we could; yet he opened them again, and, with a vault, leaps down into the garden:—the greatest and most desperate frolic that ever I saw in my life. I run to see what was become of him, and we found him crawled upon his knees, but could not rise; so we went down into the garden and dragged him to the bench, where he looked like a dead man, but could not stir; and, though he had broke nothing, yet his pain in his back was such as he could not endure. With this, my Lord (who was in the little new room) come to us in amaze, and bid us carry him up, which, by our strength, we did, and so laid him in East's bed, by the door; where he lay in great pain. We sent for a doctor and chyrurgeon, but none to be found, till by-and-by by chance comes in Dr.

---

[1] The Baron de Batteville, or Vatteville, who is said to have concealed much observant quickness and an intriguing spirit under a plain, rough, soldierlike frankness of demeanour. He was very active in opposition to the proposed marriage of Charles II. with the Infanta of Portugal.

[2] The Crown in King Street, Westminster.

Clerke, who is afeard of him.[1] So we sent to get a lodging for him, and I went up to my Lord, where Captain Cooke, Mr. Gibbons,[2] and others of the King's musicians were come to present my Lord with some songs and symphonys, which were performed very finely. Which being done I took leave and supped at my father's, where was my cozen Beck come lately out of the country. I am troubled to see my father so much decay of a suddain, as he do both in his seeing and hearing, and as much to hear of him how my brother Tom do grow disrespectful to him and my mother. I took leave and went home, where to prayers (which I have not had in my house a good while), and so to bed.

[20th]. At home all the morning; paid £50 to one Mr. Grant for Mr. Barlow, for the last half year, and was visited by Mr. Anderson, my former chamber fellow at Cambridge, with whom I parted at the Hague, but I did not go forth with him, only gave him a morning draft at home. At noon Mr. Creed came to me, and he and I to the Exchange, and so to an ordinary to dinner, and after dinner to the Mitre, and there sat drinking while it rained very much. Then to the office, where I found Sir Williams both, choosing of masters for the new fleet of ships that is ordered to be set forth, and Pen seeming to be in an ugly humour, not willing to gratify one that I mentioned to be put in, did vex me. We sat late, and so home. Mr. Moore came to me when I was going to bed, and sat with me a good while talking about my Lord's business and our own and so good night.

[21st]. Up early, and, with Sir R. Slingsby (and Major Waters the deaf gentleman, his friend, for company's sake) to the Victualling-office[3] (the first time that I ever knew where it was), and there staid while he read a commission for enquiry into some

---

[1] Captain Ferrers recovered.

[2] Christopher Gibbons, Mus. Doct. Oxon. (1664), second son of the more celebrated Dr. Orlando Gibbons (who died in 1625). Born 1615. He was appointed organist to Westminster Abbey, 1660, and composed several anthems. He died October 20th, 1676, and is buried in the cloisters of the Abbey.

[3] The Victualling Office was spoken of as on Tower Hill, but it was really at the end of East Smithfield, and occupied the site of East Minster, the Cistercian Abbey of St. Mary Graces. The Cooperage, a portion of the Victualling Office, was burnt May 18th, 1688.

of the King's lands and houses thereabouts, that are given his brother. And then we took boat to Woolwich, where we staid and gave order for the fitting out of some more ships presently. And then to Deptford, where we staid and did the same; and so took barge again, and were overtaken by the King in his barge, he having been down the river with his yacht this day for pleasure to try it; and, as I hear, Commissioner Pett's do prove better than the Dutch one, and that that his brother built. While we were upon the water, one of the greatest showers of rain fell that ever I saw. The Comptroller and I landed with our barge at the Temple, and from thence I went to my father's, and there did give order about some clothes to be made, and did buy a new hat, cost between 20 and 30 shillings, at Mr. Holden's. So home.

[22nd]. To Westminster, and there missed of my Lord, and so about noon I and W. Howe by water to the Wardrobe, where my Lord and all the officers of the Wardrobe dined, and several other friends of my Lord, at a venison pasty. Before dinner, my Lady Wright and my Lady Jem. sang songs to the harpsicon. Very pleasant and merry at dinner. And then I went away by water to the office, and there staid till it was late. At night before I went to bed the barber came to trim me and wash me, and so to bed, in order to my being clean to-morrow.

[23rd]. This day I went to my Lord, and about many other things at Whitehall, and there made even my accounts with Mr. Shepley at my Lord's, and then with him and Mr. Moore and John Bowles to the Rhenish wine house,[1] and there came Jonas Moore,[2] the mathematician, to us, and there he did by discourse make us fully believe that England and France were once the same continent, by very good arguments, and spoke very many things, not so much to prove the Scripture false as that the time therein is not well computed nor understood. From thence home by water, and there shifted myself into my black silk suit (the first day I have put it on this year), and so to my Lord Mayor's by coach, with a great deal of honourable company, and great entertain-

[1] See *ante*, February 3rd, 1659-60 (note).
[2] See *ante*, December 6th, 1660 (note).

ment. At table I had very good discourse with Mr. Ashmole, wherein he did assure me that frogs and many insects do often fall from the sky, ready formed. Dr. Bates's[1] singularity in not rising up nor drinking the King's nor other healths at the table was very much observed. From thence we all took coach, and to our office, and there sat till it was late; and so I home and to bed by day-light. This day was kept a holy-day through the town; and it pleased me to see the little boys walk up and down in procession with their broom-staffs in their hands, as I had myself long ago gone.[2]

[24th]. At home all the morning making up my private accounts, and this is the first time that I do find myself to be clearly worth £500 in money, besides all my goods in my house, &c. In the afternoon at the office late, and then I went to the Wardrobe, where I found my Lord at supper, and therefore I walked a good while till he had done, and I went in to him, and there he looked over my accounts. And they were committed to Mr. Moore to see me paid what remained due to me. Then down to the kitchen to eat a bit of bread and butter, which I did, and there I took one of the maids by the chin, thinking her to be Susan, but it proved to be her sister, who is very like her. From thence home.

[25th]. All the morning at home about business. At noon to the Temple, where I staid and looked over a book or two at Playford's, and then to the Theatre, where I saw a piece of "The Silent

---

[1] Dr. William Bates, one of the most eminent of the Puritan divines, and who took part in the Savoy Conference. His collected writings were published in 1700, and fill a large folio volume. The Dissenters called him silver-tongued Bates. Calamy affirmed that if Bates would have conformed to the Established Church he might have been raised to any bishopric in the kingdom. He died in 1699, aged seventy-four.

[2] Pepys here refers to the perambulation of parishes on Holy Thursday, still observed. This ceremony was sometimes enlivened by whipping the boys, for the better impressing on their minds the remembrance of the day, and the boundaries of the parish, instead of beating houses or stones. But this would not have harmonized well with the excellent Hooker's practice on this day, when he "always dropped some loving and *facetious* observations, to be remembered against the next year, especially by the boys and young people." Amongst Dorsetshire customs, it seems that, in perambulating a manor or parish, a boy is tossed into a stream, if that be the boundary; if a hedge, a sapling from it is applied for the purpose of flagellation.—B.

Woman,"[1] which pleased me. So homewards, and in my way bought "The Bondman"[2] in Paul's Churchyard, and so home, where I found all clean, and the hearth and range, as it is now enlarged, set up, which pleases me very much.

[26th] (Lord's day). Lay long in bed. To church and heard a good sermon at our own church, where I have not been a great many weeks. Dined with my wife alone at home pleasing myself in that my house do begin to look as if at last it would be in good order. This day the Parliament received the communion of Dr. Gunning at St. Margaret's, Westminster. In the afternoon both the Sir Williams came to church, where we had a dull stranger. After church home, and so to the Mitre, where I found Dr. Burnett,[3] the first time that ever I met him to drink with him, and my uncle Wight and there we sat and drank a great deal, and so I to Sir W. Batten's, where I have on purpose made myself a great stranger, only to get a high opinion a little more of myself in them. Here I heard how Mrs. Browne, Sir W. Batten's sister, is brought to bed, and I to be one of the godfathers, which I could not nor did deny. Which, however, did trouble me very much to be at charge to no purpose, so that I could not sleep hardly all night, but in the morning I bethought myself, and I think it is very well I should do it. Sir W. Batten told me how Mr. Prin (among the two or three that did refuse to-day to receive the sacrament upon their knees) was offered by a mistake the drink afterwards, which he did receive, being denied the drink by Dr. Gunning, unless he would take it on his knees; and after that by another the bread was brought him, and he did take it sitting, which is thought very preposterous. Home and to bed.

[27th]. To the Wardrobe, and from thence with my Lords Sandwich and Hinchinbroke to the Lords' House by boat at Westminster, and there I left them. Then to the lobby, and after waiting for Sir G. Downing's coming out, to speak with him about the

[1] Ben Jonson's "Epicene."

[2] Massinger's play was published in 1624.

[3] Alexander Burnett, M.D., who resided in Fenchurch Street, was Pepys's regular medical attendant. He died of the plague, see *post*, August 25th, 1665.

giving me up of my bond for my honesty when I was his clerk,
but to no purpose, I went to Clerke's at the Legg,[1] and there I
found both Mr. Pierces, Mr. Rolt, formerly too great a man to
meet upon such even terms, and there we dined very merry,
there coming to us Captain Ferrers, this being the first day of his
going abroad since his leap a week ago, which I was greatly glad
to see. By water to the office, and there sat late, Sir George Carteret
coming in, who among other things did inquire into the naming
of the maisters for this fleet, and was very angry that they were
named as they are, and above all to see the maister of the Adven-
ture (for whom there is some kind of difference between Sir W.
Pen and me) turned out, who has been in her list. The office done,
I went with the Comptroller to the Coffee house, and there we discoursed of this, and I seem to be fond of him, and indeed I find
I must carry fair with all as far as I see it safe, but I have got of
him leave to have a little room from his lodgings to my house, of
which I am very glad, besides I do open him a way to get lodgings
himself in the office, of which I should be very glad. Home and
to bed.

[28th]. This morning to the Wardrobe, and thence to a little alehouse hard by, to drink with John Bowles, who is now going to
Hinchinbroke this day. Thence with Mr. Shepley to the Exchange about business, and there, by Mr. Rawlinson's favour, got
into a balcone over against the Exchange; and there saw the
hangman burn, by vote of Parliament, two old acts, the one for
constituting us a Commonwealth, and the other[2] I have forgot.
Which still do make me think of the greatness of this late turn,
and what people will do to-morrow against what they all, through
profit or fear, did promise and practise this day. Then to the
Mitre with Mr. Shepley, and there dined with D. Rawlinson and
some friends of his very well. So home, and then to Cheapside
about buying a piece of plate to give away to-morrow to Mrs.

---

[1] The Leg tavern in King Street, Westminster. See *ante*, March 2nd, 1659-60
(note).

[2] It was an act for subscribing the Engagement. On the same day there had
been burned by the hangman, in Westminster Hall, the act for "erecting an
High Court of Justice for trying and judging Charles Stuart." Two more
acts were similarly burned the next day.—B.

Browne's child. So to the Star in Cheapside, where I left Mr.
Moore telling £5 out for me, who I found in a great strait for my
coming back again, and so he went his way at my coming. Then
home, where Mr. Cook I met and he paid me 30s., an old debt of
his to me. So to Sir W. Pen's, and there sat alone with him till ten
at night in talk with great content, he telling me things and persons that I did not understand in the late times, and so I home
to bed. My cozen John Holcroft[1] (whom I have not seen many
years) this morning came to see me.

[29th] (King's birth-day). Rose early and having made myself
fine, and put six spoons and a porringer of silver in my pocket to
give away to-day, Sir W. Pen and I took coach, and (the weather
and ways being foul) went to Walthamstowe; and being come
there heard Mr. Radcliffe,[2] my former school fellow at Paul's
(who is yet a mere boy), preach upon "Nay, let him take all, since
my Lord the King is returned," &c.[3] He reads all, and his sermon
very simple, but I looked for new matter. Back to dinner to Sir
William Batten's; and then, after a walk in the fine gardens, we
went to Mrs. Browne's, where Sir W. Pen and I were godfathers,
and Mrs. Jordan[4] and Shipman[5] godmothers to her boy. And
there, before and after the christening, we were with the woman
above in her chamber; but whether we carried ourselves well or
ill, I know not; but I was directed by young Mrs. Batten. One
passage of a lady that eat wafers with her dog did a little displease
me. I did give the midwife 10s. and the nurse 5s. and the maid of
the house 2s. But for as much I expected to give the name to the
child, but did not (it being called John), I forebore then to give

---

[1] John Holcraft of Balderton married Mary Pepys (born 1597), sister of Samuel's father. This John Holcraft was probably their son.

[2] Jonathan Radcliff, A.M., Vicar of Walthamstow from November, 1660, to
December, 1662.

[3] This text is from 2 Samuel xix. 30, and the true reading is—"And Mephi-
bosheth said unto the king, Yea, let him take all, forasmuch as my lord the
king is come again in peace unto his own house."

[4] The wife of Captain, afterwards Sir Joseph, Jordan.—B.

[5] Robert Shipman bought the great tithes of Walthamstow from the Argall
family in 1663; and left them by will to his wife Dorothy, from whom they
passed in 1667 to Robert Mascall, merchant.—Lysons' *Environs of London*.

my plate till another time after a little more advice. All being done, we went to Mrs. Shipman's, who is a great butter-woman, and I did see there the most of milk and cream, and the cleanest that ever I saw in my life. After we had filled our bellies with cream, we took our leaves and away. In our way, we had great sport to try who should drive fastest, Sir W. Batten's coach, or Sir W. Pen's chariott, they having four, and we two horses, and we beat them. But it cost me the spoiling of my clothes and velvet coat with dirt. Being come home I to bed, and give my breeches to be dried by the fire against to-morrow.

[30th]. To the Wardrobe and there, with my Lord, went into his new barge to try her, and found her a good boat, and like my Lord's contrivance of the door to come out round and not square as they used to do. Back to the Wardrobe with my Lord, and then with Mr. Moore to the Temple, and thence to Greatorex, who took me to Arundell-House,[1] and there showed me some fine flowers in his garden, and all the fine statues in the gallery, which I formerly had seen, and is a brave sight, and thence to a blind dark cellar, where we had two bottles of good ale, and so after giving him direction for my silver side-table, I took boat at Arundell stairs, and put in at Milford. . . . So home and found Sir Williams both and my Lady going to Deptford to christen Captain Rooth's child, and would have had me with them, but I could not go. To the office, where Sir R. Slingsby was, and he and I into his and my lodgings to take a view of them, out of a desire he has to have mine of me to join to his, and give me Mr. Turner's. To the office again, where Sir G. Carteret came and sat a while, he being angry for Sir Williams making of the maisters of this fleet upon their own heads without a full table. Then the Comptroller and I to the Coffee House, and there sat a great while talking of many things. So home and to bed. This day, I hear, the Parliament have ordered a bill to be brought in for the restoring the Bishops to the House of Lords;[2] which they had not done so soon but to spite Mr.

---

[1] Arundel House, in the Strand, was the repository of the fine collection of works of art gathered by Thomas Howard, Earl of Arundel. Arundel Street, which stands on the site, was built in 1678.

[2] A Bill for the Repeal of "An Act of Parliament intituled an Act for disen-

Prin, who is every day so bitter against them in his discourse in the House.

[31st]. I went to my father's thinking to have met with my cozen John Holcroft, but he came not, but to my great grief I found my father and mother in a great deal of discontent one with another, and indeed my mother is grown now so pettish that I know not how my father is able to bear with it. I did talk to her so as did not indeed become me, but I could not help it, she being so unsufferably foolish and simple, so that my father, poor man, is become a very unhappy man. There I dined, and so home and to the office all the afternoon till 9 at night, and then home and to supper and to bed. Great talk now how the Parliament intend to make a collection of free gifts to the King through the Kingdom; but I think it will not come to much.[1]

[June 1st]. Having taken our leaves of Sir W. Batten and my Lady, who are gone this morning to keep their Whitsuntide, Sir W. Pen and I and Mr. Gauden by water to Woolwich, and there went from ship to ship to give order for and take notice of their forwardness to go forth, and then to Deptford and did the like, having dined at Woolwich with Captain Poole at the tavern there. From Deptford we walked to Redriffe, calling at the half-way house, and there come into a room where there was infinite of new cakes placed that are made against Whitsuntide, and there we were very merry. By water home, and there did businesses of the office. Among others got my Lord's imprest of £1,000 and Mr. Creed's of £10,000 against this voyage their bills signed. Having wrote letters into the country and read some things I went to bed.

[2nd] (Whitsunday). The barber having done with me, I went to church, and there heard a good sermon of Mr. Mills, fit for the day. Then home to dinner, and then to church again, and going

---

abling all persons in holy orders to exercise any temporal jurisdiction or authority," was read a first time in the Commons on June 1st, and a third time on 13th. In the Lords it was read a first time on the 14th, and finally passed on the 18th.

[1] It will be seen from an entry further on (August 31st) that the Benevolence brought in very little.

home I found Greatorex (whom I expected to-day at dinner) come to see me, and so he and I in my chamber drinking of wine and eating of anchovies an hour or two, discoursing of many things in mathematics, and among others he showed me how it comes to pass the strength that levers have, and he showed me that what is got as to matter of strength is lost by them as to matter of time. It rained very hard, as it hath done of late so much that we begin to doubt a famine, and so he was forced to stay longer than I desired. At night after prayers to bed.

[3rd]. To the Wardrobe, where discoursing with my Lord, he did instruct me as to the business of the Wardrobe, in case, in his absence, Mr. Townsend should die, and told me that he do intend to joyne me and Mr. Moore with him as to the business, now he is going to sea, and spoke to me many other things, as to one that he do put the greatest confidence in, of which I am proud. Here I had a good occasion to tell him (what I have had long in my mind) that, since it has pleased God to bless me with something, I am desirous to lay out something for my father, and so have pitched upon Mr. Young's place in the Wardrobe, which I desired he would give order in his absence, if the place should fall that I might have the refusal. Which my Lord did freely promise me, at which I was very glad, he saying that he would do that at the least. So I saw my Lord into the barge going to Whitehall, and I and Mr. Creed home to my house, whither my father and my cozen Scott came to dine with me, and so we dined together very well, and before we had done in comes my father Bowyer and my mother and four daughters, and a young gentleman and his sister, their friends, and there staid all the afternoon, which cost me great store of wine, and were very merry. By and by I am called to the office, and there staid a little. So home again, and took Mr. Creed and left them, and so he and I to the Towre, to speak for some ammunicion for ships for my Lord; and so he and I, with much pleasure, walked quite round the Towre, which I never did before. So home, and after a walk with my wife upon the leads, I and she went to bed. This morning I and Dr. Peirce went over to the Beare at the Bridge foot, thinking to have met my Lord Hinchinbroke and his brother setting forth for France;

but they being not come we went over to the Wardrobe, and there found that my Lord Abbot Montagu[1] being not at Paris, my Lord hath a mind to have them stay a little longer before they go.

[4th]. The Comptroller came this morning to get me to go see a house or two near our office, which he would take for himself or Mr. Turner, and then he would have me have Mr. Turner's lodgings and himself mine and Mr. Davis's. But the houses did not like us, and so that design at present is stopped. Then he and I by water to the bridge, and then walked over the Bank-side till we came to the Temple, and so I went over and to my father's, where I met with my cozen J. Holcroft, and took him and my father and my brother Tom to the Bear tavern and gave them wine, my cozen being to go into the country again to-morrow. From thence to my Lord Crew's to dinner with him, and had very good discourse above having of young noblemen and gentlemen to think of going to sea, as being as honourable service as the land war. And among other things he told us how, in Queen Elizabeth's time, one young nobleman would wait with a trencher at the back of another till he came to age himself. And witnessed in my young Lord of Kent, that then was, who waited upon my Lord Bedford at table, when a letter came to my Lord Bedford that the Earldom of Kent was fallen to his servant, the young Lord; and so he rose from table, and made him sit down in his place, and took a lower for himself, for so he was by place to sit.[2] From thence to the Theatre and saw "Harry the 4th," a good play. That done I went over the water and walked over the fields to Southwark, and so home and to my lute. At night to bed.

[5th]. This morning did give my wife £4 to lay out upon lace and other things for herself. I to Wardrobe and so to Whitehall and Westminster, where I dined with my Lord and Ned Picker-

[1] Walter Montagu, second son to the first Earl of Manchester, embracing the Romish faith while on his travels, was made Abbot of Pontoise, through the influence of Mary de Medici. He afterwards became almoner to the Queen-Dowager of England, and died 1670.—B.

[2] The earldom of Kent was erected for the Grey family in 1465; that of Bedford for the Russells, in 1550. Lord Bedford was probably Francis, second earl, and Lord Grey may have been either Reginald, fifth earl, or Henry, sixth earl.

ing alone at his lodgings. After dinner to the office, where we sat and did business, and Sir W. Pen and I went home with Sir R. Slingsby to bowls in his ally, and there had good sport, and afterwards went in and drank and talked. So home Sir William and I, and it being very hot weather I took my flageolette and played upon the leads in the garden, where Sir W. Pen came out in his shirt into his leads, and there we staid talking and singing, and

drinking great drafts of claret, and eating botargo[1] and bread and butter till 12 at night, it being moonshine; and so to bed, very near fuddled.

[6th]. My head hath aked all night, and all this morning, with my last night's debauch. Called up this morning by Lieutenant Lambert, who is now made Captain of the Norwich, and he and I went down by water to Greenwich, in our way observing and

---

[1] "Botarga. The roe of the mullet pressed flat and dried; that of commerce, however, is from the tunny, a large fish of passage which is common in the Mediterranean. The best kind comes from Tunis."—Smyth's *Sailor's Word-Book*. Botargo was chiefly used to promote drinking by causing thirst, and Rabelais makes Gargantua eat it.

discoursing upon the things of a ship, he telling me all I asked him, which was of good use to me. There we went and eat and drank and heard musique at the Globe, and saw the simple motion that is there of a woman with a rod in her hand keeping time to the musique while it plays, which is simple, methinks. Back again by water, calling at Captain Lambert's house, which is very handsome and neat, and a fine prospect at top. So to the office, where we sat a little, and then the Captain and I again to Bridewell to Mr. Holland's, where his wife also, a plain dowdy, and his mother was. Here I paid Mrs. Holland the money due from me to her husband. Here came two young gentlewomen to see Mr. Holland, and one of them could play pretty well upon the viallin, but, good God! how these ignorant people did cry her up for it! We were very merry. I staid and supped there, and so home and to bed. The weather very hot, this night I left off my wastecoat.

[7th]. To my Lord's at Whitehall, but not finding him I went to the Wardrobe and there dined with my Lady, and was very kindly treated by her. After dinner to the office, and there till late at night. So home, and to Sir William Batten's, who is come this day from Chatham with my Lady, who is and has been much troubled with the toothache. Here I staid till late, and so home and to bed.

[8th]. To Whitehall to my Lord, who did tell me that he would have me go to Mr. Townsend, whom he had ordered to discover to me the whole mystery of the Wardrobe, and none else but me, and that he will make me deputy with him for fear that he should die in my Lord's absence, of which I was glad. Then to the Cook's with Mr. Shepley and Mr. Creed, and dined together, and then I went to the Theatre and there saw Bartholomew Faire,[1] the first time it was acted now-a-days. It is a most admirable play and well acted, but too much prophane and abusive. From thence, meeting Mr. Creed at the door, he and I went to the tobacco shop under Temple Bar gate, and there went up to the top of the house

---

[1] A comedy, by Ben Jonson; first acted at the Hope theatre, Bankside, October 31st, 1614.

and there sat drinking Lambeth ale a good while. Then away
home, and in my way called upon Mr. Rawlinson (my uncle
Wight being out of town), for his advice to answer a letter of
my uncle Robert, wherein he do offer me a purchase to lay some
money upon, that joynes upon some of his own lands, and plainly
telling me that the reason of his advice is the convenience that it
will give me as to his estate, of which I am exceeding glad, and
am advised to give up wholly the disposal of my money to him,
let him do what he will with it, which I shall do. So home and to
bed.

[9th] (Lord's day). This day my wife put on her black silk gown,
which is now laced all over with black gimp lace, as the fashion
is, in which she is very pretty. She and I walked to my Lady's at
the Wardrobe, and there dined and was exceeding much made
of. After dinner I left my wife there, and I walked to Whitehall,
and then went to Mr. Pierce's and sat with his wife a good while
(who continues very pretty) till he came, and then he and I, and
Mr. Symons (dancing master), that goes to sea with my Lord, to
the Swan tavern, and there drank, and so again to White Hall,
and there met with Dean Fuller, and walked a great while with
him; among other things discoursed of the liberty the Bishop (by
name he of Galloway)[1] takes to admit into orders any body that
will; among others, Roundtree, a simple mechanique that was a
person formerly in the fleet.[2] He told me he would complain of

---

[1] Murray and Heath, whose authority is generally good, assert that James
Hamilton was at this time Bishop of Galloway; but the commission for his
consecration bears date December 12th, 1661. Kennett also mentions Thomas
Sydserf, who had been deposed from the see of Galloway by the Presbyterians in 1638, as the only Scotch prelate alive at the Restoration; and adds,
that he came up to London, expecting to be advanced to the primacy. But he
had so disgusted the English bishops, that he was only removed to the See
of Orkney, which, though richly endowed, was considered at all times as a
sinecure; and he did not long survive his translation. At all events, Hamilton
was his successor, and the Bishop of Galloway mentioned in the Diary, May
15th, 1663. Lingard's testimony is in favour of Sydserf being the Bishop of
Galloway here alluded to. The death of the Bishop of Orkney (late of Galloway) is mentioned in "The Intelligencer," September 29th, 1663.—B.
[2] The reading in the early editions of the Diary is, "a person formerly of the
fleet"; in the later editions, "a parson formerly of the Fleet." The cypher for
"person" or "parson" is the same. I have preferred the reading of the early

it. By and by we went and got a sculler, and landing him at Worcester House, I and W. Howe, who came to us at Whitehall, went to the Wardrobe, where I met with Mr. Townsend, who is very willing he says to communicate anything for my Lord's advantage to me as to his business. I went up to Jane Shore's towre, and there W. Howe and I sang, and so took my wife and walked home, and so to bed. After I came home a messenger came from my Lord to bid me come to him to-morrow morning.

[10th]. Early to my Lord's, who privately told me how the King had made him Embassador in the bringing over the Queen.[1] That he is to go to Algier, &c., to settle the business, and to put the fleet in order there; and so to come back to Lisbone with three ships, and there to meet the fleet that is to follow him. He sent for me, to tell me that he do intrust me with the seeing of all things done in his absence as to this great preparation, as I shall receive orders from my Lord Chancellor and Mr. Edward Montagu. At all which my heart is above measure glad; for my Lord's honour, and some profit to myself, I hope. By and by, out with Mr. Shepley, Walden,[2] Parliament-man for Huntingdon, Rolt, Mackworth, and Alderman Backwell, to a house hard by, to drink Lambeth ale. So I back to the Wardrobe, and there found my Lord going to Trinity House, this being the solemn day of choosing Master, and my Lord is chosen, so he dines there to-day. I staid and dined with my Lady; but after we were set, comes in some persons of condition, and so the children and I rose and dined by ourselves, all the children and I, and were very merry and they mighty

editions, merely correcting "of" to "in," for two reasons—one, because the marriages were performed by clergymen, though disreputable, who would not require fresh ordination; the other because, although there were Fleet marriages at that time, yet they do not seem to be common. The date of the earliest Fleet register now preserved in the Bishop of London's Registry is 1674.—M. B.

[1] Katherine of Braganza, daughter of John IV. of Portugal, born 1638, married to Charles II., May 21st, 1662. After the death of the king she lived for some time at Somerset House, and then returned to Portugal, of which country she became Regent in 1704 on the retirement of her brother Don Pedro. She died December 31st, 1705.

[2] Lionel Walden, elected M.P. for the borough of Huntingdon, April 12th, 1661.

fond of me. Then to the office, and there sat awhile. So home and at night to bed, where we lay in Sir R. Slingsby's lodgings in the dining room there in one green bed, my house being now in its last work of painting and whiting.

[11th]. At the office this morning, Sir G. Carteret with us; and we agreed upon a letter to the Duke of York, to tell him the sad condition of this office for want of money; how men are not able to serve us more without some money; and that now the credit of the office is brought so low, that none will sell us any thing without our personal security given for the same. All the afternoon abroad about several businesses, and at night home and to bed.

[12th]. Wednesday, a day kept between a fast and a feast, the Bishops not being ready enough to keep the fast for foul weather before fair weather came; and so they were forced to keep it between both.[1] I to Whitehall, and there with Captain Rolt[2] and Ferrers we went to Lambeth to drink our morning draft, where at the Three Mariners, a place noted for their ale, we went and staid awhile very merry, and so away. And wanting a boat, we found Captain Bun going down the river, and so we went into his boat having a lady with him, and he landed them at Westminster and me at the Bridge. At home all day with my workmen, and doing several things, among others writing the letter resolved of yesterday to the Duke. Then to White Hall, where I met my Lord, who told me he must have £300 laid out in cloth, to give in Bar-

[1] A Form of Prayer was published to be used in London on the 12th, and in the country on the 19th of June, being the special days appointed for a general fast to be kept in the respective places for averting those sicknesses and diseases, that dearth and scarcity, which justly may be feared from the late immoderate rain and waters: for a thanksgiving also for the blessed change of weather; and the begging the continuance of it to us for our comfort: And likewise for beseeching a Blessing upon the High Court of Parliament now assembled: Set forth by his Majesty's authority. A sermon was preached before the Commons by Thomas Greenfield, preacher of Lincoln's Inn. The Lords taxed themselves for the poor—an earl, 30s., a baron, 20s. Those absent from prayers were to pay a forfeit.—B.

[2] Perhaps the same person who had been envoy from the Protector to the King of Sweden, and is described by Kennett, in September, 1655, as kinsman to his Highness.—B.

bary, as presents among the Turks. At which occasion of getting something I was very glad. Home to supper, and then to Sir R. Slingsby, who with his brother and I went to my Lord's at the Wardrobe, and there staid a great while, but he being now taking his leave of his friends staid out late, and so they went away. Anon came my Lord in, and I staid with him a good while, and then to bed with Mr. Moore in his chamber.

[13th]. I went up and down to Alderman Backwell's, but his servants not being up, I went home and put on my gray cloth suit and faced white coat, made of one of my wife's pettycoates, the first time I have had it on, and so in a riding garb back again and spoke with Mr. Shaw¹ at the Alderman's, who offers me £300 if my Lord pleases to buy this cloth with, which pleased me well. So to the Wardrobe and got my Lord to order Mr. Creed to imprest so much upon me to be paid by Alderman Backwell. So with my Lord to Whitehall by water, and he having taken leave of the King, comes to us at his lodgings and from thence goes to the garden stairs and there takes barge, and at the stairs was met by Sir R. Slingsby, who there took his leave of my Lord, and I heard my Lord thank him for his kindness to me, which Sir Robert answered much to my advantage. I went down with my Lord in the barge to Deptford, and there went on board the Dutch yacht and staid there a good while, W. Howe not being come with my Lord's things, which made my Lord very angry. By and by he comes and so we set sayle, and anon went to dinner, my Lord and we very merry; and after dinner I went down below and there sang, and took leave of W. Howe, Captain Rolt, and the rest of my friends, then went up and took leave of my Lord, who give me his hand and parted with great respect. So went and Captain Ferrers with me into our wherry, and my Lord did give five guns, all they had charged, which was the greatest respect my Lord could do me, and of which I was not a little proud. So with a sad and merry heart I left them sailing pleasantly from Erith, hoping to be in the Downs to-morrow early. We toward London in our boat. Pulled off our stockings and bathed our legs a great while in the river, which I had not done some years before. By and by

¹ Robin Shaw, manager of Backwell's business, who died July 25th, 1665.

we come to Greenwich, and thinking to have gone on the King's yacht, the King was in her, so we passed by, and at Woolwich went on shore, in the company of Captain Poole of Jamaica and young Mr. Kennersley, and many others, and so to the tavern where we drank a great deal both wine and beer. So we parted hence and went home with Mr. Falconer, who did give us cherrys and good wine. So to boat, and young Poole took us on board the Charity and gave us wine there, with which I had full enough, and so to our wherry again, and there fell asleep till I came almost to the Tower, and there the Captain and I parted, and I home and with wine enough in my head, went to bed.

[14th]. To Whitehall to my Lord's, where I found Mr. Edward Montagu and his family come to lie during my Lord's absence. I sent to my house by my Lord's order his shipp[1] and triangle virginall. So to my father's, and did give him order about the buying of this cloth to send to my Lord. But I could not stay with him myself, for having got a great cold by my playing the fool in the water yesterday I was in great pain, and so went home by coach to bed, and went not to the office at all, and by keeping myself warm, I broke wind and so came to some ease. Rose and eat some supper, and so to bed again.

[15th]. My father came and drank his morning draft with me, and sat with me till I was ready, and so he and I about the business of the cloth. By and by I left him and went and dined with my Lady, who, now my Lord is gone, is come to her poor housekeeping again. Then to my father's, who tells me what he has done, and we resolved upon two pieces of scarlet, two of purple, and two of black, and £50 in linen. I home, taking £300 with me home from Alderman Backwell's. After writing to my Lord to let him know what I had done I was going to bed, but there coming the purser of the King's yacht for victualls presently, for the Duke of York is to go down to-morrow, I got him to promise stowage for these things there, and so I went to bed, bidding Will go and fetch the things from the carrier's hither, which about 12 o'clock were brought to my house and laid there all night.

[1] A model of the Royal James: see *post*, October 5th, 1661.

[16th] (Lord's day). But no purser coming in the morning for them, and I hear that the Duke went last night, and so I am at a great loss what to do; and so this day (though the Lord's day) staid at home, sending Will up and down to know what to do. Sometimes thinking to continue my resolution of sending by the carrier to be at Deal on Wednesday next, sometimes to send them by sea by a vessel on purpose, but am not yet come to a resolution, but am at a very great loss and trouble in mind what in the world to do herein. The afternoon (while Will was abroad) I spent in reading "The Spanish Gypsey,"[1] a play not very good, though commended much. At night resolved to hire a Margate Hoy, who would go away to-morrow morning, which I did, and sent the things all by him, and put them on board about 12 this night, hoping to have them as the wind now serves in the Downs to-morrow night. To bed with some quiet of mind, having sent the things away.

[17th]. Visited this morning by my old friend Mr. Ch. Carter, who staid and went to Westminster with me, and there we parted, and I to the Wardrobe and dined with my Lady. So home to my painters, who are now about painting my stairs. So to the office, and at night we all went to Sir W. Pen's, and there sat and drank till 11 at night, and so home and to bed.

[18th]. All this morning at home vexing about the delay of my painters, and about four in the afternoon my wife and I by water to Captain Lambert's, where we took great pleasure in their turret-garden, and seeing the fine needle-works of his wife, the best I ever saw in my life, and afterwards had a very handsome treat and good musique that she made upon the harpsicon, and with a great deal of pleasure staid till 8 at night, and so home again, there being a little pretty witty child that is kept in their house that would not let us go without her, and so fell a-crying by the water-side. So home, where I met Jack Cole,[2] who staid with me a good while, and is still of the old good humour that we were of at school together, and I am very glad to see him. He gone, I went to bed.

---

[1] A comedy, by Thomas Middleton and William Rowley, printed 1653, and again in 1661.—B.

[2] See *post*, May 30th, 1665.

[19th]. All the morning almost at home, seeing my stairs finished by the painters, which pleases me well. So with Mr. Moore to Westminster Hall, it being term, and then by water to the Wardrobe, where very merry, and so home to the office all the afternoon, and at night to the Exchange to my uncle Wight about my intention of purchasing at Brampton. So back again home and at night to bed. Thanks be to God I am very well again of my late pain, and to-morrow hope to be out of my pain of dirt and trouble in my house, of which I am now become very weary. One thing I must observe here while I think of it that I am now become the most negligent man in the world as to matters of news, insomuch that, now-a-days, I neither can tell any, nor ask any of others.

[20th]. At home the greatest part of the day to see my workmen make an end, which this night they did to my great content.

[21st]. This morning going to my father's I met him, and so he and I went and drank our morning draft at the Samson[1] in Paul's Churchyard, and eat some gammon of bacon, &c., and then parted, having bought some green Say[2] for curtains in my parler. Home, and so to the Exchequer, where I met with my uncle Wight, and home with him to dinner, where among others (my aunt being out of town), Mr. Norbury and I did discourse of his wife's house and land at Brampton, which I find too much for me to buy. Home, and in the afternoon to the office, and much pleased at night to see my house begin to be clean after all the dirt.

[22nd]. Abroad all the morning about several businesses. At noon went and dined with my Lord Crew, where very much made of by him and his lady. Then to the Theatre, "The Alchymist,"[3] which is a most incomparable play. And that being done I met with little Luellin and Blirton, who took me to a friend's of theirs in Lincoln's Inn fields, one Mr. Hodges, where we drank

---

[1] There are tokens of the Samson in St. Paul's Churchyard (see "Boyne's Trade Tokens," ed. Williamson, vol. i., 1889, p. 735).

[2] A woollen cloth. "Saye clothe *serge*."—Palsgrave.

[3] Comedy by Ben Jonson, first printed in 1612.

great store of Rhenish wine and were very merry. So I went home, where I found my house now very clean, which was great content to me.

[23rd] (Lord's day). In the morning to church, and my wife not being well, I went with Sir W. Batten home to dinner, my Lady being out of town, where there was Sir W. Pen, Captain Allen and his daughter Rebecca, and Mr. Hempson and his wife. After dinner to church all of us and had a very good sermon of a stranger, and so I and the young company to walk first to Graye's Inn Walks, where great store of gallants, but above all the ladies that I there saw, or ever did see, Mrs. Frances Butler (Monsieur L'Impertinent's sister) is the greatest beauty. Then we went to Islington, where at the great house I entertained them as well as I could, and so home with them, and so to my own home and to bed. Pall, who went this day to a child's christening of Kate Joyce's, staid out all night at my father's, she not being well.

[24th] (Midsummer-day). We kept this a holiday, and so went not to the office at all. All the morning at home. At noon my father came to see my house now it is done, which is now yet very neat. He and I and Dr. Williams (who is come to see my wife, whose soare belly is now grown dangerous as she thinks) to the ordinary over against the Exchange, where we dined and had great wrangling with the master of the house when the reckoning was brought to us, he setting down exceeding high every thing. I home again and to Sir W. Batten's, and there sat a good while. So home.

[25th]. Up this morning to put my papers in order that are come from my Lord's, so that now I have nothing there remaining that is mine, which I have had till now. This morning came Mr. Good-groome[1] to me (recommended by Mr. Mage), with whom I agreed presently to give him 20s. entrance, which I then did, and 20s. a month more to teach me to sing, and so we began, and I hope I have come to something in it. His first song is "La cruda

---

[1] Theodore Goodgroome, Pepys's singing-master. He was probably related to John Goodgroome, a Gentleman of the Chapel Royal, who is also referred to in the Diary.

la bella."[1] He gone my brother Tom comes, with whom I made even with my father and the two drapers for the cloths I sent to sea lately. At home all day, in the afternoon came Captain Allen and his daughter Rebecca and Mr. Hempson, and by and by both Sir Williams, who sat with me till it was late, and I had a very gallant collacion for them. At night to bed.

[26th]. To Westminster about several businesses, then to dine with my Lady at the Wardrobe, taking Dean Fuller along with me; then home, where I heard my father had been to find me about special business; so I took coach and went to him, and found by a letter to him from my aunt that my uncle Robert is taken with a dizziness in his head, so that they desire my father to come down to look after his business, by which we guess that he is very ill, and so my father do think to go to-morrow. And so God's will be done. Back by water to the office, there till night, and so home to my musique and then to bed.

[27th]. To my father's, and with him to Mr. Starling's to drink our morning draft, and there I told him how I would have him speak to my uncle Robert, when he comes thither, concerning my buying of land, that I could pay ready money £600 and the rest by £150 per annum, to make up as much as will buy £50 per annum, which I do, though I not worth above £500 ready money, that he may think me to be a greater saver than I am. Here I took my leave of my father, who is going this morning to my uncle upon my aunt's letter this week that he is not well and so needs my father's help. At noon home, and then with my Lady Batten, Mrs. Rebecca Allen, Mrs. Thompson, &c., two coaches of us, we went and saw "Bartholomew Fayre" acted very well, and so home again and staid at Sir W. Batten's late, and so home to bed. This day Mr. Holden sent me a bever, which cost me £4 5s.[2]

[28th]. At home all the morning practising to sing, which is now my great trade, and at noon to my Lady and dined with her. So

---

[1] "La cruda la bella" does not appear to have been printed.

[2] Whilst a hat (see January 28th, 1660-61, *ante*) cost only 35s. See also Lord Sandwich's vexation at his beaver being stolen, and a hat only left in lieu of it, April 30th, 1661, *ante;* and April 19th and 26th, 1662, *post.*—B.

back and to the office, and there sat till 7 at night, and then Sir W. Pen and I in his coach went to Moorefields, and there walked, and stood and saw the wrestling, which I never saw so much of before, between the north and west countrymen. So home, and this night had our bed set up in our room that we called the Nursery, where we lay, and I am very much pleased with the room.

[29th]. By a letter from the Duke complaining of the delay of the ships that are to be got ready, Sir Williams both and I went to Deptford and there examined into the delays, and were satisfyed. So back again home and staid till the afternoon, and then I walked to the Bell at the Maypole[1] in the Strand, and thither came to me by appointment Mr. Chetwind, Gregory, and Hartlibb, so many of our old club, and Mr. Kipps, where we staid and drank and talked with much pleasure till it was late, and so I walked home and to bed. Mr. Chetwind by chewing of tobacco is become very fat and sallow, whereas he was consumptive, and in our discourse he fell commending of "Hooker's Ecclesiastical Polity,"[2] as the best book, and the only one that made him a Christian, which puts me upon the buying of it, which I will do shortly.

[30th] (Lord's day). To church, where we observe the trade of briefs is come now up to so constant a course every Sunday, that we resolve to give no more to them.[3] A good sermon, and then home to dinner, my wife and I all alone. After dinner Sir Williams both and I by water to Whitehall, where having walked up and down, at last we met with the Duke of York, according to an order sent us yesterday from him, to give him an account where the fault lay in the not sending out of the ships, which we

---

[1] The Maypole in the Strand was fixed on the site of the present church of St. Mary-le-Strand. It was taken away in 1718.

[2] The edition of Richard Hooker's great work, "Of the Lawes of Ecclesiastical Politie," in the Pepysian Library, is dated 1666.

[3] It appears, from an old MS. account-book of the collections in the church of St. Olave, Hart Street, beginning in 1642, still extant, that the money gathered on the 30th of June, 1661, "for several inhabitants of the parish of St. Dunstan in the West towards their losse by fire," amounted to "xxs. viii_d_." Pepys might complain of the trade in briefs, as similar contributions had been levied fourteen weeks successively, previous to the one in question at St. Olave's church. Briefs were abolished in 1828.—B.

find to be only the wind hath been against them, and so they could not get out of the river. Hence I to Graye's Inn Walk, all alone, and with great pleasure seeing the fine ladies walk there. Myself humming to myself (which now-a-days is my constant practice since I begun to learn to sing) the trillo, and found by use that it do come upon me. Home very weary and to bed, finding my wife not sick, but yet out of order, that I fear she will come to be sick. This day the Portuguese Embassador[1] came to White Hall to take leave of the King; he being now going to end all with the Queen, and to send her over. The weather now very fair and pleasant, but very hot. My father gone to Brampton to see my uncle Robert, not knowing whether to find him dead or alive. Myself lately under a great expense of money upon myself in clothes and other things, but I hope to make it up this summer by my having to do in getting things ready to send with the next fleet to the Queen. Myself in good health, but mighty apt to take cold, so that this hot weather I am fain to wear a cloth before my belly.

[July 1st]. This morning I went up and down into the city, to buy several things, as I have lately done, for my house. Among other things, a fair chest of drawers for my own chamber, and an Indian gown for myself. The first cost me 33s., the other 34s. Home and dined there, and Theodore Goodgroome, my singing master, with me, and then to our singing. After that to the office, and then home.

[2nd]. To Westminster Hall and there walked up and down, it being Term time. Spoke with several, among others my cozen Roger Pepys, who was going up to the Parliament House, and inquired whether I had heard from my father since he went to Brampton, which I had done yesterday, who writes that my uncle is by fits stupid, and like a man that is drunk, and sometimes speechless. Home, and after my singing master had done, took coach and went to Sir William Davenant's[2] Opera; this being the

---

[1] Don Francisco de Mello, Conde de Ponte.—B.

[2] This clashes with the statement of Downes, who says that his company being complete, Davenant opened his house in Lincoln's Inn Fields with the two parts of the "Siege of Rhodes," in the spring of 1662. Messrs. Maidment

fourth day that it hath begun, and the first that I have seen it.
To-day was acted the second part of "The Siege of Rhodes."[1] We
staid a very great while for the King and the Queen of Bohemia.
And by the breaking of a board over our heads, we had a great
deal of dust fell into the ladies' necks and the men's hair, which
made good sport. The King being come, the scene opened; which
indeed is very fine and magnificent, and well acted, all but the
Eunuch, who was so much out that he was hissed off the stage.
Home and wrote letters to my Lord at sea, and so to bed.

[3rd]. To Westminster to Mr. Edward Montagu about business
of my Lord's, and so to the Wardrobe, and there dined with my
Lady, who is in some mourning for her brother, Mr. Saml. Crew,
who died yesterday of the spotted fever. So home through Duck
Lane[2] to inquire for some Spanish books, but found none that
pleased me. So to the office, and that being done to Sir W. Batten's with the Comptroller, where we sat late talking and dis-
puting with Mr. Mills the parson of our parish. This day my
Lady Batten and my wife were at the burial of a daughter of
Sir John Lawson's, and had rings for themselves and their hus-
bands. Home and to bed.

[4th]. At home all the morning; in the afternoon I went to the
Theatre, and there I saw "Claracilla"[3] (the first time I ever saw
it), well acted. But strange to see this house, that used to be so
thronged, now empty since the Opera begun; and so will continue
for a while, I believe. Called at my father's, and there I heard that
my uncle Robert[4] continues to have his fits of stupefaction every
day for 10 or 12 hours together. From thence to the Exchange at
night, and then went with my uncle Wight to the Mitre and were

---

and Logan, in their edition of Davenant's Dramatic Works, state that this
performance was at Salisbury Court.

[1] Davenant's opera of the "Siege of Rhodes" was published in 1656. The
author afterwards wrote a second part, which Pepys saw. The two parts, as
altered, and as acted at Lincoln's Inn Fields, were published in 1663.

[2] Duck Lane was largely inhabited by booksellers. It is now renamed Little
Britain.

[3] A tragi-comedy, by Thomas Killigrew, first published in 1641.

[4] Robert Pepys died on the following day.

merry, but he takes it very ill that my father would go out of
town to Brampton on this occasion and would not tell him of it,
which I endeavoured to remove but could not. Here Mr. Batersby
the apothecary was, who told me that if my uncle had the
emerods[1] (which I think he had) and that now they are stopped,
he will lay his life that bleeding behind by leeches will cure him,
but I am resolved not to meddle in it. Home and to bed.

[5th]. At home, and in the afternoon to the office, and that being
done all went to Sir W. Batten's and there had a venison pasty,
and were very merry. At night home and to bed.

[6th]. Waked this morning with news, brought me by a messenger on purpose, that my uncle Robert is dead, and died yesterday; so I rose sorry in some respect, glad in my expectations
in another respect. So I made myself ready, went and told my
uncle Wight, my Lady, and some others thereof, and bought me
a pair of boots in St. Martin's, and got myself ready, and then
to the Post House and set out about eleven and twelve o'clock,
taking the messenger with me that came to me, and so we rode
and got well by nine o'clock to Brampton, where I found my
father well. My uncle's corps in a coffin standing upon joynt-
stools in the chimney in the hall; but it begun to smell, and so
I caused it to be set forth in the yard all night, and watched by
two men. My aunt I found in bed in a most nasty ugly pickle,
made me sick to see it. My father and I lay together to-night, I
greedy to see the will, but did not ask to see it till to-morrow.

[7th] (Lord's day). In the morning my father and I walked in
the garden and read the will; where, though he gives me nothing
at present till my father's death, or at least very little, yet I am
glad to see that he hath done so well for us all, and well to the
rest of his kindred. After that done, we went about getting things,
as ribbands and gloves, ready for the burial. Which in the afternoon was done; where, it being Sunday, all people far and near
come in; and in the greatest disorder that ever I saw, we made
shift to serve them what we had of wine and other things; and
then to carry him to the church, where Mr. Taylor buried him,

---

[1] Hæmorrhoids or piles.

and Mr. Turner[1] preached a funerall sermon, where he spoke
not particularly of him anything, but that he was one so well
known for his honesty, that it spoke for itself above all that he
could say for it. And so made a very good sermon. Home with
some of the company who supped there, and things being quiet,
at night to bed.

[8th, 9th, 10th, 11th, 12th, 13th]. I fell to work, and my father
to look over my uncle's papers and clothes, and continued all this

week upon that business, much troubled with my aunt's base,
ugly humours. We had news of Tom Trice's putting in a caveat
against us, in behalf of his mother, to whom my uncle hath not
given anything, and for good reason therein expressed, which
troubled us also. But above all, our trouble is to find that his estate
appears nothing as we expected, and all the world believes; nor
his papers so well sorted as I would have had them, but all in
confusion, that break my brains to understand them. We missed

[1] Rev. John Turner.

also the surrenders of his copyhold land, without which the land would not come to us, but to the heir at law, so that what with this, and the badness of the drink and the ill opinion I have of the meat, and the biting of the gnats by night and my disappointment in getting home this week, and the trouble of sorting all the papers, I am almost out of my wits with trouble, only I appear the more contented, because I would not have my father troubled. The latter end of the week Mr. Philips[1] comes home from London, and so we advised with him and have the best counsel he could give us, but for all that we were not quiet in our minds.

[14th] (Lord's day). At home, and Robert Barnwell with us, and dined, and in the evening my father and I walked round Portholme and viewed all the fields, which was very pleasant. Thence to Hinchingbroke, which is now all in dirt, because of my Lord's building, which will make it very magnificent. Back to Brampton, and to supper and to bed.

[15th]. Up by three o'clock this morning, and rode to Cambridge, and was there by seven o'clock, where, after I was trimmed, I went to Christ College, and found my brother John at eight o'clock in bed, which vexed me. Then to King's College chappell, where I found the scholars in their surplices at the service with the organs, which is a strange sight to what it used in my time to be here. Then with Dr. Fairbrother (whom I met there) to the Rose tavern, and called for some wine, and there met fortunately with Mr. Turner of our office, and sent for his wife, and were very merry (they being come to settle their son here), and sent also for Mr. Sanchy, of Magdalen, with whom and other gentlemen, friends of his, we were very merry, and I treated them as well as I could, and so at noon took horse again, having taken leave of my cozen Angier, and rode to Impington, where I found my old uncle[2] sitting all alone, like a man out of the world: he

---

[1] Lewis Phillips.

[2] Talbot Pepys, sixth son of John Pepys of Impington, was born 1583, and therefore at this time he was seventy-eight years of age. He was educated at Trinity Hall, Cambridge, and called to the bar at the Middle Temple in 1605. He was M.P. for Cambridge in 1625, and Recorder of Cambridge from 1624 to 1660, in which year he was succeeded by his son Roger. He died of the plague, March, 1666, aged eighty-three.

can hardly see; but all things else he do pretty lively. Then with Dr. John Pepys and him, I read over the will, and had their advice therein, who, as to the sufficiency thereof confirmed me, and advised me as to the other parts thereof. Having done there, I rode to Gravely[1] with much ado to inquire for a surrender of my uncle's in some of the copyholders' hands there, but I can hear of none, which puts me into very great trouble of mind, and so with a sad heart rode home to Brampton, but made myself as cheerful as I could to my father, and so to bed.

[16th, 17th, 18th, 19th]. These four days we spent in putting things in order, letting of the crop upon the ground, agreeing with Stankes[2] to have a care of our business in our absence, and we think ourselves in nothing happy but in lighting upon him to be our bayly; in riding to Offord and Sturtlow, and up and down all our lands, and in the evening walking, my father and I about the fields talking, and had advice from Mr. Moore from London, by my desire, that the three witnesses of the will being all legatees, will not do the will any wrong. To-night Serjeant Bernard,[3] I hear, is come home into the country. To supper and to bed. My aunt continuing in her base, hypocritical tricks, which both Jane Perkin (of whom we make great use), and the maid do tell us every day.

[20th]. Up to Huntingdon this morning to Sir Robert Bernard, with whom I met Jaspar Trice.[4] So Sir Robert caused us to sit down together and began discourse very fairly between us, so I drew out the Will and show it him, and [he] spoke between us as well as I could desire, but could come to no issue till Tom Trice comes. Then Sir Robert and I fell to talk about the money due to us upon surrender from Piggott, £164, which he tells me will go with

---

[1] Gravely is in Cambridgeshire, although it is contiguous to Hunts.

[2] William Stankes, bailiff of Robert Pepys's land.

[3] Sir Robert Bernard, Sergeant-at-Law, of Huntingdon, created baronet 1662, and died 1666. His second wife, here mentioned, was Elizabeth, relict of George, Lord Digby, died January, 1662.—B.

[4] There is a monument to "Jasper Trice, gent.," in Brampton Church, Hunts, from which it appears that he died October 27th, 1675. He is referred to on March 8th, 1659-60, as "Jasper" without a surname. Apparently he was brother of Tom Trice.

debts to the heir at law, which breaks my heart on the other side. Here I staid and dined with Sir Robert Bernard and his lady, my Lady Digby, a very good woman. After dinner I went into the town and spent the afternoon, sometimes with Mr. Phillips, sometimes with Dr. Symcottes, Mr. Vinter, Robert Ethell, and many more friends, and at last Mr. Davenport, Phillips, Jaspar Trice, myself and others at Mother — over against the Crown we sat and drank ale and were very merry till 9 at night, and so broke up. I walked home, and there found Tom Trice come, and he and my father gone to Goody Gorum's, where I found them and Jaspar Trice got before me, and Mr. Greene, and there had some calm discourse, but came to no issue, and so parted. So home and to bed, being now pretty well again of my left hand, which lately was stung and very much swelled.

[21st] (Lord's day). At home all the morning, putting my papers in order against my going to-morrow and doing many things else to that end. Had a good dinner, and Stankes and his wife with us. To my business again in the afternoon, and in the evening came the two Trices, Mr. Greene, and Mr. Philips, and so we began to argue. At last it came to some agreement that for our giving of my aunt £10 she is to quit the house, and for other matters they are to be left to the law, which do please us all, and so we broke up, pretty well satisfyed. Then came Mr. Barnwell and J. Bowles and supped with us, and after supper away, and so I having taken leave of them and put things in the best order I could against to-morrow I went to bed. Old William Luffe having been here this afternoon and paid up his bond of £20, and I did give him into his hand my uncle's surrender of Sturtlow to me before Mr. Philips, R. Barnwell, and Mr. Pigott, which he did acknowledge to them my uncle did in his lifetime deliver to him.

[22nd]. Up by three, and going by four on my way to London; but the day proves very cold, so that having put on no stockings but thread ones under my boots, I was fain at Bigglesworth[1] to buy a pair of coarse woollen ones, and put them on. So by degrees till I come to Hatfield before twelve o'clock, where I had a very

---

[1] Biggleswade, the largest town in Bedfordshire after Bedford.

good dinner with my hostess at my Lord of Salisbury's Inn, and
after dinner though weary I walked all alone to the Vineyard,
which is now a very beautiful place again;[1] and coming back I
met with Mr. Looker, my Lord's gardener (a friend of Mr.
Eglin's), who showed me the house, the chappell with brave pictures, and, above all, the gardens, such as I never saw in all my
life; nor so good flowers, nor so great gooseberrys, as big as nut-
megs. Back to the inn, and drank with him, and so to horse again,
and with much ado got to London, and set him up at Smithfield;
so called at my uncle Fenner's, my mother's, my Lady's, and so
home, in all which I found all things as well as I could expect. So
weary and to bed.

[23rd]. Put on my mourning. Made visits to Sir W. Pen and Batten. Then to Westminster, and at the Hall staid talking with
Mrs. Michell, a good while, and in the afternoon, finding myself
unfit for business, I went to the Theatre, and saw "Brenoralt,"[2]
I never saw before. It seemed a good play, but ill acted; only I sat
before Mrs. Palmer, the King's mistress, and filled my eyes with
her, which much pleased me. Then to my father's, where by
my desire I met my uncle Thomas, and discoursed of my uncle's
will to him, and did satisfy [him] as well as I could. So to my
uncle Wight's, but found him out of doors, but my aunt I saw and
staid a while, and so home and to bed. Troubled to hear how
proud and idle Pall is grown, that I am resolved not to keep her.

[24th]. This morning my wife in bed tells me of our being robbed
of our silver tankard, which vexed me all day for the negligence
of my people to leave the door open. My wife and I by water to

---

[1] Hatfield or Bishop's Hatfield, Herts. In 1109, when the abbey of Ely was
erected into a bishopric, Hatfield became an episcopal residence, and a
sumptuous palace was built there. In 1538 the manor was conveyed to Henry
VIII. by Thomas Goodrich, Bishop of Ely, in exchange for lands in Cambridge, Essex, and Norfolk, and the palace became a royal abode. James I. in
1607 exchanged it with Lord Salisbury for Theobalds, and built a new mansion for his minister, who died the year after it was finished. The inn mentioned by Pepys was the Salisbury Arms. The vineyard is still carefully kept,
and is one of the last of its age existing. William Cecil, second Earl of Salisbury, succeeded his father in 1612, and died December 3rd, 1668.
[2] "Brennoralt, or the Discontented Colonel," a tragedy, by Sir John Suckling.
Written about 1639, and first published in Suckling's Works, 1646.

Whitehall, where I left her to her business, and I to my cozen
Thomas Pepys, and discoursed with him at large about our business of my uncle's will. He can give us no light at all into his
estate, but upon the whole tells me that he do believe that he has
left but little money, though something more than we have
found, which is about £500. Here came Sir G. Lane by chance,
seeing a bill upon the door to hire the house, with whom my coz
and I walked all up and down, and indeed it is a very pretty place,
and he do intend to leave the agreement for the House, which is
£400 fine, and £46 rent a year to me between them. Then to the
Wardrobe, but come too late, and so dined with the servants. And
then to my Lady, who do shew my wife and me the greatest
favour in the world, in which I take great content. Home by
water and to the office all the afternoon, which is a great pleasure
to me again, to talk with persons of quality and to be in command, and I give it out among them that the estate left me is
£200 a year in land, besides moneys, because I would put an
esteem upon myself. At night home and to bed after I had set
down my Journals ever since my going from London this journey
to this house. This afternoon I hear that my man Will hath lost
his clock with my tankard, at which I am very glad.

[25th]. This morning came my box of papers from Brampton of
all my uncle's papers, which will now set me at work enough. At
noon I went to the Exchange, where I met my uncle Wight, and
found him so discontented about my father (whether that he
takes it ill that he has not been acquainted with things, or whether
he takes it ill that he has nothing left him, I cannot tell), for
which I am much troubled, and so staid not long to talk with him.
Thence to my mother's, where I found my wife and my aunt Bell
and Mrs. Ramsey, and great store of tattle there was between the
old women and my mother, who thinks that there is, God knows
what fallen to her, which makes me mad, but it was not a proper
time to speak to her of it, and so I went away with Mr. Moore,
and he and I to the Theatre, and saw "The Jovial Crew,"[1] the
first time I saw it, and indeed it is as merry and the most inno-

---

[1] "The Jovial Crew, or the Merry Beggars," a comedy, by Richard Brome,
acted at the Cockpit, Drury Lane, in 1641.

cent play that ever I saw, and well performed. From thence home, and wrote to my father and so to bed. Full of thoughts to think of the trouble that we shall go through before we come to see what will remain to us of all our expectations.

[26th]. At home all the morning, and walking met with Mr. Hill of Cambridge at Pope's Head Alley with some women with him whom he took and me into the tavern there, and did give us wine, and would fain seem to be very knowing in the affairs of state, and tells me that yesterday[1] put a change to the whole state of England as to the Church; for the King now would be forced to favour Presbytery, or the City would leave him: but I heed not what he says, though upon enquiry I do find that things in the Parliament are in a great disorder. Home at noon and there found Mr. Moore, and with him to an ordinary alone and dined, and there he and I read my uncle's will, and I had his opinion on it, and still find more and more trouble like to attend it. Back to the office all the afternoon, and that done home for all night. Having the beginning of this week made a vow to myself to drink no wine this week (finding it to unfit me to look after business), and this day breaking of it against my will, I am much troubled for it, but I hope God will forgive me.

[27th]. To Westminster, where at Mr. Montagu's chamber I heard a Frenchman play, a friend of Monsieur Eschar's, upon the guitar, most extreme well, though at the best methinks it is but a bawble. From thence to Westminster Hall, where it was expected that the Parliament was to have been adjourned for two or three months, but something hinders it for a day or two. In the lobby I spoke with Mr. George Montagu, and advised about a ship to carry my Lord Hinchingbroke and the rest of the young gentlemen to France, and they have resolved of going in a hired vessell from Rye, and not in a man of war. He told me in discourse that my Lord Chancellor is much envied, and that many great men, such as the Duke of Buckingham and my Lord of Bristoll,[2] do endeavour to undermine him, and that he believes it

---

[1] When the Savoy Conference ended, the Royal Commission having expired on that day.—B.

[2] George Digby, second Earl of Bristol. Died March 20th, 1678.

will not be done; for that the King (though he loves him not in the way of a companion, as he do these young gallants that can answer him in his pleasures), yet cannot be without him, for his policy and service. From thence to the Wardrobe, where my wife met me, it being my Lord of Sandwich's birthday, and so we had many friends here, Mr. Townsend and his wife, and Captain Ferrers' lady and Captain Isham, and were very merry, and had a good venison pasty. Mr. Pargiter, the merchant, was with us also. After dinner Mr. Townsend was called upon by Captain Cooke: so we three went to a tavern hard by, and there he did give us a song or two; and without doubt he hath the best manner of singing in the world. Back to my wife, and with my Lady Jem. and Pall[1] by water through bridge, and showed them the ships with great pleasure, and then took them to my house to show it them (my Lady their mother having been lately all alone to see it and my wife, in my absence in the country), and we treated them well, and were very merry. Then back again through bridge, and set them safe at home, and so my wife and I by coach home again, and after writing a letter to my father at Brampton, who, poor man, is there all alone, and I have not heard from him since my coming from him, which troubles me. To bed.

[28th] (Lord's day). This morning as my wife and I were going to church, comes Mrs. Ramsay to see us, so we sent her to church, and we went too, and came back to dinner, and she dined with us and was wellcome. To church again in the afternoon, and then come home with us Sir W. Pen, and drank with us, and then went away, and my wife after him to see his daughter[2] that is lately come out of Ireland. I staid at home at my book; she came back again and tells me that whereas I expected she should have been a great beauty, she is a very plain girl. This evening my wife gives me all my linen, which I have put up, and intend to keep it now in my own custody. To supper and to bed.

[29th]. This morning we began again to sit in the mornings at

---

[1] Lady Jemima Montagu and Lady Paulina Montagu, daughters of the Earl of Sandwich.

[2] Margaret Penn, only daughter of Sir William Penn, was married to Anthony Lowther, of Mask, in the county of York, in February, 1666-67.

the office, but before we sat down Sir R. Slingsby and I went to
Sir R. Ford's to see his house, and we find it will be very convenient for us to have it added to the office if he can be got to part
with it. Then we sat down and did business in the office. So home
to dinner, and my brother Tom dined with me, and after dinner
he and I alone in my chamber had a great deal of talk, and I find
that unless my father can forbear to make profit of his house in
London and leave it to Tom, he has no mind to set up the trade

any where else, and so I know not what to do with him. After this
I went with him to my mother, and there told her how things do
fall out short of our expectations, which I did (though it be true)
to make her leave off her spending, which I find she is now-a-days
very free in, building upon what is left to us by my uncle to bear
her out in it, which troubles me much. While I was here word is
brought that my aunt Fenner is exceeding ill, and that my
mother is sent for presently[1] to come to her: also that my cozen
Charles Glassecocke,[2] though very ill himself, is this day gone to
the country to his brother, John Glassecocke, who is a-dying
there. Home.

[30th]. After my singing-master had done with me this morn-

[1] Immediately.

[2] Pepys was very lax in his use of the term cousin. Charles Glasscocke was
brother-in-law of Judith Pepys, *née* Cutter.

ing, I went to White Hall and Westminster Hall, where I found
the King expected to come and adjourn the Parliament. I found
the two Houses at a great difference, about the Lords challenging
their privileges not to have their houses searched, which makes
them deny to pass the House of Commons' Bill for searching for
pamphlets and seditious books. Thence by water to the Wardrobe (meeting the King upon the water going in his barge to adjourn the House) where I dined with my Lady, and there met
Dr. Thomas Pepys, who I found to be a silly talking fellow, but
very good-natured. So home to the office, where we met about
the business of Tangier this afternoon. That done, at home I
found Mr. Moore, and he and I walked into the City and there
parted. To Fleet Street to find when the Assizes begin at Cambridge and Huntingdon, in order to my going to meet with Roger
Pepys for counsel. So in Fleet Street I met with Mr. Salisbury,
who is now grown in less than two years' time so great a limner
that he is become excellent, and gets a great deal of money at it.
I took him to Hercules Pillars to drink, and there came Mr.
Whore (whom I formerly have known), a friend of his to him,
who is a very ingenious fellow, and there I sat with them a good
while, and so home and wrote letters late to my Lord and to my
father, and then to bed.

[31st]. Singing-master came to me this morning; then to the
office all the morning. In the afternoon I went to the Theatre, and
there I saw "The Tamer Tamed"[1] well done. And then home,
and prepared to go to Walthamstow to-morrow. This night I was
forced to borrow £40 of Sir W. Batten.

[August 1st]. This morning Sir Williams both, and my wife and
I and Mrs. Margarett Pen (this first time that I have seen her
since she came from Ireland) went by coach to Walthamstow,
a-gossiping to Mrs. Browne, where I did give her six silver
spoons[2] for her boy. Here we had a venison pasty, brought hot
from London, and were very merry. Only I hear how nurse's
husband has spoken strangely of my Lady Batten how she was

[1] On October 30th, 1660, Pepys saw this play at the Cockpit theatre.
[2] But not the porringer of silver. See May 29th, 1661.—M. B.

such a man's whore, who indeed is known to leave her her estate, which we would fain have reconciled to-day, but could not and indeed I do believe that the story is true. Back again at night home.

[2d]. At the office all the morning. At noon Dr. Thos. Pepys dined with me, and after dinner my brother Tom came to me and then I made myself ready to get a-horseback for Cambridge. So I set out and rode to Ware, this night, in the way having much discourse with a fell-monger,[1] a Quaker, who told me what a wicked man he had been all his life-time till within this two years. Here I lay, and

[3rd]. Got up early the next morning and got to Barkway, where I staid and drank, and there met with a letter-carrier of Cambridge, with whom I rode all the way to Cambridge, my horse being tired, and myself very wet with rain. I went to the Castle Hill, where the Judges were at the Assizes; and I staid till Roger Pepys rose and went with him, and dined with his brother, the Doctor, and Claxton[2] at Trinity Hall. Then parted, and I went to the Rose, and there with Mr. Pechell,[3] Sanchy, and others, sat and drank till night and were very merry, only they tell me how high the old doctors are in the University over those they found there, though a great deal better scholars than themselves; for which I am very sorry, and, above all, Dr. Gunning. At night I took horse, and rode with Roger Pepys and his two brothers to Impington, and there with great respect was led up by them to the best chamber in the house, and there slept.

[4th] (Lord's day). Got up, and by and by walked into the orchard with my cozen Roger, and there plucked some fruit, and then discoursed at large about the business I came for, that is, about my uncle's will, in which he did give me good satisfaction, but tells me I shall meet with a great deal of trouble in it. However, in all things he told me what I am to expect and what to do.

---

[1] A dealer in hides.

[2] Paulina Pepys, sister of Roger Pepys and Talbot Pepys, M.D., married Hammond Claxton of Booton, co. Norfolk.

[3] See *ante*, February 26th, 1659-60 (note).

To church, and had a good plain sermon, and my uncle Talbot went with us and at our coming in the country-people all rose with so much reverence; and when the parson begins, he begins "Right worshipfull and dearly beloved" to us. Home to dinner, which was very good, and then to church again, and so home and to walk up and down and so to supper, and after supper to talk about publique matters, wherein Roger Pepys (who I find a very sober man, and one whom I do now honour more than ever before for this discourse sake only) told me how basely things have been carried in Parliament by the young men, that did labour to oppose all things that were moved by serious men. That they are the most prophane swearing fellows that ever he heard in his life, which makes him think that they will spoil all, and bring things into a warr again if they can. So to bed.

[5th]. Early to Huntingdon, but was fain to stay a great while at Stanton because of the rain, and there borrowed a coat of a man for 6d., and so he rode all the way, poor man, without any. Staid at Huntingdon for a little, but the judges are not come hither: so I went to Brampton, and there found my father very well, and my aunt gone from the house, which I am glad of, though it costs us a great deal of money, viz., £10. Here I dined, and after dinner took horse and rode to Yelling, to my cozen Nightingale's, who hath a pretty house here, and did learn of her all she could tell me concerning my business, and has given me some light by her discourse how I may get a surrender made for Graveley lands. Hence to Graveley, and there at an alehouse met with Chancler and Jackson (one of my tenants for Cotton closes) and another with whom I had a great deal of discourse, much to my satisfaction. Hence back again to Brampton and after supper to bed, being now very quiet in the house, which is a content to us.

[6th]. Up early and went to Mr. Phillips, but lost my labour, he lying at Huntingdon last night, so I went back again and took horse and rode thither, where I staid with Thos. Trice and Mr. Philips drinking till noon, and then Tom Trice and I to Brampton, where he to Goody Gorum's and I home to my father, who could discern that I had been drinking, which he did never see or

hear of before, so I eat a bit of dinner and went with him to Gorum's, and there talked with Tom Trice, and then went and took horse for London, and with much ado, the ways being very bad, got to Baldwick,¹ and there lay and had a good supper by myself. The landlady being a pretty woman, but I durst not take notice of her, her husband being there. Before supper I went to see the church, which is a very handsome church, but I find that both here, and every where else that I come, the Quakers do still continue, and rather grow than lessen. To bed.

[7th]. Called up at three o'clock, and was a-horseback by four; and as I was eating my breakfast I saw a man riding by that rode a little way upon the road with me last night; and he being going with venison in his pan-yards² to London, I called him in and did give him his breakfast with me, and so we went together all the way. At Hatfield we bayted and walked into the great house through all the courts; and I would fain have stolen a pretty dog that followed me, but I could not, which troubled me. To horse again, and by degrees with much ado got to London, where I found all well at home and at my father's and my Lady's, but no news yet from my Lord where he is. At my Lady's (whither I went with Dean Fuller, who came to my house to see me just as I was come home) I met with Mr. Moore, who told me at what a loss he was for me, for to-morrow is a Seal day at the Privy Seal, and it being my month, I am to wait upon my Lord Roberts,³ Lord Privy Seal, at the Seal. Home and to bed.

[8th]. Early in the morning to Whitehall, but my Lord Privy Seal came not all the morning. At noon Mr. Moore and I to the Wardrobe to dinner, where my Lady and all merry and well. Back again to the Privy Seal; but my Lord comes not all the

¹ Baldock, Herts, in the district of Hitchin. It belonged at one time to the Knights Templars, who built a church there.

² Panyards = panniers.

³ John, second Lord Robartes, created Viscount Bodmin and Earl of Radnor in July, 1679. At the Restoration William Viscount Say and Sele was appointed Lord Privy Seal, but he was succeeded in May, 1661, by Lord Robartes, who held the office until April, 1673. Lord Radnor died July 17th, 1685.

afternoon, which made me mad and gives all the world reason to talk of his delaying of business, as well as of his severity and ill using of the Clerks of the Privy Seal. In the evening I took Mons. Eschar and Mr. Moore and Dr. Pierce's brother (the souldier) to the tavern next the Savoy, and there staid and drank with them. Here I met with Mr. Mage,¹ and discoursing of musique Mons. Eschar spoke so much against the English and in praise of the French that made him mad, and so he went away. After a stay with them a little longer we parted and I home.

[9th]. To the office, where word is brought me by a son-in-law of Mr. Pierce's,² the purser, that his father is a dying and that he desires that I would come to him before he dies. So I rose from the table and went, where I found him not so ill as I thought that he had been ill. So I did promise to be a friend to his wife and family if he should die, which was all he desired of me, but I do believe he will recover. Back again to the office, where I found Sir G. Carteret had a day or two ago invited some of the officers to dinner to-day at Deptford. So at noon, when I heard that he was a-coming, I went out, because I would see whether he would send to me or no to go with them; but he did not, which do a little trouble me till I see how it comes to pass. Although in other things I am glad of it because of my going again to-day to the Privy Seal. I dined at home, and having dined news is brought by Mr. Hater that his wife is now falling into labour, so he is come for my wife, who presently went with him. I to White Hall, where, after four o'clock, comes my Lord Privy Seal, and so we went up to his chamber over the gate at White Hall,³ where he asked me what deputacion I had from my Lord. I told him none; but that I am sworn my Lord's deputy by both of the Secretarys, which did satisfy him. So he caused Mr. Moore to read over all the bills as is the manner, and all ended very well. So that I see the Lyon is not so fierce as he is painted. That being

---

¹ Probably Humphry Madge, who was one of the King's twenty-four fiddlers in 1674.

² Mr. Pierce did not die at this time, and is mentioned in the Diary on September 18th, 1665.

³ The Signet and Privy Seal office was situated in what is now Whitehall Yard, a little north of the site of the United Service Institution.

done Mons. Eschar (who all this afternoon had been waiting at the Privy Seal for the Warrant for £5,000 for my Lord of Sandwich's preparation for Portugal) and I took some wine with us and went to visit la belle Pierce, who we find very big with child, and a pretty lady, one Mrs. Clifford, with her, where we staid and were extraordinary merry. From thence I took coach to my father's, where I found him come home this day from Brampton (as I expected) very well, and after some discourse about business and it being very late I took coach again home, where I hear by my wife that Mrs. Hater is not yet delivered, but continues in her pains. So to bed.

[10th]. This morning came the maid that my wife hath lately hired for a chamber maid. She is very ugly, so that I cannot care for her, but otherwise she seems very good. But however she do come about three weeks hence, when my wife comes back from Brampton, if she go with my father. By and by came my father to my house, and so he and I went and found out my uncle Wight at the Coffee House, and there did agree with him to meet the next week with my uncle Thomas and read over the Captain's will before them both for their satisfaction. Having done with him I went to my Lady's and dined with her, and after dinner took the two young gentlemen and the two ladies and carried them and Captain Ferrers to the Theatre, and shewed them "The merry Devill of Edmunton,"[1] which is a very merry play, the first time I ever saw it, which pleased me well. And that being done I took them all home by coach to my house and there gave them fruit to eat and wine. So by water home with them, and so home myself.

[11th] (Lord's day). To our own church in the forenoon, and in the afternoon to Clerkenwell Church,[2] only to see the two fayre

---

[1] A comedy acted at the Globe, and first printed in 1608. In the original entry in the Stationers' books it is said to be by T. B., which may stand for Tony or Anthony Brewer. The play has been attributed without authority both to Shakespeare and to Drayton.

[2] The old parish church of St. James the Less, Clerkenwell, was pulled down in 1788, and the first stone of the present church was laid on December 16th of that year. The church was completed in 1792.

Botelers;[1] and I happened to be placed in the pew where they afterwards came to sit, but the pew by their coming being too full, I went out into the next, and there sat, and had my full view of them both, but I am out of conceit now with them, Colonel Dillon being come back from Ireland again, and do still court them, and comes to church with them, which makes me think they are not honest. Hence to Graye's-Inn walks, and there staid a good while; where I met with Ned Pickering, who told me what a great match of hunting of a stagg the King had yesterday; and how the King tired all their horses, and come home with not above two or three able to keep pace with him. So to my father's, and there supped, and so home.

[12th]. At the office this morning. At home in the afternoon, and had notice that my Lord Hinchingbroke is fallen ill, which I fear is with the fruit that I did give them on Saturday last at my house: so in the evening I went thither and there found him very ill, and in great fear of the small-pox. I supped with my Lady, and did consult about him, but we find it best to let him lie where he do; and so I went home with my heart full of trouble for my Lord Hinchingbroke's sickness, and more for my Lord Sandwich's himself, whom we are now confirmed is sick ashore at Alicante, who, if he should miscarry, God knows in what condition would his family be. I dined to-day with my Lord Crew, who is now at Sir H. Wright's, while his new house is making fit for him, and he is much troubled also at these things.

[13th]. To the Privy Seal in the morning, then to the Wardrobe to dinner, where I met my wife, and found my young Lord very ill. So my Lady intends to send her other three sons, Sidney, Oliver, and John,[2] to my house, for fear of the small-pox. After dinner I went to my father's, where I found him within, and went up to him, and there found him settling his papers against his removal, and I took some old papers of difference between

---

[1] Mrs. Frances Butler and her sister.

[2] Hon. Sidney Montagu assumed the name of Wortley, and was father of Edward Wortley Montagu (husband of Lady Mary Wortley Montagu). He died in 1727.

me and my wife and took them away. After that Pall being there
I spoke to my father about my intention not to keep her longer
for such and such reasons, which troubled him and me also,
and had like to have come to some high words between my
mother and me, who is become a very simple woman. By and by
comes in Mrs. Cordery to take her leave of my father, thinking
he was to go presently into the country, and will have us to come
and see her before he do go. Then my father and I went forth to
Mr. Rawlinson's, where afterwards comes my uncle Thomas[1]
and his two sons, and then my uncle Wight by appointment of us
all, and there we read the will and told them how things are, and
what our thoughts are of kindness to my uncle Thomas if he do
carry himself peaceable, but otherwise if he persist to keep his
caveat up against us. So he promised to withdraw it, and seemed
to be very well contented with things as they are. After a while
drinking, we paid all and parted, and so I home, and there found
my Lady's three sons come, of which I am glad that I am in condition to do her and my Lord any service in this kind, but my
mind is yet very much troubled about my Lord of Sandwich's
health, which I am afeard of.

[14th]. This morning Sir W. Batten and Sir W. Pen and I,
waited upon the Duke of York in his chamber, to give him an
account of the condition of the Navy for lack of money, and how
our own very bills are offered upon the Exchange, to be sold at 20
in the 100 loss. He is much troubled at it, and will speak to the
King and Council of it this morning. So I went to my Lady's and
dined with her, and found my Lord Hinchingbroke somewhat
better. After dinner Captain Ferrers and I to the Theatre, and
there saw "The Alchymist"; and there I saw Sir W. Pen, who
took us when the play was done and carried the Captain to Paul's
and set him down, and me home with him, and he and I to the
Dolphin, but not finding Sir W. Batten there, we went and carried a bottle of wine to his house, and there sat a while and talked,
and so home to bed. At home I found a letter from Mr. Creed of
the 15th of July last, that tells me that my Lord is rid of his pain

---

[1] Thomas Pepys of London, next brother to Robert Pepys of Brampton. His
two sons were Thomas and Charles.

(which was wind got into the muscles of his right side) and his feaver, and is now in hopes to go aboard in a day or two, which do give me mighty great comfort.

[15th]. To the Privy Seal and Whitehall, up and down, and at noon Sir W. Pen carried me to Paul's, and so I walked to the Wardrobe and dined with my Lady, and there told her of my Lord's sickness (of which though it hath been the town-talk this fortnight, she had heard nothing[1]) and recovery, of which she was glad, though hardly persuaded of the latter. I found my Lord Hinchingbroke better and better, and the worst past. Thence to the Opera, which begins again to-day with "The Witts,"[2] never acted yet with scenes; and the King and Duke and Duchess were there (who dined to-day with Sir H. Finch,[3] reader at the Temple, in great state); and indeed it is a most excellent play, and admirable scenes. So home and was overtaken by Sir W. Pen in his coach, who has been this afternoon with my Lady Batten, &c., at the Theatre. So I followed him to the Dolphin, where Sir W. Batten was, and there we sat awhile, and so home after we had made shift to fuddle Mr. Falconer of Woolwich. So home.

[16th]. At the office all the morning, though little to be done; because all our clerks are gone to the buriall of Tom Whitton, one of the Controller's clerks, a very ingenious, and a likely young man to live, as any in the Office. But it is such a sickly time both in City and country every where (of a sort of fever), that never was heard of almost, unless it was in a plague-time. Among others, the famous Tom Fuller is dead of it;[4] and Dr.

---

[1] So of the Emperor Claudius:

> "Dabitur mora parvula dum res
> Nota urbi et populo contingat Principis aures.
> Dedecus ille domus sciet ultimus."
>
> Juv., *Sat.*, x. 340.—M. B.

[2] A comedy, by Sir W. Davenant, licensed in January, 1633-34.

[3] Sir Heneage Finch, the Solicitor-General, was treasurer of the Inner Temple, and was selected as autumn reader, when he revived the splendid festivities which had long been discontinued.

[4] Dr. Thomas Fuller, who died on this day, was buried at Cranford, Middlesex, by his patron, Lord Berkeley. Dr. Hardy, Dean of Rochester, preached his funeral sermon.—Smyth's *Obituary*, p. 54.

Nichols,[1] Dean of Paul's; and my Lord General Monk is very dangerously ill. Dined at home with the children and were merry, and my father with me, who after dinner he and I went forth about business. Among other things we found one Dr. John Williams at an alehouse, where we staid till past nine at night, in Shoe Lane, talking about our country business, and I found him so well acquainted with the matters of Gravely that I expect he will be of great use to me. So by link home. I understand my Aunt Fenner is upon the point of death.

[17th]. At the Privy Seal, where we had a seal this morning. Then met with Ned Pickering, and walked with him into St. James's Park (where I had not been a great while), and there found great and very noble alterations. And, in our discourse, he was very forward to complain and to speak loud of the lewdness and beggary of the Court, which I am sorry to hear, and which I am afeard will bring all to ruin again. So he and I to the Wardrobe to dinner, and after dinner Captain Ferrers and I to the Opera, and saw "The Witts" again, which I like exceedingly. The Queen of Bohemia was here, brought by my Lord Craven.[2] So the Captain and I and another to the Devil tavern and drank, and so by coach home. Troubled in mind that I cannot bring myself to mind my business, but to be so much in love of plays. We have been at a great loss a great while for a vessel that I sent about a month ago with things of my Lord's to Lynn, and cannot till now hear of them, but now we are told that they are put into Soale Bay, but to what purpose I know not.

[18th] (Lord's day). To our own church in the morning and so

---

[1] Matthew Nicholas, LL.D., installed Dean of St. Paul's, July, 1660. Died August 14th, 1661, and was buried at Winterbourn-Erles, Wilts. He was brother to Sir Edward Nicholas, Secretary of State.

[2] William, first Earl of Craven, eldest son of Sir William Craven, born 1606. Knighted by Charles I. in 1627, and a few days later created Baron Craven of Hampstead Marshall, Berks. He was rich, and aided the king with money; but in 1649 his estates were confiscated. He recovered them at the Restoration, and in 1664 he was created Earl of Craven. High Steward of the University of Cambridge, 1667, and Master of the Trinity House, 1670-71. He was a devoted adherent of the Queen of Bohemia, and was supposed to be married to her, but there is no direct evidence of such marriage. He died April 9th, 1697.

home to dinner, where my father and Dr. Tom Pepys came to me to dine, and were very merry. After dinner I took my wife and Mr. Sidney to my Lady to see my Lord Hinchingbroke, who is now pretty well again, and sits up and walks about his chamber. So I went to White Hall, and there hear that my Lord General Monk continues very ill: so I went to la belle Pierce and sat with

ELIZABETH PEPYS

her; and then to walk in St. James's Park, and saw great variety of fowl which I never saw before and so home. At night fell to read in "Hooker's Ecclesiastical Polity," which Mr. Moore did give me last Wednesday very handsomely bound; and which I shall read with great pains and love for his sake. So to supper and to bed.

[19th]. At the office all the morning; at noon the children are sent for by their mother my Lady Sandwich to dinner, and my wife goes along with them by coach, and she to my father's and dines

there, and from thence with them to see Mrs. Cordery, who do invite them before my father goes into the country, and thither I should have gone too but that I am sent for to the Privy Seal, and there I found a thing of my Lord Chancellor's[1] to be sealed this afternoon, and so I am forced to go to Worcester House, where severall Lords are met in Council this afternoon. And while I am waiting there, in comes the King in a plain common riding-suit and velvet cap, in which he seemed a very ordinary man to one that had not known him. Here I staid till at last, hearing that my Lord Privy Seal had not the seal here, Mr. Moore and I hired a coach and went to Chelsy,[2] and there at an alehouse sat and drank and past the time till my Lord Privy Seal came to his house, and so we to him and examined and sealed the thing, and so homewards, but when we came to look for our coach we found it gone, so we were fain to walk home afoot and saved our money. We met with a companion that walked with us, and coming among some trees near the Neate[3] houses, he began to whistle, which did give us some suspicion, but it proved that he that answered him was Mr. Marsh[4] (the Lutenist) and his wife, and so we all walked to Westminster together, in our way drinking a while at my cost, and had a song of him, but his voice is quite lost.

[1] This "thing" was probably one of those large grants which Clarendon quietly, or, as he himself says, "without noise or scandal," procured from the king. Besides lands and manors, Clarendon states at one time that the king gave him a "little billet into his hand, that contained a warrant of his own hand-writing to Sir Stephen Fox to pay to the Chancellor the sum of £20,000, of which nobody could have notice." In 1662 he received £25,000 out of the money voted to the king by the Parliament of Ireland, as he mentions in his vindication of himself against the impeachment of the Commons; and we shall see that Pepys, in February, 1664, names another sum of £20,000 given to the Chancellor to clear *the* mortgage upon Clarendon Park; and this last sum, it was believed, was paid from the money received from France by the sale of Dunkirk.—B.

[2] The Lord Privy Seal was John, Lord Robartes, and his house stood at the corner of Paradise Row and Robinson's Lane. Lord Robartes was created Earl of Radnor in 1679, and one of the streets in the neighbourhood of his house is called Radnor Street.

[3] Houses at Chelsea situated on the low ground on the banks of the Thames. The church of St. Gabriel's, Pimlico, marks the site.

[4] Alphonso, son of Robert Marsh, one of the musicians in ordinary to Charles I., baptized at St. Margaret's, Westminster, January 28th, 1627.

So walked home, and there I found that my Lady do keep the children at home, and lets them not come any more hither at present, which a little troubles me to lose their company. This day my aunt Fenner dyed.

[20th]. At the office in the morning and all the afternoon at home to put my papers in order. This day we come to some agreement with Sir R. Ford for his house to be added to the office to enlarge our quarters.

[21st]. This morning by appointment I went to my father, and after a morning draft he and I went to Dr. Williams, but he not within we went to Mrs. Terry, a daughter of Mr. Whately's, who lately offered a proposal of her sister for a wife for my brother Tom, and with her we discoursed about and agreed to go to her mother this afternoon to speak with her, and in the meantime went to Will. Joyce's and to an alehouse, and drank a good while together, he being very angry that his father Fenner will give him and his brother no more for mourning than their father did give him and my aunt at their mother's death, and a very troublesome fellow I still find him to be, that his company ever wearys me. From thence about two o'clock to Mrs. Whately's, but she being going to dinner we went to Whitehall and there staid till past three, and here I understand by Mr. Moore that my Lady Sandwich[1] is brought to bed yesterday of a young Lady, and is very well. So to Mrs. Whately's again, and there were well received, and she desirous to have the thing go forward, only is afeard that her daughter is too young and portion not big enough, but offers £200 down with her. The girl is very well favoured, and a very child, but modest, and one I think will do very well for my brother: so parted till she hears from Hatfield from her husband, who is there; but I find them very desirous of it, and so am I. Hence home to my father's, and I to the Wardrobe, where I supped with the ladies,[2] and hear their mother is well and the young child, and so home.

[22nd]. To the Privy Seal, and sealed; so home at noon, and

---

[1] The child was christened Katherine, see *post*, September 3rd, 1661.
[2] Lady Jemima and Lady Paulina Montagu.

there took my wife by coach to my uncle Fenner's, where there was both at his house and the Sessions, great deal of company, but poor entertainment, which I wonder at; and the house so hot, that my uncle Wight, my father and I were fain to go out, and stay at an alehouse awhile to cool ourselves. Then back again and to church, my father's family being all in mourning, doing him the greatest honour, the world believing that he did give us it: so to church, and staid out the sermon, and then with my aunt Wight, my wife, and Pall and I to her house by coach, and there staid and supped upon a Westphalia ham, and so home and to bed.

[23rd]. This morning I went to my father's, and there found him and my mother in a discontent, which troubles me much, and indeed she is become very simple and unquiet. Hence he and I to Dr. Williams, and found him within, and there we sat and talked a good while, and from him to Tom Trice's to an alehouse near, and there sat and talked, and finding him fair we examined my uncle's will before him and Dr. Williams, and had them sign the copy and so did give T. Trice the original to prove, so he took my father and me to one of the Judges of the Court, and there we were sworn, and so back again to the alehouse and drank and parted. Dr. Williams and I to a cook's where we eat a bit of mutton, and away, I to W. Joyce's, where by appointment my wife was, and I took her to the Opera, and shewed her "The Witts," which I had seen already twice, and was most highly pleased with it. So with my wife to the Wardrobe to see my Lady, and then home.

[24th]. At the office all the morning and did business; by and by we are called to Sir W. Batten's to see the strange creature that Captain Holmes hath brought with him from Guiny; it is a great baboon, but so much like a man in most things, that though they say there is a species of them, yet I cannot believe but that it is a monster got of a man and she-baboon. I do believe that it already understands much English, and I am of the mind it might be taught to speak or make signs. Hence the Comptroller and I to Sir Rd. Ford's and viewed the house again, and are come to a com-

plete end with him to give him £200 per an. for it. Home and there met Capt. Isham inquiring for me to take his leave of me, he being upon his voyage to Portugal, and for my letters to my Lord which are not ready. But I took him to the Mitre and gave him a glass of sack, and so adieu, and then straight to the Opera, and there saw "Hamlet, Prince of Denmark," done with scenes very well, but above all, Betterton[1] did the prince's part beyond imagination. Hence homeward, and met with Mr. Spong and took him to the Sampson in Paul's churchyard, and there staid till late, and it rained hard, so we were fain to get home wet, and so to bed.

[25th] (Lord's day). At church in the morning, and dined at home alone with my wife very comfortably, and so again to church with her, and had a very good time and pungent sermon of Mr. Mills, discoursing the necessity of restitution. Home, and I found my Lady Batten and her daughter to look something askew upon my wife, because my wife do not buckle to them, and is not solicitous for their acquaintance, which I am not troubled at at all. By and by comes in my father (he intends to go into the country to-morrow), and he and I among other discourse at last called Pall up to us, and there in great anger told her before my father that I would keep her no longer, and my father he said he would have nothing to do with her. At last, after we had brought down her high spirit, I got my father to yield that she should go into the country with my mother and him, and stay there awhile to see how she will demean herself. That being done, my father and I to my uncle Wight's, and there supped, and he took his leave of them, and so I walked with [him] as far as Paul's and there parted, and I home, my mind at some rest upon this making an end with Pall, who do trouble me exceedingly.

[26th]. This morning before I went out I made even with my maid Jane, who has this day been my maid three years, and is this day to go into the country to her mother. The poor girl cried,

---

[1] Sir William Davenant introduced the use of scenery. The character of Hamlet was one of Betterton's masterpieces. Downes tells us that he was taught by Davenant how the part was acted by Taylor of the Blackfriars, who was instructed by Shakespeare himself.

and I could hardly forbear weeping to think of her going, for though she be grown lazy and spoilt by Pall's coming, yet I shall never have one to please us better in all things, and so harmless, while I live. So I paid her her wages and gave her 2s. 6d. over, and bade her adieu, with my mind full of trouble at her going. Hence to my father, where he and I and Thomas together setting things even, and casting up my father's accounts, and upon the whole I find that all he hath in money of his own due to him in the world is but £45, and he owes about the same sum: so that I cannot but think in what a condition he had left my mother if he should have died before my uncle Robert. Hence to Tom Trice for the probate of the will and had it done to my mind, which did give my father and me good content. From thence to my Lady at the Wardrobe and thence to the Theatre, and saw the "Antipodes,"[1] wherein there is much mirth, but no great matter else. Hence with Mr. Bostock whom I met there (a clerk formerly of Mr. Phelps) to the Devil tavern, and there drank and so away. I to my uncle Fenner's, where my father was with him at an alehouse, and so we three went by ourselves and sat talking a great while about a broker's daughter that he do propose for a wife for Tom, with a great portion, but I fear it will not take, but he will do what he can. So we broke up, and going through the street we met with a mother and son, friends of my father's man, Ned's, who are angry at my father's putting him away, which troubled me and my father, but all will be well as to that. We have news this morning of my uncle Thomas and his son Thomas being gone into the country without giving notice thereof to anybody, which puts us to a stand, but I fear them not. At night at home I found a letter from my Lord Sandwich, who is now very well again of his feaver, but not yet gone from Alicante, where he lay sick, and was twice let blood. This letter dated the 22nd July last, which puts me out of doubt of his being ill. In my coming home I called in at the 3 Crane tavern[2] at the Stocks by appointment,

---

[1] A comedy, by Richard Brome, first acted at Salisbury Court, 1638, and published in 1640.

[2] This Three Cranes tavern was situated in the Poultry. There is a token of George Twine, dated 1665 (see "Boyne's Trade Tokens," ed. Williamson, vol. i., 1889, p. 704).

and there met and took leave of Mr. Fanshaw, who goes to-morrow and Captain Isham toward their voyage to Portugal. Here we drank a great deal of wine, I too much and Mr. Fanshaw till he could hardly go. So we took leave one of another.

[27th]. This morning to the Wardrobe, and there took leave of my Lord Hinchingbroke and his brother, and saw them go out by coach toward Rye in their way to France, whom God bless. Then I was called up to my Lady's bedside, where we talked an hour about Mr. Edward Montagu's disposing of the £5,000 for my Lord's departure for Portugal, and our fears that he will not do it to my Lord's honour, and less to his profit, which I am to enquire a little after. Hence to the office, and there sat till noon, and then my wife and I by coach to my cozen, Thos. Pepys, the Executor, to dinner, where some ladies and my father and mother, where very merry, but methinks he makes but poor dinners for such guests, though there was a poor venison pasty. Hence my wife and I to the Theatre, and there saw "The Joviall Crew,"[1] where the King, Duke and Duchess, and Madame Palmer, were; and my wife, to her great content, had a full sight of them all the while. The play full of mirth. Hence to my father's, and there staid to talk a while and so by foot home by moonshine. In my way and at home, my wife making a sad story to me of her brother Balty's[2] condition, and would have me to do something for him, which I shall endeavour to do, but am afeard to meddle therein for fear I shall not be able to wipe my hands of him again, when I once concern myself for him. I went to bed, my wife all the while telling me his case with tears, which troubled me.

[28th]. At home all the morning setting papers in order. At noon to the Exchange, and there met with Dr. Williams by appointment, and with him went up and down to look for an attorney, a friend of his, to advise with about our bond of my aunt Pepys of £200, and he tells me absolutely that we shall not be forced to pay interest for the money yet. I do doubt it very much. I spent

---

[1] "The Jovial Crew, or the Merry Beggars," a comedy, by Richard Brome, first acted at the Cockpit, Drury Lane, in 1641. Published in 1652.
[2] Balthazar St. Michel, see *ante*, February 8th, 1659-60 (note).

the whole afternoon drinking with him and so home. This day I counterfeited a letter to Sir W. Pen, as from the thief that stole his tankard lately, only to abuse and laugh at him.

[29th]. At the office all the morning, and at noon my father, mother, and my aunt Bell (the first time that ever she was at my house) come to dine with me, and were very merry. After dinner the two women went to visit my aunt Wight, &c., and my father about other business, and I abroad to my bookseller, and there staid till four o'clock, at which time by appointment I went to meet my father at my uncle Fenner's. So thither I went and with him to an alehouse, and there came Mr. Evans, the taylor, whose daughter we have had a mind to get for a wife for Tom, and then my father, and there we sat a good while and talked about the business; in fine he told us that he hath not to except against us or our motion, but that the estate that God hath blessed him with is too great to give where there is nothing in present possession but a trade and house; and so we friendly ended. There parted, my father and I together, and walked a little way, and then at Holborn he and I took leave of one another, he being to go to Brampton (to settle things against my mother comes) to-morrow morning. So I home.

[30th]. At noon my wife and I met at the Wardrobe, and there dined with the children, and after dinner up to my Lady's bedside, and talked and laughed a good while. Then my wife and I to Drury Lane to the French comedy,[1] which was so ill done, and the scenes and company and everything else so nasty and out of order and poor, that I was sick all the while in my mind to be there. Here my wife met with a son of my Lord Somersett,[2] whom she knew in France, a pretty man; I showed him no great countenance, to avoyd further acquaintance. That done, there being nothing pleasant but the foolery of the farce, we went home.

---

[1] The French comedians acted at the Cockpit. The Theatre Royal on the site of the present Drury Lane Theatre was not built till 1663.

[2] Lord John Somerset, second son of the first Marquis of Worcester, had himself three sons, Henry, Thomas, and Charles, but it is uncertain which is here meant. There was no other Lord Somerset to whom the passage could apply. It was probably Thomas, as the other brothers were married.—B.

[31st]. At home and the office all the morning, and at noon comes Luellin to me, and he and I to the tavern and after that to Bartholomew fair, and there upon his motion to a pitiful alehouse, where we had a dirty slut or two come up that were whores, but my very heart went against them, so that I took no pleasure but a great deal of trouble in being there and getting from thence for fear of being seen. From hence he and I walked towards Ludgate and parted. I back again to the fair all alone, and there met with my Ladies Jemimah and Paulina, with Mr. Pickering and Madamoiselle,[1] at seeing the monkeys dance, which was much to see, when they could be brought to do so, but it troubled me to sit among such nasty company. After that with them into Christ's Hospitall, and there Mr. Pickering bought them some fairings, and I did give every one of them a bauble, which was the little globes of glass with things hanging in them, which pleased the ladies very well. After that home with them in their coach, and there was called up to my Lady, and she would have me stay to talk with her, which I did I think a full hour. And the poor lady did with so much innocency tell me how Mrs. Crispe had told her that she did intend, by means of a lady that lies at her house, to get the King to be godfather to the young lady that she is in child-bed now of; but to see in what a manner my Lady told it me, protesting that she sweat in the very telling of it, was the greatest pleasure to me in the world to see the simplicity and harmlessness of a lady. Then down to supper with the ladies, and so home, Mr. Moore (as he and I cannot easily part) leading me as far as Fenchurch Street to the Mitre, where we drank a glass of wine and so parted, and I home and to bed.

Thus ends the month. My maid Jane newly gone, and Pall left now to do all the work till another maid comes, which shall not be till she goes away into the country with my mother. Myself and wife in good health. My Lord Sandwich in the Straits and newly recovered of a great sickness at Alicante. My father gone to settle at Brampton, and myself under much business and trouble for to settle things in the estate to our content. But what is worst, I find myself lately too much given to seeing of plays,

---

[1] The young ladies' governess.

and expense, and pleasure, which makes me forget my business, which I must labour to amend. No money comes in, so that I have been forced to borrow a great deal for my own expenses, and to furnish my father, to leave things in order. I have some trouble about my brother Tom, who is now left to keep my father's trade, in which I have great fears that he will miscarry for want of brains and care. At Court things are in very ill condition, there being so much emulacion, poverty, and the vices of drinking, swearing, and loose amours, that I know not what will be the end of it, but confusion. And the Clergy so high, that all people that I meet with do protest against their practice. In short, I see no content or satisfaction any where, in any one sort of people. The Benevolence[1] proves so little, and an occasion of so much discontent every where, that it had better it had never been set up. I think to subscribe £20. We are at our Office quiet, only for lack of money all things go to rack. Our very bills offered to be sold upon the Exchange at 10 per cent. loss. We are upon getting Sir R. Ford's house added to our Office. But I see so many difficulties will follow in pleasing of one another in the dividing of it, and in becoming bound personally to pay the rent of £200 per annum, that I do believe it will yet scarce come to pass. The season very sickly every where of strange and fatal fevers.

[September 1st] (Lord's day). Last night being very rainy [the rain] broke into my house, the gutter being stopped, and spoiled all my ceilings almost. At church in the morning, and dined at home with my wife. After dinner to Sir W. Batten's, where I found Sir W. Pen and Captain Holmes. Here we were very merry with Sir W. Pen about the loss of his tankard, though all be but a cheat, and he do not yet understand it; but the tankard was stole by Sir W. Batten, and the letter, as from the thief, wrote by me, which makes very good sport. Here I staid all the afternoon, and then Captain Holmes and I by coach to White Hall; in our way, I found him by discourse, to be a great friend of my Lord's, and he told me there was many did seek to remove him; but they were old seamen, such as Sir J. Minnes (but he would name no

---

[1] A voluntary contribution made by the subjects to their sovereign. Upon this occasion the clergy alone gave £33,743. See May 31st, 1661.—B.

more, though I do believe Sir W. Batten is one of them that do envy him), but he says he knows that the King do so love him, and the Duke of York too, that there is no fear of him. He seems to be very well acquainted with the King's mind, and with all the several factions at Court, and spoke all with so much frankness, that I do take him to be my Lord's good friend, and one able to do

SIR WILLIAM PENN

him great service, being a cunning fellow, and one (by his own confession to me) that can put on two several faces, and look his enemies in the face with as much love as his friends. But, good God! what an age is this, and what a world is this! that a man cannot live without playing the knave and dissimulation. At Whitehall we parted, and I to Mrs. Pierce's, meeting her and Madam Clifford in the street, and there staid talking and laughing with them a good while, and so back to my mother's, and there supped, and so home and to bed.

[2nd]. In the morning to my cozen Thos. Pepys, executor, and there talked with him about my uncle Thomas, his being in the country, but he could not advise me to anything therein, not knowing what the other has done in the country, and so we parted. And so to Whitehall, and there my Lord Privy Seal, who has been out of town this week, not being yet come, we can have no seal, and therefore meeting with Mr. Battersby the apothecary in Fenchurch Street to the King's Apothecary's chamber in Whitehall, and there drank a bottle or two of wine, and so he and I by water towards London. I landed at Blackfriars and so to the Wardrobe and dined, and then back to Whitehall with Captain Ferrers, and there walked, and thence to Westminster Hall, where we met with Mr. Pickering, and so all of us to the Rhenish wine house (Prior's), where the master of the house is laying out some money in making a cellar with an arch in his yard, which is very convenient for him. Here we staid a good while, and so Mr. Pickering and I to Westminster Hall again, and there walked an hour or two talking, and though he be a fool, yet he keeps much company, and will tell all he sees or hears, and so a man may understand what the common talk of the town is, and I find by him that there are endeavours to get my Lord out of play at sea, which I believe Mr. Coventry and the Duke do think will make them more absolute; but I hope, for all this, they will not be able to do it. He tells me plainly of the vices of the Court, and how the pox is so common there, and so I hear on all hands that it is as common as eating and swearing. From him by water to the bridge, and thence to the Mitre, where I met my uncle and aunt Wight come to see Mrs. Rawlinson (in her husband's absence out of town), and so I staid with them and Mr. Lucas and other company, very merry, and so home, where my wife has been busy all the day making of pies, and had been abroad and bought things for herself, and tells me that she met at the Change with my young ladies of the Wardrobe, and there helped them to buy things, and also with Mr. Somersett, who did give her a bracelet of rings, which did a little trouble me, though I know there is no hurt yet in it, but only for fear of further acquaintance. So to bed. This night I sent another letter to Sir W.

Pen to offer him the return of his tankard upon his leaving of 30*s.* at a place where it should be brought. The issue of which I am to expect.

[3rd]. This day some of us Commissioners went down to Deptford to pay off some ships, but I could not go, but staid at home all the morning setting papers to rights, and this morning Mr. Howell, our turner, sent me two things to file papers on very handsome. Dined at home, and then with my wife to the Wardrobe, where my Lady's child was christened (my Lord Crew and his Lady, and my Lady Montagu, my Lord's mother-in-law, were the witnesses), and named Katherine[1] (the Queen elect's name); but to my and all our trouble, the Parson of the parish christened her, and did not sign the child with the sign of the cross. After that was done, we had a very fine banquet, the best I ever was at, and so (there being very little company) we by and by broke up, and my wife and I to my mother, who I took a liberty to advise about her getting things ready to go this week into the country to my father, and she (being become now-a-days very simple) took it very ill, and we had a great deal of noise and wrangling about it. So home by coach.

[4th]. In the morning to the Privy Seal to do some things of the last month, my Lord Privy Seal having been some time out of town. Then my wife came to me to Whitehall, and we went and walked a good while in St. James's Park to see the brave alterations, and so to Wilkinson's, the Cook's, to dinner, where we sent for Mrs. Sarah and there dined and had oysters, the first I have eat this year, and were pretty good. After dinner by agreement to visit Mrs. Symonds, but she is abroad, which I wonder at, and so missing her my wife again to my mother's (calling at Mrs. Pierce's who we found brought to bed of a girl last night) and there staid and drank, and she resolves to be going to-morrow without fail. Many friends come in to take their leave of her, but a great deal of stir I had again to-night about getting her to go to

---

[1] Lady Katherine Montagu, youngest daughter of Lord Sandwich, married, first, Nicholas Bacon, eldest son and heir of Sir Nicholas Bacon, K.B., of Shrubland Hall, co. Suffolk; and, secondly, the Rev. Balthazar Gardeman. She died January 15th, 1757, æt. ninety-six years, four months.—B.

see my Lady Sandwich before she goes, which she says she will do to-morrow. So I home.

[5th]. To the Privy Seal this morning about business, in my way taking leave of my mother, who goes to Brampton to-day. But doing my business at the Privy Seal pretty soon, I took boat and went to my uncle Fenner's, and there I found my mother and my wife and Pall (of whom I had this morning at my own house taken leave, and given her 20s. and good counsel how to carry herself to my father and mother), and so I took them, it being late, to Beard's, where they were staid for, and so I put them into the waggon, and saw them going presently, Pall crying exceedingly. Then in with my wife, my aunt Bell and Charles Pepys, whom we met there, and drank, and so to my uncle Fenner's to dinner (in the way meeting a French footman[1] with feathers, who was in quest of my wife, and spoke with her privately, but I could not tell what it was, only my wife promised to go to some place to-morrow morning, which do trouble my mind how to know whither it was), where both his sons and daughters were, and there we were merry and dined. After dinner news was brought that my aunt Kite, the butcher's widow in London, is sick ready to die and sends for my uncle and me to come to take charge of things, and to be intrusted with the care of her daughter. But I through want of time to undertake such a business, I was taken up by Antony Joyce, which came at last to very high words, which made me very angry, and I did not think that he would ever have been such a fool to meddle with other people's business, but I saw he spoke worse to his father than to me, and therefore I bore it the better, but all the company was offended with him, so we parted angry he and I, and so my wife and I to the fair, and I showed her the Italians dancing the ropes, and the women that do strange tumbling tricks, and so by foot home vexed in my mind about Antony Joyce.

[6th]. This morning my uncle Fenner by appointment came and drank his morning draft with me, and from thence he and I to see my aunt Kite (my wife holding her resolution to go this morn-

[1] Apparently a servant of Mr. Somerset's.—B.

ing as she resolved yesterday, and though there could not be much hurt in it, yet my own jealousy put a hundred things into my mind, which did much trouble me all day), whom we found in bed and not like to live as we think, and she told us her mind was that if she should die she should give all she had to her daughter, only £5 apiece to her second husband's children, in case they live to come out of their apprenticeships, and that if her daughter should die before marrying, then £10 to be divided between Sarah Kite's children and the rest as her own daughter shall dispose of it, and this I set down that I may be able to swear in case there should be occasion. From thence to an alehouse while it rained, which kept us there I think above two hours, and at last we were fain to go through the rainy street home, calling on his sister Utbeck and drank there. Then I home to dinner all alone, and thence my mind being for my wife's going abroad much troubled and unfit for business, I went to the Theatre, and saw "Elder Brother"[1] ill acted; that done, meeting here with Sir G. Askew,[2] Sir Theophilus Jones,[3] and another Knight, with Sir W. Pen, we to the Ship tavern, and there staid and were merry till late at night, and so got a coach, and Sir Wm. and I home, where my wife had been long come home, but I seemed very angry, as indeed I am, and did not all night show her any countenance, neither before nor in bed, and so slept and rose discontented.

[7th]. At the office all the morning. At noon Mr. Moore dined with me, and then in comes Wm. Joyce to answer a letter of mine I wrote this morning to him about a maid of his that my wife had hired, and she sent us word that she was hired to stay longer with her master, which mistake he came to clear himself of, and I took it very kindly. So I having appointed the young ladies at the

---

[1] A comedy, by John Fletcher, acted at the Blackfriars. It was published first in 1637.

[2] Admiral Sir George Ayscue, knighted by Charles I., but appointed Admiral of the Fleet in the Irish Seas in 1649 "for his fidelity and good affection to the Parliament." Vice-Admiral of the Blue Squadron under the Duke of York in the action with the Dutch fleet on June 3rd, 1665, and Admiral of the White under Prince Rupert and the Duke of Albemarle in 1666, when he was taken prisoner by the Dutch (see Diary, June 7th, 1666).

[3] Sir Theophilus Jones had represented the county of Dublin in Parliament, and served as a Colonel in the Commonwealth army.—B.

Wardrobe to go with them to a play to-day, I left him and my brother Tom who came along with him to dine, and my wife and I took them to the Theatre, where we seated ourselves close by the King, and Duke of York, and Madame Palmer, which was great content; and, indeed, I can never enough admire her beauty. And here was "Bartholomew Fayre," with the puppet-show, acted to-day, which had not been these forty years (it being so satyricall against Puritanism, they durst not till now, which is strange they should already dare to do it, and the King do countenance it), but I do never a whit like it the better for the puppets, but rather the worse. Thence home with the ladies, it being by reason of our staying a great while for the King's coming, and the length of the play, near nine o'clock before it was done, and so in their coach home, and still in discontent with my wife, to bed, and rose so this morning also.

[8th] (Lord's day). To church, it being a very wet night last night and to-day, dined at home, and so to church again with my wife in the afternoon, and coming home again found our new maid Doll[1] asleep, that she could not hear to let us in, so that we were fain to send the boy in at a window to open the door to us. So up to my chamber all alone, and troubled in mind to think how much of late I have addicted myself to expense and pleasure, that now I can hardly reclaim myself to look after my great business of settling Gravely business, till it is now almost too late. I pray God give me grace to begin now to look after my business, but it always was, and I fear will ever be, my foible that after I am once got behindhand with business, I am hard to set to it again to recover it. In the evening I begun to look over my accounts, and upon the whole I do find myself, by what I can yet see, worth near £600, for which God be blessed, which put me into great comfort. So to supper and to bed.

[9th]. To the Privy Seal in the morning, but my Lord did not come, so I went with Captain Morrice at his desire into the King's Privy Kitchen to Mr. Sayres, the Master Cook, and there we had

---

[1] Dorothy or Doll did not stay long, for on November 27th we find that Mrs. Pepys parted with her.

a good slice of beef or two to our breakfast, and from thence he took us into the wine cellar where, by my troth, we were very merry, and I drank too much wine, and all along had great and particular kindness from Mr. Sayres, but I drank so much wine that I was not fit for business, and therefore at noon I went and walked in Westminster Hall a while, and thence to Salisbury Court play house, where was acted the first time " 'Tis pity Shee's a Whore,"[1] a simple play and ill acted, only it was my fortune to sit by a most pretty and most ingenious lady, which pleased me much. Thence home, and found Sir Williams both and much more company gone to the Dolphin to drink the 30s. that we got the other day of Sir W. Pen about his tankard. Here was Sir R. Slingsby, Holmes, Captn. Allen, Mr. Turner, his wife and daughter, my Lady Batten, and Mrs. Martha, &c., and an excellent company of fiddlers; so we exceeding merry till late; and then we begun to tell Sir W. Pen the business, but he had been drinking to-day, and so is almost gone, that we could not make him understand it, which caused us more sport. But so much the better, for I believe when he do come to understand it he will be angry, he has so talked of the business himself and the letter up and down that he will be ashamed to be found abused in it. So home and to bed.

[10th]. At the office all the morn, dined at home; then my wife into Wood Street to buy a chest, and thence to buy other things at my uncle Fenner's (though by reason of rain we had ill walking), thence to my brother Tom's, and there discoursed with him about business, and so to the Wardrobe to see my Lady, and after supper with the young ladies, bought a link and carried it myself till I met one that would light me home for the link. So he light me home with his own, and then I did give him mine. This night I found Mary, my cozen W. Joyce's maid, come to me to be my cook maid, and so my house is full again. So to bed.

[11th]. Early to my cozen Thomas Trice to discourse about our affairs, and he did make demand of the £200 and the interest

---

[1] A tragedy, by John Ford, acted at the Phœnix, Drury Lane, and printed 1633.

thereof. But for the £200 I did agree to pay him, but for the other I did desire to be advised. So from him to Dr. Williams,[1] who did carry me into his garden, where he hath abundance of grapes; and did show me how a dog that he hath do kill all the cats that come thither to kill his pigeons, and do afterwards bury them; and do it with so much care that they shall be quite covered; that if but the tip of the tail hangs out he will take up the cat again, and dig the hole deeper. Which is very strange; and he tells me that he do believe that he hath killed above 100 cats. After he was ready we went up and down to inquire about my affairs and then parted and to the Wardrobe, and there took Mr. Moore to Tom Trice, who promised to let Mr. Moore have copies of the bond and my aunt's deed of gift, and so I took him home to my house to dinner, where I found my wife's brother, Balty, as fine as hands could make him, and his servant, a Frenchman, to wait on him, and come to have my wife to visit a young lady which he is a servant to, and have hope to trepan and get for his wife. I did give way for my wife to go with him, and so after dinner they went, and Mr. Moore and I out again, he about his business and I to Dr. Williams to talk with him again, and he and I walking through Lincoln's Inn Fields observed at the Opera a new play, "Twelfth Night,"[2] was acted there, and the King there; so I, against my own mind and resolution, could not forbear to go in, which did make the play seem a burthen to me, and I took no pleasure at all in it; and so after it was done went home with my mind troubled for my going thither, after my swearing to my wife that I would never go to a play without her. So that what with this and things going so cross to me as to matters of my uncle's estate, makes me very much troubled in my mind, and so to bed. My wife was with her brother to see his mistress to-day, and says she is young, rich, and handsome, but not likely for him to get.

[12th]. Though it was an office day, yet I was forced to go to the Privy Seal, at which I was all the morning, and from thence to

---

[1] Dr. Williams's house was in Holborn.

[2] Pepys seldom liked any play of Shakespeare's, and he sadly blundered when he supposed "Twelfth Night" was a new play.

my Lady's to dinner at the Wardrobe; and in my way upon the Thames, I saw the King's new pleasure-boat that is come now for the King to take pleasure in above bridge; and also two Gundaloes[1] that are lately brought which are very rich and fine. After dinner I went into my Lady's chamber where I found her up now out of her child-bed, which I was glad to see, and after an hour's talk with her I took leave and to Tom Trice again, and sat talking and drinking with him about our business a great while. I do find I am likely to be forced to pay interest for the £200. By and by in comes my uncle Thomas, and as he was always a close cunning fellow, so he carries himself to me, and says nothing of what his endeavours are, though to my trouble I know that he is about recovering of Gravely, but neither I nor he began any discourse of the business. From thence to Dr. Williams (at the little blind alehouse in Shoe Lane, at the Gridiron, a place I am ashamed to be seen to go into), and there with some bland counsel of his we discuss our matters, but I find men of so different minds that by my troth I know not what to trust to. It being late I took leave, and by link home and called at Sir W. Batten's, and there hear that Sir W. Pen do take our jest of the tankard very ill, which I am sorry for.

[13th]. This morning I was sent for by my uncle Fenner to come and advise about the buriall of my aunt, the butcher, who died yesterday; and from thence to the Anchor, by Doctor's Commons, and there Dr. Williams and I did write a letter for my purpose to Mr. Sedgewick, of Cambridge, about Gravely business, and after that I left him and an attorney with him and went to the Wardrobe, where I found my wife, and thence she and I to the water to spend the afternoon in pleasure; and so we went to old George's, and there eat as much as we would of a hot shoulder of mutton, and so to boat again and home. So to bed, my mind very full of business and trouble.

---

[1] "Two long boats that were made in Venice, called gondolas, were by the Duke of Venice (Dominico Contareni) presented to His Majesty; and the attending watermen, being four, were in very rich clothes, crimson satin; very big were their breeches and doublets; they wore also very large shirts of the same satin, very richly laced."—Rugge's *Diurnal.*—B.

[14th]. At the office all the morning, at noon to the Change, and then home again. To dinner, where my uncle Fenner by appointment came and dined with me, thinking to go together to my aunt Kite's that is dead; but before we had dined comes Sir R. Slingsby and his lady, and a great deal of company, to take my wife and I out by barge to shew them the King's and Duke's yachts. So I was forced to leave my uncle and brother Tom at dinner and go forth with them, and we had great pleasure, seeing all four yachts, viz., these two and the two Dutch ones. And so home again, and after writing letters by post, to bed.

[15th] (Lord's day). To my aunt Kite's in the morning to help my uncle Fenner to put things in order against anon for the buriall, and at noon home again; and after dinner to church, my wife and I, and after sermon with my wife to the buriall of my aunt Kite, where besides us and my uncle Fenner's family, there was none of any quality, but poor rascally people. So we went to church with the corps, and there had service read at the grave, and back again with Pegg Kite, who will be, I doubt, a troublesome carrion to us executors; but if she will not be ruled, I shall fling up my executorship. After that home, and Will Joyce along with me, where we sat and talked and drank and ate an hour or two, and so he went away and I up to my chamber and then to prayers and to bed.

[16th]. This morning I was busy at home to take in my part of our freight of Coles, which Sir G. Carteret, Sir R. Slingsby, and myself sent for, which is ten Chaldron, 8 of which I took in, and with the other to repay Sir W. Pen what I borrowed of him a little while ago. So that from this day I should see how long 10 chaldron of coals will serve my house, if it please the Lord to let me live to see them burned. In the afternoon by appointment to meet Dr. Williams and his attorney, and they and I to Tom Trice, and there got him in discourse to confess the words that he had said that his mother did desire him not to see my uncle about her £200 bond while she was alive. Here we were at high words with T. Trice and then parted, and we to Standing's, in Fleet Street, where we sat and drank and talked a great while about my going

157

down to Gravely Court,[1] which will be this week, whereof the Doctor had notice in a letter from his sister this week. In the middle of our discourse word was brought me from my brother's that there is a fellow come from my father out of the country, on purpose to speak to me, so I went to him and he made a story how he had lost his letter, but he was sure it was for me to go into the country, which I believed, and thought it might be to give me notice of Gravely Court, but I afterwards found that it was a rogue that did use to play such tricks to get money of people, but he got none of me. At night I went home, and there found letters from my father informing me of the Court, and that I must come down and meet him at Impington, which I presently resolved to do.

[17th]. And the next morning got up, telling my wife of my journey, and she with a few words got me to hire her a horse to go along with me. So I went to my Lady's and elsewhere to take leave, and of Mr. Townsend did borrow a very fine side-saddle for my wife; and so after all things were ready, she and I took coach to the end of the town towards Kingsland, and there got upon my horse and she upon her pretty mare that I hired for her, and she rides very well. By the mare at one time falling she got a fall, but no harm; so we got to Ware, and there supped, and to bed very merry and pleasant.

[18th]. The next morning up early and begun our march; the way about Puckridge[2] very bad, and my wife, in the very last dirty place of all, got a fall, but no hurt, though some dirt. At last she begun, poor wretch, to be tired, and I to be angry at it, but I was to blame; for she is a very good companion as long as she is well. In the afternoon we got to Cambridge, where I left my wife at my cozen Angier's while I went to Christ's College, and there found my brother in his chamber, and talked with him; and so to the barber's, and then to my wife again, and remounted for Impington, where my uncle received me and my wife very

---

[1] The manorial court of Gravely, in Huntingdonshire, to which Impington owed suit or service, and under which the Pepys's copyhold estates were held. See July 8th, 1661, *ante.*—B.

[2] Puckeridge, a village in Hertfordshire six and a half miles N.N.E. of Ware.

kindly. And by and by in comes my father, and we supped and talked and were merry, but being weary and sleepy my wife and I to bed without talking with my father anything about our business.

[19th]. Up early, and my father and I alone into the garden, and there talked about our business, and what to do therein. So after I had talked and advised with my coz Claxton, and then with my uncle by his bedside, we all horsed away to Cambridge, where my father and I, having left my wife at the Beare with my brother, went to Mr. Sedgewicke, the steward of Gravely, and there talked with him, but could get little hopes from anything that he would tell us, but at last I did give him a fee, and then he was free to tell me what I asked, which was something, though not much comfort. From thence to our horses, and with my wife went and rode through Sturbridge[1] fair, but the fair was almost done. So we did not 'light there at all, but went back to Cambridge, and there at the Beare had some herrings, we and my brother, and after dinner set out for Brampton, where we come in very good time, and found all things well, and being somewhat weary, after some talk about to-morrow's business with my father, we went to bed.

[20th]. Will Stankes and I set out in the morning betimes for Gravely, where to an ale-house and drank, and then, going towards the Court House, met my uncle Thomas and his son Thomas, with Bradly, the rogue that had betrayed us, and one Young, a cunning fellow, who guides them. There passed no unkind words at all between us, but I seemed fair and went to drink with them. I said little till by and by that we come to the Court, which was a simple meeting of a company of country rogues, with the Steward, and two Fellows of Jesus College, that are lords of the town where the jury were sworn; and I producing no surrender, though I told them I was sure there is and must be one

---

[1] Sturbridge fair is of great antiquity. The first trace of it is found in a charter granted about 1211 by King John to the Lepers of the Hospital of St. Mary Magdalen at Sturbridge by Cambridge, a fair to be held in the close of the hospital on the vigil and feast of the Holy Cross (see Cornelius Walford's "Fairs Past and Present," 1883, p. 54).

somewhere, they found my uncle Thomas heir at law,[1] as he is, and so, though I did tell him and his son that they would find themselves abused by these fellows, and did advise them to forbear being admitted this Court (which they could have done, but that these rogues did persuade them to do it now), my uncle was admitted, and his son also, in reversion after his father, which he did well in to secure his money. The father paid a year and a half for his fine, and the son half a year, in all £48, besides about £3 fees; so that I do believe the charges of his journeys, and what he gives those two rogues, and other expenses herein, cannot be less than £70, which will be a sad thing for them if a surrender be found. After all was done, I openly wished them joy in it, and so rode to Offord with them and there parted fairly without any words. I took occasion to bid them money for their half acre of land, which I had a mind to do that in the surrender I might secure Piggott's, which otherwise I should be forced to lose. So with Stankes home and supped, and after telling my father how things went, I went to bed with my mind in good temper, because I see the matter and manner of the Court and the bottom of my business, wherein I was before and should always have been ignorant.

[21st]. All the morning pleasing myself with my father, going up and down the house and garden with my father and my wife, contriving some alterations. After dinner (there coming this morning my aunt Hanes and her son from London, that is to live with my father) I rode to Huntingdon, where I met Mr. Philips, and there put my Bugden[2] matter in order against the Court, and so to Hinchingbroke, where Mr. Barnwell shewed me the condition of the house, which is yet very backward, and I fear will be very dark in the cloyster when it is done. So home and to supper and to bed, very pleasant and quiet.

[22nd] (Lord's day). Before church time walking with my father in the garden contriving. So to church, where we had common prayer, and a dull sermon by one Mr. Case,[3] who yet I heard

---

[1] To Robert Pepys of Brampton, his eldest brother.

[2] Bugden, or Buckden, a village and parish in the St. Neots district of Huntingdonshire, four miles S.W. of Huntingdon.

[3] Probably Thomas Case, see *ante*, May 15th, 1660.

sing very well. So to dinner, and busy with my father about his accounts all the afternoon, and people came to speak with us about business. Mr. Barnwell at night came and supped with us. So after setting matters even with my father and I, to bed.

BRAMPTON

[23rd]. Up, and sad to hear my father and mother wrangle as they used to do in London, of which I took notice to both, and told them that I should give over care for anything unless they would spend what they have with more love and quiet. So (John Bowles coming to see us before we go) we took horse and got early to Baldwick,¹ where there was a fair, and we put in and eat a mouthfull of pork, which they made us pay 14*d*. for, which vexed us much. And so away to Stevenage, and staid till a showre was over, and so rode easily to Welling, where we supped well, and had two beds in the room and so lay single, and still remember it that of all the nights that ever I slept in my life I never did pass a night with more epicurism of sleep; there being now and then a noise of people stirring that waked me, and then it was a very rainy night, and then I was a little weary, that what between waking and then sleeping again, one after another, I never had

¹ Baldock, a town, parish, and sub-district in the district of Hitchin, Herts.

so much content in all my life, and so my wife says it was with her.

[24th]. We rose, and set forth, but found a most sad alteration in the road by reason of last night's rains, they being now all dirty and washy, though not deep. So we rode easily through, and only drinking at Holloway, at the sign of a woman with cakes in one hand and a pot of ale in the other,[1] which did give good occasion of mirth, resembling her to the maid that served us, we got home very timely and well, and finding there all well, and letters from sea, that speak of my Lord's being well, and his action, though not considerable of any side, at Argier.[2] I went straight to my Lady, and there sat and talked with her, and so home again, and after supper we to bed somewhat weary, hearing of nothing ill since my absence but my brother Tom, who is pretty well though again.

[25th]. By coach with Sir W. Pen to Covent Garden. By the way, upon my desire, he told me that I need not fear any reflection upon my Lord for their ill success at Argier, for more could not be done than was done. I went to my cozen, Thos. Pepys, there, and talked with him a good while about our country business, who is troubled at my uncle Thomas his folly, and so we parted; and then meeting Sir R. Slingsby in St. Martin's Lane, he and I in his coach through the Mewes,[3] which is the way that now all coaches are forced to go, because of a stop at Charing Cross, by reason of a drain there to clear the streets. To Whitehall, and there to Mr. Coventry, and talked with him, and thence to my Lord Crew's and dined with him, where I was used with all imaginable kindness both from him and her. And I see that he is afraid that my Lord's reputacion will a little suffer in common talk by this late success; but there is no help for it now. The Queen

---

[1] Probably the original of the well-known Mother Red-Cap at Upper Holloway.

[2] Algiers.

[3] The Mews stood on the site of the present National Gallery. The place was originally occupied by the king's falcons, but in the reign of Henry VIII. it was turned into a stable. After the battle of Naseby it was used as a prison for a time. The Mews was rebuilt in 1732, and taken down in 1830.

of England (as she is now owned and called) I hear doth keep open Court, and distinct at Lisbon. Hence, much against my nature and will, yet such is the power of the Devil over me I could not refuse it, to the Theatre, and saw "The Merry Wives of Windsor," ill done. And that ended, with Sir W. Pen and Sir G. More to the tavern, and so home with him by coach, and after supper to prayers and to bed. In full quiet of mind as to thought, though full of business, blessed be God.

[26th]. At the office all the morning, so dined at home, and then abroad with my wife by coach to the Theatre to shew her "King and no King,"[1] it being very well done. And so by coach, though hard to get it, being rainy, home. So to my chamber to write letters and the Journal for these six last days past.

[27th]. By coach to Whitehall with my wife (where she went to see Mrs. Pierce, who was this day churched, her month of childbed being out). I went to Mrs. Montagu and other businesses, and at noon met my wife at the Wardrobe; and there dined, where we found Captain Country[2] (my little Captain that I loved, who carried me to the Sound), come with some grapes and millons[3] from my Lord at Lisbon, the first that ever I saw any, and my wife and I eat some, and took some home; but the grapes are rare things. Here we staid, and in the afternoon comes Mr. Edwd. Montagu (by appointment this morning) to talk with my Lady and me about the provisions fit to be bought, and sent to my Lord along with him. And told us, that we need not trouble ourselves how to buy them, for the King would pay for all, and that he would take care to get them: which put my Lady and me into a great deal of ease of mind. Here we staid and supped too, and, after my wife had put up some of the grapes in a basket for to be sent to the King, we took coach and home, where we found a hampire of millons sent to me also.

---

[1] Pepys saw this play acted well on March 14th, 1660-61.

[2] Richard Country, captain of the "Hind," a vessel of six guns and thirty-five men, in the fleet at Scheveling.

[3] The antiquity of the cultivation of the melon is very remote. Both the melon (*cucumis melo*) and the water-melon (*cucumis citrullus*) were introduced into England at the end of the sixteenth century. See *ante*, August 23rd, 1660.

[28th]. At the office in the morning, dined at home, and then Sir W. Pen and his daughter and I and my wife to the Theatre, and there saw "Father's own Son,"[1] a very good play, and the first time I ever saw it, and so at night to my house, and there sat and talked and drank and merrily broke up, and to bed.

[29th] (Lord's day). To church in the morning, and so to dinner, and Sir W. Pen and daughter, and Mrs. Poole, his kinswoman, Captain Poole's wife, came by appointment to dinner with us, and a good dinner we had for them, and were very merry, and so to church again, and then to Sir W. Pen's and there supped, where his brother,[2] a traveller, and one that speaks Spanish very well, and a merry man, supped with us, and what at dinner and supper I drink I know not how, of my own accord, so much wine, that I was even almost foxed, and my head aked all night; so home and to bed, without prayers, which I never did yet, since I came to the house, of a Sunday night: I being now so out of order that I durst not read prayers, for fear of being perceived by my servants in what case I was. So to bed.

[30th]. This morning up by moon-shine, at 5 o'clock, to White Hall, to meet Mr. Moore at the Privy Seal, but he not being come as appointed, I went into King Street to the Red Lyon[3] to drink my morning draft, and there I heard of a fray between the two Embassadors of Spain[4] and France;[5] and that, this day, being

---

[1] The only mention of this piece occurs in a MS. list of plays belonging to Will. Beeston, as governor of the Cockpit, in Drury Lane, preserved in the Lord Chamberlain's office. The list is dated August 10th, 1639. Mr. Halliwell-Phillipps states that a small portion of the piece formed into a droll under the title of "The Doctors of Dullhead College," is printed in the "Wits, or Sport upon Sport," 1672.

[2] George Penn, elder brother of Sir William, was a merchant at San Lucar.

[3] The Red Lion in King Street is not mentioned in the "List of Taverns in London and Westminster in 1698" (Harl. MS. 4716).

[4] The Baron de Batteville, or, as is more often written, Vatteville. See *ante*, May 19th, 1661.

[5] Godefroi, Comte d'Estrades, Marshal of France, and Viceroy of America. He proved himself, upon many occasions, an able diplomatist, and particularly at the conferences of Nimeguen when acting as plenipotentiary in 1678. Died February 26th, 1686, aged seventy-nine.

the day of the entrance of an Embassador from Sweden,[1] they intended to fight for the precedence.[2] Our King, I heard, ordered
that no Englishman should meddle in the business,[3] but let them
do what they would. And to that end all the soldiers in the town
were in arms all the day long, and some of the train-bands in the
City; and a great bustle through the City all the day. Then I to
the Privy Seal, and there Mr. Moore and a gentleman being come
with him, we took coach (which was the business I come for) to
Chelsy, to my Lord Privy Seal, and there got him to seal the
business. Here I saw by day-light two very fine pictures in the
gallery, that a little while ago I saw by night; and did also go all
over the house, and found it to be the prettiest contrived house
that ever I saw in my life. So to coach back again; and at White
Hall 'light, and saw the soldiers and people running up and down
the streets. So I went to the Spanish Embassador's and the French,
and there saw great preparations on both sides; but the French
made the most noise and vaunted most, the other made no stir
almost at all; so that I was afraid the other would have had too
great a conquest over them. Then to the Wardrobe, and dined
there, and then abroad and in Cheapside hear that the Spanish
hath got the best of it, and killed three of the French coach-horses
and several men, and is gone through the City next to our King's
coach; at which, it is strange to see how all the City did rejoice.
And indeed we do naturally all love the Spanish, and hate the

---

[1] The Count Brahé.

[2] This had been a frequent source of contention, and many absurd incidents
had occurred. In 1618, Gaspar Dauvet, Comte des Marets, ambassador to
James I., left our court in dissatisfaction upon a point of precedence claimed
by him over Gondomar, which was not allowed by James. The question now
came to a crisis, and was settled. See Evelyn's account, drawn up by royal
command, printed at the end of his Diary.—B.

[3] The Comte de Brienne insinuates, in his "Memoirs," that Charles purposely
abstained from interfering, in the belief that it was for his interest to let
France and Spain quarrel, in order to further his own designs in the match
with Portugal. Louis certainly held that opinion; and he afterwards instructed D'Estrades to solicit from the English court the punishment of those
Londoners who had insulted his ambassador, and to demand the dismissal of
De Batteville. Either no Londoner had interfered, or Louis's demand had not
in England the same force as in Spain; for no one was punished. The latter
part of his request it was clearly not for Charles to entertain, much less enforce.—B.

French. But I, as I am in all things curious, presently got to the
water-side, and there took oars to Westminster Palace, thinking
to have seen them come in thither with all the coaches, but they
being come and returned, I ran after them with my boy after me
through all the dirt and the streets full of people; till at last, at
the Mewes, I saw the Spanish coach go, with fifty drawn swords
at least to guard it, and our soldiers shouting for joy. And so I
followed the coach, and then met it at York House,[1] where the
embassador lies; and there it went in with great state. So then I
went to the French house, where I observe still, that there is no
men in the world of a more insolent spirit where they do well,
nor before they begin a matter, and more abject if they do miscarry, than these people are; for they all look like dead men, and
not a word among them, but shake their heads. The truth is, the
Spaniards were not only observed to fight most desperately, but
also they did outwitt them; first in lining their own harness with
chains of iron that they could not be cut, then in setting their
coach in the most advantageous place, and to appoint men to
guard every one of their horses, and others for to guard the coach,
and others the coachmen. And, above all, in setting upon the
French horses and killing them, for by that means the French
were not able to stir. There were several men slain of the French,
and one or two of the Spaniards, and one Englishman by a bul-
let.[2] Which is very observable, the French were at least four to
one in number,[3] and had near 100 case of pistols among them, and
the Spaniards had not one gun among them; which is for their
honour for ever, and the others' disgrace. So, having been very
much daubed with dirt, I got a coach, and home; where I vexed
my wife in telling of her this story, and pleading for the Spaniards against the French. So ends this month; myself and family
in good condition of health, but my head full of my Lord's and

[1] See *ante*, May 19th.

[2] This fray was the occasion of a good joke at the French court, thus related
in the "Menagiana," vol. ii., p. 336:—"Lors qu'on demandoit, 'Que fait Batteville en Angleterre?' on repondoit, '*Il bat L'Estrade*'." This expression, as is
well known, means "battre la campagne avec de la cavalerie pour avoir des
nouvelles des ennemis."—Chambaud's *Dictionary*.—B.

[3] The French accounts swell the number of the Spanish ambassador's attend-
ants to two thousand; two hundred would, perhaps, be the truth.—B.

my own and the office business; where we are now very busy about the business of sending forces to Tangier,[1] and the fleet to my Lord of Sandwich, who is now at Lisbon to bring over the Queen, who do now keep a Court as Queen of England. The business of Argier hath of late troubled me, because my Lord hath not done what he went for, though he did as much as any man in the world could have done. The want of money puts all things, and above all things the Navy, out of order; and yet I do not see that the King takes care to bring in any money, but thinks of new designs to lay out money.

[October 1st]. This morning my wife and I lay long in bed, and among other things fell into talk of musique, and desired that I would let her learn to sing, which I did consider, and promised her she should. So before I rose, word was brought me that my singing master, Mr. Goodgroome, was come to teach me; and so she rose and this morning began to learn also. To the office, where busy all day. So to dinner and then to the office again till night, and then to my study at home to set matters and papers in order, which, though I can hardly bring myself to do, yet do please me much when it is done. So eat a bit of bread and cheese, and to bed.

[2nd]. All this morning at Pegg Kite's with my uncle Fenner, and two friends of his, appraising her goods that her mother has

---

[1] This place, so often mentioned, was first given up to the English fleet under Lord Sandwich, by the Portuguese, January 30th, 1662; and Lord Peterborough left governor, with a garrison. The greatest pains were afterwards taken to preserve the fortress, and a fine mole was constructed at a vast expense, to improve the harbour. At length, after immense sums of money had been wasted there, the House of Commons expressed a dislike to the management of the garrison, which they suspected to be a nursery for a popish army, and seemed disinclined to maintain it any longer. The king consequently, in 1683, sent Lord Dartmouth to bring home the troops, and destroy the works; which he performed so effectually, that it would puzzle all our engineers to restore the harbour. It were idle to speculate on the benefits which might have accrued to England, by its preservation and retention; Tangier fell into the hands of the Moors, its importance having ceased with the demolition of the mole. Many curious views of Tangier were taken by Hollar, during its occupation by the English; and his drawings are preserved in the British Museum. Some have been engraved by himself; but the impressions are of considerable rarity.—B.

left; but the slut is like to prove so troublesome that I am out of heart with troubling myself in her business. After we had done we all went to a cook's shop in Bishopsgate Street and dined, and then I took them to the tavern and did give them a quart of sack, and so parted. I home and then took my wife out, and in a coach of a gentlewoman's that had been to visit my Lady Batten and was going home again our way, we went to the Theatre, but coming late, and sitting in an ill place, I never had so little pleasure in a play in my life, yet it was the first time that ever I saw it, "Victoria Corombona."[1] Methinks a very poor play. Then at night troubled to get my wife home, it being very dark, and so we were forced to have a coach. So to supper and to bed.

[3rd]. At the office all the morning; dined at home, and in the afternoon Mr. Moore came to me, and he and I went to Tower Hill to meet with a man, and so back all three to my house, and there I signed a bond to Mr. Battersby, a friend of Mr. Moore's, who lends me £50, the first money that ever I borrowed upon bond for my own occasion, and so I took them to the Mitre and a Portugal millon with me; there sat and discoursed in matters of religion till night with great pleasure, and so parted, and I home, calling at Sir W. Batten's, where his son and his wife were, who had yesterday been at the play where we were, and it was good sport to hear how she talked of it with admiration like a fool. So home, and my head was not well with the wine that I drank to-day.

[4th]. By coach to White Hall with Sir W. Pen. So to Mr. Montagu, where his man, Mons. Eschar, makes a great complaint against the English, that they did help the Spaniards against the French the other day; and that their Embassador do demand justice of our King,[2] and that he do resolve to be gone for France the

---

[1] "The White Devil; or, the Tragedie of Paulo Giordano Ursini, Duke of Brachiano, with the Life and Death of Vittoria Corombona, the famous Venetian Courtezan," by John Webster. Acted at the Phœnix, in Drury Lane, and first printed in 1612.

[2] The courier sent by D'Estrades to Paris, with the news of his discomfiture, arrived at the hôtel of the Comte de Brienne (Louis-Henri de Lomenie, who had succeeded his father, Henri-Auguste, as Secretary of State) at eleven at night. Brienne instantly repaired to the king, then at supper with the queen-

next week; which I, and all that I met with, are very glad of. Thence to Paternoster Row, where my Will did receive the £50 I borrowed yesterday. I to the Wardrobe to dinner, and there staid most of the afternoon very merry with the ladies. Then Captain Ferrers and I to the Theatre, and there came too late, so we staid and saw a bit of "Victoria," which pleased me worse

mother, his own queen, and his brother, Philippe of Anjou (Monsieur); and, requesting Louis to appear composed before the numerous spectators, he told him that the Spanish ambassador's people had cut the traces of his ambassador's coach, killed two coachmen, and cut the horses' bridles; and that the Spanish ambassador's coach had taken precedence of that of D'Estrades, whose own son had also been wounded in the affray. In spite of the caution which he had received, Louis rose up in such agitation, as nearly to overturn the table; seized Brienne by the arm, led him into the queen-mother's chamber, and bade him read D'Estrades's despatch. The queen-mother followed in haste. "What is the matter?" said she. "It is," replied the king, "an attempt to embroil the King of Spain and myself." The queen-mother begged him to return to the company. "I have supped, madam," said he, raising his voice. "I will be righted in this affair, or I will declare war against the King of Spain; and I will force him to yield precedence to my ambassadors in every court in Europe." "Oh, my son!" replied the queen-mother, "break not a peace which has cost me so dear; and remember, that the King of Spain is my brother." "Leave me, madam," rejoined Louis, "to hear D'Estrades's despatch. Return to the table, and let some fruit only be prepared for me." Anne of Austria having retired, Louis listened to the despatch, and instantly gave his commands to Brienne; which were, in substance, to order the Conde de Fuensaldagna, the Spanish ambassador, to quit France instantly, and to forbid the Marques de las Fuentes, his intended successor, to set foot on the French territory—to recall his commissioners on the boundary question, as well as the Archbishop of Embrum, his ambassador at Madrid—to demand from the King of Spain an apology proportionable to the offence; that De Batteville should be punished in person; and that in all the courts of Europe the Spanish ambassador should give place to the French; and, on the refusal of any part of his demands, to declare war. Louis gained all and every point. After much paper war, and many protocols, Spain gave way. The Baron de Batteville was recalled; the Marques de las Fuentes was sent ambassador extraordinary to Paris, to tender apologies; and on March 24th, 1662, in the presence of twenty-seven ambassadors and envoys from various courts of Europe, the Marques de las Fuentes declared to Louis XIV. that the king, his master, had sent orders to all his ambassadors and ministers to abstain from all rivalry with those of Louis. Louis, turning to the foreign ministers, desired them to communicate this declaration to their masters. The Dutch ambassador drily remarked, that he had heard of embassies to tender obedience to the Pope, but that he had never before known of such from one prince to another. An amusing volume might be written on the absurd punctilios of the ambassadors of the seventeenth century. A medal was struck by the French to commemorate this great event.—B.

than it did the other day. So we staid not to see it out, but went out and drank a bottle or two of China ale, and so home, where I found my wife vexed at her people for grumbling to eat Suffolk Cheese,[1] which I also am vexed at. So to bed.

[5th]. At the office all the morning, then dined at home, and so staid at home all the afternoon putting up my Lord's model of the Royal James, which I borrowed of him long ago to hang up in my room. And at night Sir W. Pen and I alone to the Dolphin, and there eat some bloat-herrings[2] and drank good sack. Then came in Sir W. Warren and another and staid a while with us, and then Sir Arnold Brames, with whom we staid late and till we had drank too much wine. So home and I to bed pleased at my afternoon's work in hanging up the ship. So to bed.

[6th] (Lord's day). To church in the morning; Mr. Mills preached, who, I expect, should take in snuffe[3] that my wife did not come to his child's christening the other day. The winter coming on, many of parish ladies are come home and appear at church again; among others, the three sisters of the Thornbury's,[4] very fine, and the most zealous people that ever I saw in my life, even to admiration, if it were true zeal. There was also my pretty black girl, Mrs. Dekins[5] and Mrs. Margaret Pen, this

---

[1] This prejudice extended to the days of Pope, whose country mouse entertained his courtly guest with

"Cheese *such as men in Suffolk make,*
But wished it Stilton for his sake."
Imitations of Horace, Sat. vi., b. ii.

See also Shadwell's "Works," vol. iv., p. 350.—B.

[2] To bloat is to dry by smoke, a method chiefly used to cure herrings or bloaters. "I have more smoke in my mouth than would *blote* a hundred herrings."—Beaumont and Fletcher, *Island Princess.* "Why, you stink like so many bloat-herrings newly taken out of the chimney."—Ben Jonson, *Masque of Augurs.*

[3] Snuff, anger.

"Who therewith angry, when it next came there,
Took it in snuff."
Shakespeare, 1 *Henry IV.,* act i., sc. 3.—M. B.

[4] Mr. Thornbury was yeoman of the wine cellar to the king. See *ante,* April 23, 1661.

[5] Elizabeth Dekins or Dickins, sometimes styled *Morena* (or brunette), daughter of John Dekins. She died in October, 1662 (see *post,* Oct. 3, 1662).

day come to church in a new flowered satin suit that my wife helped to buy her the other day. So home to dinner, and to church in the afternoon to St. Gregory's,[1] by Paul's, where I saw Mr. Moore in the gallery and so went up to him and heard a good sermon of Dr. Buck's,[2] one I never heard before, a very able man. So home, and in the evening I went to my Valentine, her father and mother being out of town, to fetch her to supper to my house, and then came Sir W. Pen and would have her to his, so with much sport I got them all to mine, and we were merry, and so broke up and to bed.

[7th]. Up in the morning and to my uncle Fenner's, thinking to have met Peg Kite about her business but she comes not, so I went to Dr. Williams, where I found him sick in bed and was sorry for it. So about business all day, troubled in my mind till I can hear from Brampton, how things go on at Sturtlow, at the Court, which I was cleared in at night by a letter, which tells me that my cozen Tom was there to be admitted, in his father's name, as heir-at-law, but that he was opposed, and I was admitted by proxy, which put me out of great trouble of mind.

[8th]. At the office all the morning. After office done, went and eat some Colchester oysters with Sir W. Batten at his house, and there, with some company, dined and staid there talking all the afternoon; and late after dinner took Mrs. Martha out by coach, and carried her to the Theatre in a frolique, to my great expense, and there shewed her part of the "Beggar's Bush," without much pleasure, but only for a frolique, and so home again.

[9th]. This morning went out about my affairs, among others to put my Theorbo out to be mended, and then at noon home again, thinking to go with Sir Williams both to dinner by invitation to

---

[1] St. Gregory's Church was at the west end of old St. Paul's. It was destroyed in the Great Fire, and not rebuilt. The parish was then joined to that of St. Mary Magdalen's, Knightrider Street, and is now united to St. Martin's, Ludgate Hill.

[2] James Buck, D.D., afterwards preacher at the Temple, a man of great learning, and rector of St. James's, Garlickhithe, from 1661 till his death, at an advanced age, in 1685.—B.

Sir W. Rider's,[1] but at home I found Mrs. Pierce la belle, and
Madam Clifford, with whom I was forced to stay, and made them
the most welcome I could; and I was (God knows) very well
pleased with their beautiful company, and after dinner took
them to the Theatre, and shewed them "The Chances"; and so
saw them both at home and back to the Fleece tavern, in Covent
Garden, where Luellin and Blurton, and my old friend Frank
Bagge, was to meet me, and there staid till late very merry. Frank
Bagge tells me a story of Mrs. Pepys that lived with my Lady
Harvy,[2] Mr. Montagu's sister, a good woman; that she had been
very ill, and often asked for me; that she is in good condition, and
that nobody could get her to make her will; but that she did still
enquire for me, and that now she is well she desires to have a
chamber at my house. Now I do not know whether this is a trick
of Bagge's, or a goood will of her's to do something for me; but I
will not trust her, but told him I should be glad to see her, and
that I would be sure to do all that I could to provide a place for
her. So by coach home late.

[10th]. At the office all the morning; dined at home, and after
dinner Sir W. Pen and my wife and I to the Theatre (she first
going into Covent Garden to speak a word with a woman to enquire of her mother, and I in the meantime with Sir W. Pen's
coach staying at W. Joyce's), where the King came to-day, and
there was "The Traytor"[3] most admirably acted; and a most excellent play it is. So home, and intended to be merry, being my
sixth wedding night; but by a late bruise . . . I am in so much
pain that I eat my supper and in pain to bed, yet my wife and I
pretty merry.

[11th]. All day in bed with a cataplasm . . . and at night rose a
little, and to bed again in more ease than last night. This noon

---

[1] Sir William Rider's house was at Bethnal Green, and was popularly associ-
ated with the ballad of the "Beggar's Daughter of Bethnal Green." It was
long known as the "Blind Beggar's House."

[2] Elizabeth Montagu, wife of Sir Daniel Harvey, who was appointed ambassador to Constantinople in 1668.

[3] Pepys had seen Shirley's "Traitor" on November 22nd, 1660.

there came my brother and Dr. Tom and Snow to dinner, and by themselves were merry.

[12th]. In bed the greatest part of this day also, and my swelling in some measure gone. I received a letter this day from my father, that Sir R. Bernard do a little fear that my uncle has not observed exactly the custom of Brampton in his will about his lands there, which puts me to a great trouble in mind, and at night wrote to him and to my father about it, being much troubled at it.

[13th] (Lord's day). Did not stir out all day, but rose and dined below, and this day left off half skirts and put on a wastecoat, and my false taby wastecoat with gold lace; and in the evening there came Sir W. Batten to see me, and sat and supped very kindly with me, and so to prayers and to bed.

[14th]. This morning I ventured by water abroad to Westminster, but lost my labour, for Mr. Montagu was not in town. So to the Wardrobe, and there dined with my Lady, which is the first time I have seen her dine abroad since her being brought to bed of my Lady Katherine. In the afternoon Captain Ferrers and I walked abroad to several places, among others to Mr. Pim's, my Lord's taylour's, and there he went out with us to the Fountain tavern and did give us store of wine, and it being the Duke of York's birthday, we drank the more to his health. But, Lord! what a sad story he makes of his being abused by a Dr. of Physique who is in one part of the tenement wherein he dwells. It would make one laugh, though I see he is under a great trouble in it. Thence home by link and found a good answer from my father that Sir R. Bernard do clear all things as to us and our title to Brampton, which puts my heart in great ease and quiet.

[15th]. At the office all the morning, and in the afternoon to Paul's Churchyard to a blind place, where Mrs. Goldsborough was to meet me (who dare not be known where she lives) to treat about the difference which remains between my uncle and her. But, Lord! to hear how she talks and how she rails against my uncle would make one mad. But I seemed not to be troubled at it,

173

but would indeed gladly have an agreement with her. So I appoint Mr. Moore and she another against Friday next to look into our papers and to see what can be done to conclude the matter. So home in much pain by walking too much yesterday . . . which much troubles me.

[16th]. In bed till 12 o'clock. This morning came several maids to my wife to be hired, and at last she pitched upon one Nell, whose mother, an old woman, came along with her, but would not be hired under half a year, which I am pleased at their drollness. This day dined by appointment with me, Dr. Thos. Pepys and my Coz. Snow, and my brother Tom, upon a fin of ling and some sounds, neither of which did I ever know before, but most excellent meat they are both, that in all my life I never eat the like fish. So after dinner came in W. Joyce and eat and drank and were merry. So up to my chamber and put all my papers at rights, and in the evening our maid Mary (who was with us upon trial for a month) did take leave of us, going as we suppose to be married, for the maid liked us and we her, but all she said was that she had a mind to live in a tradesman's house where there was but one maid. So to supper and to bed.

[17th]. At the office all the morning, at noon my wife being gone to my coz Snow's with Dr. Thomas Pepys and my brother Tom to a venison pasty (which proved a pasty of salted pork), by appointment I went with Captain David Lambert to the Exchequer, and from thence by appointment he and I were to meet at a cook's shop to dine. But before I went to him Captain Cock,[1] a merchant I had not long known, took me to the Sun tavern and gave me a glass of sack, and being a man of great observation and repute, did tell me that he was confident that the Parliament, when it comes the next month to sit again, would bring trouble with it, and enquire how the King had disposed of offices and

[1] Captain George Cock, a merchant possessed of large tanning works in Limerick. On July 31st, 1660, he was rewarded for his services during the Civil War with the office of searcher of the port of Newcastle, his native place; commissioner for inspecting the chest; and in November, 1664, steward for sick and wounded seamen. Elected a Fellow of the Royal Society, 1666, and died 1679.

money, before they will raise more; which, I fear, will bring all things to ruin again. Thence to the Cook's and there dined with Captain Lambert and his father-in-law, and had much talk of Portugall; from whence he is lately come, and he tells me it is a very poor dirty place; I mean the City and Court of Lisbon; that the King[1] is a very rude and simple fellow; and, for reviling of somebody a little while ago, and calling of him cuckold, was run into . . . with a sword and had been killed, had he not told them that he was their king. That there are there no glass windows, nor will they have any; which makes sport among our merchants there to talk of an English factor that, being newly come thither, writ into England that glass would be a good commodity to send thither, &c. That the King has his meat sent up by a dozen of lazy guards and in pipkins, sometimes, to his own table; and sometimes nothing but fruits, and, now and then, half a hen. And now that the Infanta is become our Queen, she is come to have a whole hen or goose to her table, which is not ordinary. So home and to look over my papers that concern the difference between Mrs. Goldsborough and us, which cost me much pains, but contented me much after it was done. So at home all the evening and to supper and to bed.

[18th]. To White Hall, to Mr. Montagu's, where I met with Mr. Pierce, the purser, to advise about the things to be sent to my Lord for the Queen's provision, and was cleared in it, and now there is all haste made, for the fleet's going. At noon to my Lord's to dinner, and in the afternoon, leaving my wife there, Mr. Moore and I to Mrs. Goldsborough, who sent for a friend to meet with us, and so we were talking about the difference between us till 10 at night. I find it very troublesome, and have brought it into some hopes of an agreement, I offering to forgive her £10 that is yet due according to my uncle's accounts to us. So we left her friend to advise about it, and I hope to hear of her, for I would not by any means go to law with a woman of so devilish a tongue as she has. So to my Lady's, where I left my wife to lie with Mademoiselle all night, and I by link home and to bed. This

---

[1] The King of Portugal was Alfonso VI., who ascended the throne in 1656, and was deposed in 1667.

night lying alone, and the weather cold, and having this last 7 or 8 days been troubled with a tumor . . . which is now abated by a poultice of a good handful of bran with half a pint of vinegar and a pint of water boiled till it be thick, and then a spoonful of honey put to it and so spread in a cloth and laid to it, I first put on my waistcoat to lie in all night this year, and do not intend to put it off again till spring. I met with complaints at home that my wife left no victuals for them all this day.

[19th]. At the office all the morning, and at noon Mr. Coventry, who sat with us all the morning, and Sir G. Carteret, Sir W. Pen, and myself, by coach to Captain Marshe's, at Limehouse, to a house that hath been their ancestors' for this 250 years, close by the lime-house[1] which gives the name to the place. Here they have a design to get the King to hire a dock for the herring busses,[2] which is now the great design on foot, to lie up in. We had a very good and handsome dinner, and excellent wine. I not being neat in clothes, which I find a great fault in me, could not be so merry as otherwise, and at all times I am and can be, when I am in good habitt, which makes me remember my father Osborne's[3] rule for a gentleman to spare in all things rather than in that. So by coach home, and so to write letters by post, and so to bed.

[20th] (Lord's day). At home in bed all the morning to ease my late tumour, but up to dinner and much offended in mind at a proud trick my man Will hath got, to keep his hat on in the house, but I will not speak of it to him to-day; but I fear I shall be troubled with his pride and laziness, though in other things he is good enough. To church in the afternoon, where a sleepy Presbyter preached, and then to Sir W. Batten who is to go to Portsmouth to-morrow to wait upon the Duke of York, who goes

---

[1] A part of the main river-side road was long known as Limekiln Hill, after this lime-house.

[2] A peculiar boat of ten or fifteen tons, for the herring fishery.—Smyth's *Sailor's Word-Book*.

[3] "Wear your clothes neat, exceeding rather than coming short of others of like fortune; a charge borne out by acceptance where ever you come. Therefore spare all other ways rather than prove defective in this."—*Advice to a Son*, by Francis Osborn, i. 23.

to take possession and to set in order the garrison there. Supped at home and to bed.

[21st]. Early with Mr. Moore by coach to Chelsy, to my Lord Privy Seal's, but have missed of coming time enough; and having taken up Mr. Pargiter, the goldsmith (who is the man of the world that I do most know and believe to be a cheating rogue), we drank our morning draft there together of cake and ale, and did make good sport of his losing so much by the King's coming

in, he having bought much of Crown lands, of which, God forgive me! I am very glad. At Whitehall, at the Privy Seal, did with Sir W. Pen take advice about passing of things of his there that concern his matters of Ireland. Thence to the Wardrobe and dined, and so against my judgment and conscience (which God forgive, for my very heart knows that I offend God in breaking my vows herein) to the Opera, which is now newly begun to act again, after some alteracion of their scene, which do make it very much worse; but the play, "Love and Honour,"[1] being the first time of their acting it, is a very good plot, and well done. So on foot home, and after a little business done in my study and supper, to bed.

[22nd]. At the office all the morning, where we had a deputation from the Duke in his absence, he being gone to Portsmouth, for us to have the whole disposal and ordering of the Fleet. In the afternoon about business up and down, and at night to visit Sir R. Slingsby, who is fallen sick of this new disease,[2] an ague and fever. So home after visiting my aunt Wight and Mrs. Norbury (who continues still a very pleasant lady), and to supper, and so to bed.

[23rd]. To Whitehall, and there, to drink our morning, Sir W. Pen and I to a friend's lodging of his (Col. Pr. Swell), and at noon he and I dined together alone at the Legg in King Street, and so by coach to Chelsy to my Lord Privy Seal's about business of Sir William's, in which we had a fair admittance to talk with my Lord, and had his answer, and so back to the Opera, and there I saw again "Love and Honour," and a very good play it is. And thence home, calling by the way to see Sir Robert Slingsby, who continues ill, and so home. This day all our office is invited against Tuesday next, my Lord Mayor's day, to dinner with him at Guildhall. This evening Mr. Holliard came and sat with us, and gave us both directions to observe.

[24th]. At the office all morning, at noon Luellin dined with me,

---

[1] A tragi-comedy by Sir William Davenant. It was originally acted at the Blackfriars, and printed in 1649. "This play was richly cloath'd; the King gave Mr. Betterton his Coronation suit, in which he acted the part of Prince Alvaro; the Duke of York giving Mr. Harris his, who did Prince Prospero; and my Lord of Oxford gave Mr. Joseph Price his, who did Lionel, the Duke of Parma's son. The Duke was acted by Mr. Lilliston; Evandra by Mrs. Davenport, and all the other parts being very well done. The play having a great run produc'd the Company great gain and estimation from the Town." —Downes, *Roscius Anglicanus,* 1708, pp. 21, 22.

[2] This complaint is referred to in Ben Jonson's "Every Man in His Humour," and in 1659 H. Whitmore published a little book entitled "Febris Anomala, or the New Disease that now rageth throughout England." It appears to have been somewhat similar to subsequent epidemics of influenza.

178

and then abroad to Fleet Street, leaving my wife at Tom's while I went out and did a little business. So home again, and went to see Sir Robert [Slingsby], who continues ill, and this day has not spoke at all, which makes them all afeard of him. So home.

[25th]. To Whitehall, and so to dinner at the Wardrobe, where my wife met me, and there we met with a venison pasty, and my Lady very merry and very handsome, methought. After dinner my wife and I to the Opera, and there saw again "Love and Honour," a play so good that it has been acted but three times and I have seen them all, and all in this week; which is too much, and more than I will do again a good while. Coming out of the house we met Mrs. Pierce and her comrade Mrs. Clifford, and I seeming willing to stay with them to talk my wife grew angry, and whether she be jealous or no I know not, but she loves not that I should speak of Mrs. Pierce. Home on foot very discontented, in my way I calling at the Instrument maker, Hunt's, and there saw my lute, which is now almost done, it being to have a new neck to it and to be made to double strings. So home and to bed. This day I did give my man Will a sound lesson about his forbearing to give us the respect due to a master and mistress.

[26th]. This morning Sir W. Pen and I should have gone out of town with my Lady Batten, to have met Sir William coming back from Portsmouth, at Kingston, but could not, by reason that my Lord of Peterborough[1] (who is to go Governor of Tangier[2]) came this morning, with Sir G. Carteret, to advise with us about completing of the affairs and preparacions for that place. So at the office all the morning, and in the afternoon Sir W. Pen, my wife and I to the Theatre, and there saw "The Country Captain,"[3] the first time it hath been acted this twenty-five years, a

---

[1] Henry Mordaunt, second Earl of Peterborough, born November 16th, 1621; Captain-General of the Forces in Tangier, Fez, and Morocco, and Chief Governor of Tangier from September 6th, 1661, to June, 1663; Privy Councillor, 1674-79, 1683; and in 1685 made Groom of the Stole to James II. He was created K.G. 1685, and died June 19th, 1697.

[2] For note on Tangier, see *ante*, September 30th, 1661.

[3] A comedy by the Duke of Newcastle, which was originally played at the Blackfriars, and printed in 1649.

play of my Lord Newcastle's, but so silly a play as in all my life I never saw, and the first that ever I was weary of in my life. So home again, and in the evening news was brought that Sir R. Slingsby, our Comptroller (who hath this day been sick a week), is dead; which put me into so great a trouble of mind, that all the night I could not sleep, he being a man that loved me, and had many qualitys that made me to love him above all the officers and commissioners in the Navy. Coming home we called at Dan Rawlinson's,[1] and there drank good sack, and so home.

[27th] (Lord's day). At church in the morning; where in the pew both Sir Williams and I had much talk about the death of Sir Robert, which troubles me much; and them in appearance, though I do not believe it; because I know that he was a cheque to their engrossing the whole trade of the Navy-office. Home to dinner, and in the afternoon to church again, my wife with me, whose mourning is now grown so old that I am ashamed to go to church with her. And after church to see my uncle and aunt Wight, and there staid and talked and supped with them, and were merry as we could be in their company. Among other things going up into their chamber to see their two pictures, which I am forced to commend against my judgment, and also she showed us her cabinet, where she had very pretty medals and good jewels. So home and to prayers and to bed.

[28th]. At the office all the morning, and dined at home, and so to Paul's Churchyard to Hunt's,[2] and there found my Theorbo done, which pleases me very well, and costs me 26s. to the altering. But now he tells me it is as good a lute as any is in England, and is worth well £10. Hither I sent for Captain Ferrers to me, who comes with a friend of his, and they and I to the Theatre, and there saw "Argalus and Parthenia,"[3] where a woman acted Parthenia, and came afterwards on the stage in men's clothes, and had the best legs that ever I saw, and I was very well pleased with it. Thence to the Ringo alehouse, and thither sent for a belt-

[1] Host of the Mitre in Fenchurch Street.
[2] Hunt was a musical instrument maker. See *ante*, October 25th.
[3] Henry Glapthorne's tragi-comedy. See *ante*, January 31st, 1660-61 (note).

maker, and bought of him a handsome belt for second mourning, which cost me 24*s.*, and is very neat.

[29th]. This day I put on my half cloth black stockings and my new coat of the fashion, which pleases me well, and with my beaver[1] I was (after office was done) ready to go to my Lord Mayor's feast, as we are all invited; but the Sir Williams were both loth to go, because of the crowd, and so none of us went, and I staid and dined with them, and so home, and in the evening, by consent, we met at the Dolphin, where other company came to us, and should have been merry, but their wine was so naught, and all other things out of order, that we were not so, but staid long at night, and so home and to bed. My mind not pleased with the spending of this day, because I had proposed a great deal of pleasure to myself this day at Guildhall. This Lord Mayor,[2] it seems, brings up again the custom of Lord Mayors going the day of their instalment to Paul's, and walking round about the Cross, and offering something at the altar.

[30th]. All the morning at the office. At noon played on my Theorbo, and much pleased therewith; it is now altered with a new neck. In the afternoon Captain Lambert called me out by appointment, and we walked together to Deptford, and there in his ship, the Norwich, I got him to shew me every hole and corner of the ship, much to my information, and the purpose of my going. So home again, and at Sir W. Batten's heard how he had been already at Sir R. Slingsby's, as we were all invited, and I intended this night to go, and there he finds all things out of order, and no such thing done to-night, but pretending that the corps stinks, they will bury it to-night privately, and so will un-bespeak all their guests, and there shall be no funerall, which I am sorry for, that there should be nothing done for the honour of

---

[1] Doubtless the same mentioned June 27th, 1661. It was a *chapeau de poil*, a mark of some distinction in those days, and which gave name to Rubens's famous picture, formerly in Sir Robert Peel's collection (now at the National Gallery), of a lady in a beaver hat, or *chapeau de poil*. This having been corrupted into *chapeau de paille*, has led to many mistakes and conjectures.

[2] Sir John Frederick, educated at Christ's Hospital, and afterwards its president.

Sir Robert, but I fear he hath left his family in great distraction.
Here I staid till late at cards with my Lady and Mrs. Martha,
and so home. I sent for a bottle or two of wine thither. At my coming home I am sorry to find my wife displeased with her maid
Doll, whose fault is that she cannot keep her peace, but will always be talking in an angry manner, though it be without any
reason and to no purpose, which I am sorry for and do see the
inconvenience that do attend the increase of a man's fortune by
being forced to keep more servants, which brings trouble. Sir
Henry Vane, Lambert, and others, are lately sent suddenly away
from the Tower, prisoners to Scilly; but I do not think there is
any plot as is said, but only a pretence; as there was once pre-
tended often against the Cavaliers.

[31st]. This morning comes Prior of Brampton to me about the
house he has to buy of me, but I was forced to be at the office all
the morning, and so could not talk with him. And so, after the
office was done, and dined at home, I went to my brother Tom's,
and there met him. He demanded some abatement, he having
agreed with my father for Barton's house, at a price which I told
him I could not meddle with, but that as for anything to secure
his title to them I was ready, and so we parted. Thence to Sir
Robert Bernard, and as his client did ask his advice about my
uncle Thomas's case and ours as to Gravely, and in short he tells
me that there is little hopes of recovering it or saving his annuity,
which do trouble me much, but God's will be done. Hence, with
my mind full of trouble, to my uncle Fenner's, when at the alehouse I found him drinking and very jolly and youthsome, and
as one that I believe will in a little time get a wife. So home.

[November 1st]. I went this morning with Sir W. Pen by coach
to Westminster, and having done my business at Mr. Montagu's,
I went back to him at Whitehall, and from thence with him to
the 3 Tun Tavern, at Charing Cross, and there sent for up the
maister of the house's dinner, and dined very well upon it, and
afterwards had him and his fayre sister (who is very great with
Sir W. Batten and Sir W. Pen in mirth) up to us, and looked over
some medals that they shewed us of theirs, and so went away to

the Theatre, to "The Joviall Crew," and from hence home, and at my house we were very merry till late, having sent for his son, Mr. William Pen,[1] lately come from Oxford. And after supper parted, and to bed.

[2d]. At the office all the morning; where Sir John Minnes, our new comptroller, was fetched by Sir Wm. Pen and myself from Sir Wm. Batten's, and led to his place in the office. The first time that he had come hither, and he seems a good fair condition man, and one that I am glad hath the office. After the office done, I to the Wardrobe, and there dined, and in the afternoon had an hour or two's talk with my Lady with great pleasure. And so with the two young ladies by coach to my house, and gave them some entertainment, and so late at night sent them home with Captain Ferrers by coach. This night my boy Wayneman, as I was in my chamber, I overheard him let off some gun-powder, and hearing my wife chide him below for it, and a noise made, I call him up, and find that it was powder that he had put in his pocket, and a match carelessly with it, thinking that it was out, and so the match did give fire to the powder, and had burnt his side and his hand that he put into his pocket to put out the fire. But upon examination, and finding him in a lie about the time and place that he bought it, I did extremely beat him, and though it did trouble me to do it, yet I thought it necessary to do it. So to write by the post, and to bed.

[3rd] (Lord's day). This day I stirred not out, but took physique, and it did work very well, and all the day as I was at leisure I did read in Fuller's Holy Warr,[2] which I have of late bought, and did try to make a song in the praise of a liberall genius (as I take my own to be) to all studies and pleasures, but it not proving to my mind I did reject it and so proceeded not in it. At night my wife and I had a good supper by ourselves of a pullet hashed, which pleased me much to see my condition come to allow ourselves a dish like that, and so at night to bed.

---

[1] The celebrated Quaker, and founder of Pennsylvania.

[2] Fuller's "Historie of the Holy Warre," fourth edition, folio, Cambridge, 1651, is in the Pepysian Library.

[4th]. In the morning, being very rainy, by coach with Sir W. Pen and my wife to Whitehall, and sent her to Mrs. Hunt's, and he and I to Mr. Coventry's about business, and so sent for her again, and all three home again, only I to the Mitre (Mr. Rawlinson's), where Mr. Pierce, the Purser, had got us a most brave chine of beef, and a dish of marrowbones. Our company my uncle Wight, Captain Lambert, one Captain Davies, and purser Barter, Mr. Rawlinson, and ourselves, and very merry. After dinner I took coach, and called my wife at my brother's, where I left her, and to the Opera, where we saw "The Bondman," which of old we both did so doat on, and do still; though to both our thinking not so well acted here (having too great expectations), as formerly at Salisbury-court. But for Betterton[1] he is called by us both the best actor in the world. So home by coach, I 'lighting by the way at my uncle Wight's and staid there a little, and so home after my wife, and to bed.

[5th]. At the office all the morning. At noon comes my brother Tom and Mr. Armiger to dine with me, and did, and we were very merry. After dinner, I having drunk a great deal of wine, I went away, seeming to go about business with Sir W. Pen, to my Lady Batten's (Sir William being at Chatham), and there sat a good while, and then went away (before I went I called at home to see whether they were gone, and found them there, and Armiger inviting my wife to go to a play, and like a fool would be courting her, but he is an ass, and lays out money with Tom, otherwise I should not think him worth half this respect I shew him). To the Dolphin, where he and I and Captain Cocke sat late and drank much, seeing the boys in the streets flying their crack-

---

[1] Thomas Betterton, the celebrated actor, born in Westminster and baptized on August 11th, 1635, was the son of Matthew Betterton, an under-cook to Charles I., and first appeared on the stage at the Cockpit in Drury Lane, in 1659-60. After the Restoration, two distinct companies were established by royal authority: one called the King's Company, under a patent granted to Thomas Killigrew; the other styled the Duke's Company, the patentee of which was Sir William Davenant, who engaged Betterton. Mr. Robert W. Lowe, in his valuable little work, "Thomas Betterton," 1891, states his belief that the character of Archas in "The Loyal Subject" was taken by Betterton in 1660. Betterton died April 28th, 1710, and was buried in the cloisters of Westminster Abbey.

ers, this day being kept all the day very strictly in the City. At last broke up, and called at my Lady Batten's again and would have gone to cards, but Sir W. Pen was so fuddled that we could not try him to play, and therefore we parted, and I home and to bed.

[6th]. Going forth this morning I met Mr. Davenport and a friend of his, one Mr. Furbisher, to drink their morning draft with me, and I did give it them in good wine, and anchovies, and pickled oysters, and took them to the Sun in Fish Street, there did give them a barrel of good ones, and a great deal of wine, and sent for Mr. W. Bernard (Sir Robert's son), a grocer thereabouts, and were very merry, and cost me a good deal of money, and at noon left them, and with my head full of wine, and being invited by a note from Luellin, that came to my hands this morning in bed, I went to Nick Osborne's at the Victualling Office, and there saw his wife, who he has lately married, a good sober woman, and new come to their home. We had a good dish or two of marrowbones and another of neats' tongues to dinner, and that being done I bade them adieu and hastened to Whitehall (calling Mr. Moore by the way) to my Lord Privy Seal, who will at last force the clerks to bring in a table of their fees, which they have so long denied, but I do not join with them, and so he is very respectful to me. So he desires me to bring in one which I observe in making of fees, which I will speedily do. So back again, and endeavoured to speak with Tom Trice (who I fear is hatching some mischief), but could not, which vexed me, and so I went home and sat late with pleasure at my lute, and so to bed.

[7th]. This morning came one Mr. Hill (sent by Mr. Hunt, the Instrument maker), to teach me to play on the Theorbo, but I do not like his play nor singing, and so I found a way to put him off. So to the office. And then to dinner, and got Mr. Pett the Commissioner to dinner with me, he and I alone, my wife not being well, and so after dinner parted. And I to Tom Trice, who in short, shewed me a writt he had ready for my father, and I promise to answer it. So I went to Dr. Williams (who is now pretty well got up after his sickness), and after that to Mr. Moore

to advise, and so returned home late on foot, with my mind
cleared, though not satisfied. I met with letters at home from my
Lord from Lisbone, which speak of his being well; and he tells
me he had seen at the court there the day before he wrote this
letter, the Juego de Toro.[1] So fitted myself for bed. Coming home
I called at my uncle Fenner's, who tells that Peg Kite now hath
declared she will have the beggarly rogue the weaver, and so we
are resolved neither to meddle nor make with her.

[8th]. This morning up early, and to my Lord Chancellor's with
a letter to him from my Lord, and did speak with him; and he did
ask me whether I was son to Mr. Talbot Pepys[2] or no (with whom
he was once acquainted in the Court of Requests),[3] and spoke to
me with great respect. Thence to Westminster Hall (it being
Term time) and there met with Commissioner Pett, and so at
noon he and I by appointment to the Sun in New Fish Street,
where Sir J. Minnes, Sir W. Batten, and we all were to dine, at
an invitation of Captain Stoaks and Captain Clerk, and were very
merry, and by discourse I found Sir J. Minnes a fine gentleman
and a very good scholler. After dinner to the Wardrobe, and
thence to Dr. Williams, who went with me (the first time that
he has been abroad a great while) to the Six Clerks Office to find
me a clerk there able to advise me in my business with Tom
Trice, and after I had heard them talk, and had given me some
comfort, I went to my brother Tom's, and took him with me
to my coz. Turner[4] at the Temple, and had his opinion that I
should not pay more than the principal £200, with which I was
much pleased, and so home.

[9th]. At the office all the morning. At noon Mr. Davenport,
Phillips, and Mr. Wm. Bernard and Furbisher, came by appointment and dined with me, and we were very merry. After dinner

---

[1] A bull fight. See May 24th, 1662.—B.

[2] Of Impington, great-uncle to Samuel and father of Roger Pepys, M.P., and
Thomas Pepys, M.D. He died March, 1665-66 (see March 12th, 1665-66).

[3] The Court of Requests was abolished by act of Parliament, 16-17 Car. I. c.
10. It was held in a part of the old Westminster Palace, and adjoined St.
Stephen's Chapel.

[4] Sergeant John Turner, husband of Jane Pepys, who lived in Salisbury Court.

I to the Wardrobe, and there staid talking with my Lady all the afternoon till late at night. Among other things my Lady did mightily urge me to lay out money upon my wife, which I perceived was a little more earnest than ordinary, and so I seemed to be pleased with it, and do resolve to bestow a lace upon her, and what with this and other talk, we were exceeding merry. So home at night.

[10th] (Lord's day). At our own church in the morning, where Mr. Mills preached. Thence alone to the Wardrobe to dinner with my Lady, where my Lady continues upon yesterday's discourse still for me to lay out money upon my wife, which I think it is best for me to do for her honour and my own. Last night died Archibald, my Lady's butler and Mrs. Sarah's brother, of a dropsy, which I am troubled at. In the afternoon went and sat with Mr. Turner in his pew at St. Gregory's, where I hear our Queen Katherine, the first time by name as such, publickly prayed for,[1] and heard Dr. Buck[2] upon "Woe unto thee, Corazin,"[3] &c., where he started a difficulty, which he left to another time to answer, about why God should give means of grace to those people which he knew would not receive them, and deny to others which he himself confesses, if they had had them, would have received them, and they would have been effectual too. I would I could hear him explain this, when he do come to it. Thence home to my wife, and took her to my Aunt Wight's, and there sat a while with her (my uncle being at Katharine hill), and so home, and I to Sir W. Batten's, where Captain Cock was, and we sent for two bottles of Canary to the Rose, which did do me a great deal of hurt, and did trouble me all night, and, indeed, came home so out of order that I was loth to say prayers to-night as I am used ever to do on Sundays, which my wife took notice of and people of the house, which I was sorry for.

---

[1] The King's letter to the Council for this purpose was read on November 19th.—B.

[2] Lord Braybrooke says probably John Buck, D.D., who was vicar of Stradbrook, Suffolk, and published, in 1660, a Thanksgiving Sermon, preached at St. Paul's, but see *ante*, Oct. 6th (note), for Dr. James Buck.

[3] "Woe unto thee, Chorazin! woe unto thee, Bethsaida!" &c., St. Matthew xi, 21; St. Luke x. 13.

[11th]. To the Wardrobe, and with Mr. Townsend and Moore to the Saracen's Head to a barrel of oysters, and so Mr. Moore and I to Tom Trice's, with whom I did first set my hand to answer to a writt of his this tearm. Thence to the Wardrobe to dinner, and there by appointment met my wife, who had by my direction brought some laces for my Lady to choose one for her. And after dinner I went away, and left my wife and ladies together, and all their work was about this lace of hers. Captain Ferrers and I went together, and he carried me the first time that ever I saw any gaming house, to one, entering into Lincoln's-Inn-Fields, at the end of Bell Yard, where strange the folly of men to lay and lose so much money, and very glad I was to see the manner of a gamester's life, which I see is very miserable, and poor, and unmanly. And thence he took me to a dancing school in Fleet Street, where we saw a company of pretty girls dance, but I do not in myself like to have young girls exposed to so much vanity. So to the Wardrobe, where I found my Lady had agreed upon a lace for my wife of £6, which I seemed much glad of that it was no more, though in my mind I think it too much, and I pray God keep me so to order myself and my wife's expenses that no inconvenience in purse or honour follow this my prodigality. So by coach home.

[12th]. At the office all the morning. Dined at home alone. So abroad with Sir W. Pen. My wife and I to "Bartholomew Fayre," with puppets which I had seen once before, and the play without puppets often, but though I love the play as much as ever I did, yet I do not like the puppets at all, but think it to be a lessening to it. Thence to the Greyhound in Fleet Street, and there drank some raspberry sack and eat some sasages, and so home very merry. This day Holmes come to town; and we do expect hourly to hear what usage he hath from the Duke and the King about this late business of letting the Swedish Embassador[1] go by him without striking his flag.[2]

---

[1] The Count Brahé.

[2] And that, too, in the River Thames itself. The right of obliging ships of all nations to lower topsails, and strike their flag to the English, whilst in the British seas, and even on the French coasts, had, up to this time, been rigidly

[13th]. By appointment, we all went this morning to wait upon the Duke of York, which we did in his chamber, as he was dressing himself in his riding suit to go this day by sea to the Downs. He is in mourning for his wife's grandmother,[1] which is thought a great piece of fondness.[2] After we had given him our letter relating the bad condition of the Navy for want of money, he referred it to his coming back and so parted, and I to Whitehall and to see la belle Pierce, and so on foot to my Lord Crew's, where I found him come to his new house, which is next to that he lived in last; here I was well received by my Lord and Sir Thomas, with whom I had great talk: and he tells me in good earnest that he do believe the Parliament (which comes to sit again the next week), will be troublesome to the Court and Clergy, which God

enforced. When Sully was sent by Henry IV., in 1603, to congratulate James I. on his accession, and in a ship commanded by a vice-admiral of France, he was fired upon by the English Admiral Mansel, for daring to hoist the flag of France in the presence of that of England, although within sight of Calais. The French flag was lowered, and all Sully's remonstrances could obtain no redress for the alleged injury. According to Rugge, Holmes had insisted upon the Swede's lowering his flag, and had even fired a shot to enforce the observance of the usual tribute of respect, but the ambassador sent his secretary and another gentleman on board the English frigate, to assure the captain, *upon the word and honour of an ambassador*, that the king, by a verbal order, had given him leave and a dispensation in that particular, and upon this false representation he was allowed to proceed on his voyage without further question. This want of caution, and disobedience of orders, fell heavily on Holmes, who was imprisoned for two months, and not re-appointed to the same ship. Brahé afterwards made a proper submission for the fault he had committed, at his own court. His conduct reminds us of Sir Henry Wotton's definition of an ambassador—*that he is an honest man sent to* lie *abroad for the good of his country*. A pun upon the term *lieger*-ambassador.—B.

[1] Edward Hyde, first Earl of Clarendon, was twice married. His first wife was Anne, daughter of Sir George Ayliffe, Bart., of Gretenham, in the county of Wilts. He married her in 1628, when he was only twenty years old, and she died of the small-pox six months afterwards, before any child was born. In 1634 he married Frances, daughter of Sir Thomas and Lady Aylesbury, by whom he had four sons and two daughters. Sir Thomas Aylesbury, Bart., had been secretary to George, Duke of Buckingham, and through his influence was made Master of Requests and Master of the Mint. He died at Breda in 1657, aged eighty-one.

[2] Fondness, foolishness.

> "Fondness it were for any, being free,
> To covet fetters, tho' they golden be."
>
> Spenser, *Sonnet* 37.—M. B.

forbid! But they see things carried so by my Lord Chancellor and some others, that get money themselves, that they will not endure it. From thence to the Theatre, and there saw "Father's own Son" again, and so it raining very hard I went home by coach, with my mind very heavy for this my expensefull life, which will undo me, I fear, after all my hopes, if I do not take up, for

THE EARL OF CLARENDON

now I am coming to lay out a great deal of money in clothes for my wife, I must forbear other expenses. To bed, and this night began to lie in the little green chamber, where the maids lie, but we could not a great while get Nell to lie there, because I lie there and my wife, but at last, when she saw she must lie there or sit up, she, with much ado, came to bed.

[14th]. At the office all the morning. At noon I went by appointment to the Sun in Fish Street to a dinner of young Mr. Bernard's

for myself, Mr. Phillips, Davenport, Weaver, &c., where we had a most excellent dinner, but a pie of such pleasant variety of good things, as in all my life I never tasted. Hither came to me Captain Lambert to take his leave of me, he being this day to set sail for the Straights. We drank his farewell and a health to all our friends, and were very merry, and drank wine enough. Hence to the Temple to Mr. Turner about drawing up my bill in Chancery against T. Trice, and so to Salisbury Court, where Mrs. Turner is come to town to-night, but very ill still of an ague, which I was sorry to see. So to the Wardrobe and talked with my Lady, and so home and to bed.

[15th]. At home all the morning, and at noon with my wife to the Wardrobe to dinner, and there did shew herself to my Lady in the handkercher that she bought the lace for the other day, and indeed it is very handsome. Here I left my wife and went to my Lord Privy Seal to Whitehall, and there did give him a copy of the Fees of the office as I have received them, and he was well pleased with it. So to the Opera, where I met my wife and Captain Ferrers and Madamoiselle Le Blanc, and there did see the second part of "The Siege of Rhodes" very well done; and so by coach set her home, and the coach driving down the hill through Thames Street, which I think never any coach did before from that place to the bridge-foot, but going up Fish Street Hill his horses were so tired, that they could not be got to go up the hill, though all the street boys and men did beat and whip them. At last I was fain to send my boy for a link, and 'light out of the coach till we got to another at the corner of Fenchurch Street, and so home, and to bed.

[16th]. At the office all the morning. Dined at home, and so about my business in the afternoon to the Temple, where I found my Chancery bill drawn against T. Trice, which I read and like it, and so home.

[17th] (Lord's day). To our own church, and at noon, by invitation, Sir W. Pen dined with me, and I took Mrs. Hester, my Lady Batten's kinswoman, to dinner from church with me, and we were very merry. So to church again, and heard a simple fellow

upon the praise of Church musique, and exclaiming against men's wearing their hats on in the church, but I slept part of the sermon, till latter prayer and blessing and all was done without waking which I never did in my life. So home, and by and by comes my uncle Wight and my aunt and Mr. Norbury and his lady, and we drank hard and were very merry till supper time, and then we parted, my wife and I being invited to Sir W. Pen's, where we also were very merry, and so home to prayers and to bed.

[18th]. By coach with Sir W. Pen, my wife and I toward Westminster, but seeing Mr. Moore in the street I 'light and he and I went to Mr. Battersby's the minister, in my way I putting in at St. Paul's, where I saw the quiristers in their surplices going to prayers, and a few idle poor people and boys to hear them, which is the first time I have seen them, and am sorry to see things done so out of order, and there I received £50 more, which make up £100 that I now have borrowed of him, and so I did burn the old bond for £50, and paying him the use of it did make a new bond for the whole £100. Here I dined and had a good dinner, and his wife a good pretty woman. There was a young Parson at the table that had got himself drunk before dinner, which troubled me to see. After dinner to Mr. Bowers at Westminster for my wife, and brought her to the Theatre to see "Philaster,"[1] which I never saw before, but I found it far short of my expectations. So by coach home.

[19th]. At the office all the morning, and coming home found Mr. Hunt with my wife in the chamber alone, which God forgive me did trouble my head, but remembering that it was washing and that there was no place else with a fire for him to be in, it being also cold weather, I was at ease again. He dined with us, and after dinner took coach and carried him with us as far as my cozen Scott's, where we set him down and parted, and my wife and I staid there at the christening of my cozen's boy, where my cozen Samuel Pepys, of Ireland,[2] and I were godfathers, and I did name

---

[1] "Philaster; or, Love lies a-bleeding," a tragi-comedy, by Beaumont and Fletcher, acted at court in 1613.

[2] Samuel, son of Lord Chief Justice Pepys.

the child Samuel. There was a company of pretty women there
in the chamber, but we staid not, but went with the minister into
another room and eat and drank, and at last, when most of the
women were gone, Sam and I went into my cozen Scott, who was
got off her bed, and so we staid and talked and were very merry,
my she-cozen, Stradwick, being godmother. And then I left my
wife to go home by coach, and I walked to the Temple about my
law business, and there received a subpœna for T. Trice. I carried it myself to him at the usual house at Doctors Commons and
did give it him, and so home and to bed. It cost me 20*s.* between
the midwife and the two nurses to-day.

[20th]. To Westminster Hall by water in the morning, where I
saw the King going in his barge to the Parliament House; this
being the first day of their meeting again. And the Bishops, I hear,
do take their places in the Lords' House this day. I walked long
in the Hall, but hear nothing of news, but what Ned Pickering
tells me, which I am troubled at, that Sir J. Minnes should send
word to the King, that if he did not remove all my Lord Sandwich's captains out of this fleet, he believed the King would not
be master of the fleet at its coming again: and so do endeavour to
bring disgrace upon my Lord. But I hope all that will not do, for
the King loves him. Hence by water to the Wardrobe, and dined
with my Lady, my Lady Wright being there too, whom I find
to be a witty but very conceited woman and proud. And after
dinner Mr. Moore and I to the Temple, and there he read my bill
and likes it well enough, and so we came back again, he with me
as far as the lower end of Cheapside, and there I gave him a pint
of sack and parted, and I home, and went seriously to look over
my papers touching T. Trice, and I think I have found some that
will go near to do me more good in this difference of ours than
all I have before. So to bed with my mind cheery upon it, and lay
long reading "Hobbs his Liberty and Necessity,"[1] and a little but
very shrewd piece, and so to sleep.

[21st]. In the morning again at looking over my last night's
papers, and by and by comes Mr. Moore, who finds that my

---

[1] "Letter on Liberty and Necessity," by Thomas Hobbes, 1654.

papers may do me much good. He staid and dined with me, and we had a good surloyne of rost beefe, the first that ever I had of my own buying since I kept house; and after dinner he and I to the Temple, and there showed Mr. Smallwood[1] my papers, who likes them well, and so I left them with him, and went with Mr. Moore to Gray's Inn to his chamber, and there he shewed me his old Camden's "Britannica,"[2] which I intend to buy of him, and so took it away with me, and left it at St. Paul's Churchyard to be bound, and so home and to the office all the afternoon; it being the first afternoon that we have sat, which we are now to do always, so long as the Parliament sits, who this day have voted the King £120,000[3] to be raised to pay his debts. And after the office with Sir W. Batten to the Dolphin, and drank and left him there, and I again to the Temple about my business, and so on foot home again and to bed.

[22nd]. Within all the morning, and at noon with my wife, by appointment to dinner at the Dolphin, where Sir W. Batten, and his lady and daughter Matt,[4] and Captain Cocke and his lady, a German lady, but a very great beauty, and we dined together, at the spending of some wagers won and lost between him and I; and there we had the best musique and very good songs, and were very merry and danced, but I was most of all taken with Madam Cocke and her little boy, which in mirth his father had given to me. But after all our mirth comes a reckoning of £4, besides 40s. to the musicians, which did trouble us, but it must be paid, and so I took leave and left them there about eight at night. And on foot went to the Temple, and then took my cozen Turner's man Roger, and went by his advice to Serjeant Fountaine and told him our case, who gives me good comfort in it, and I gave him 30s. fee. So home again and to bed. This day a good

---

[1] Smallwood, poser at St. Paul's School (see February 4th, 1663-64).

[2] The edition of Camden's "Britannia," now in the Pepysian Library, is that of London, 1695.

[3] A mistake. According to the journals, £1,200,000. And see Diary, February 29th, 1663-64.—M. B.

[4] Martha Batten, afterwards married to Mr. Castle.

pretty maid was sent my wife by Mary Bowyer, whom my wife has hired.

[23rd]. To Westminster with my wife (she to her father's), and about 10 o'clock back again home, and there I to the office a little, and thence by coach with Commissioner Pett to Cheapside to one Savill,[1] a painter, who I intend shall do my picture and my wife's. Thence I to dinner at the Wardrobe, and so home to the office, and there all the afternoon till night, and then both Sir Williams to my house, and in comes Captain Cock, and they to cards. By and by Sir W. Batten and Cock, after drinking a good deal of wine, went away, and Sir W. Pen staid with my wife and I to supper, very pleasant, and so good night. This day I have a chine of beef sent home, which I bespoke to send, and did send it as a present to my uncle Wight.

[24th] (Lord's day). Up early, and by appointment to St. Clement Danes[2] to church, and there to meet Captain Cocke, who had often commended Mr. Alsopp, their minister, to me, who is indeed an able man, but as all things else did not come up to my expectations. His text was that all good and perfect gifts are from above.[3] Thence Cocke and I to the Sun tavern behind the Exchange, and there met with others that are come from the same church, and staid and drank and talked with them a little, and so broke up, and I to the Wardrobe and there dined, and staid all the afternoon with my Lady alone talking, and thence to see Madame Turner, who, poor lady, continues very ill, and I begin to be afraid of her. Thence homewards, and meeting Mr. Yong, the upholster, he and I to the Mitre, and with Mr. Rawlinson sat and drank a quart of sack, and so I to Sir W. Batten's and there staid and supped, and so home, where I found an invitation sent my wife and I to my uncle Wight's on Tuesday next to the chine of beef which I presented them with yesterday. So to prayers and to bed.

[25th]. To Westminster Hall in the morning with Captain Lam-

---

[1] Savill, the painter of Cheapside, is not mentioned by Walpole.
[2] Richard Dukeson was the rector of the parish at this time.
[3] "Every good gift and every perfect gift is from above," Epistle of *James* i. 17.

bert, and there he did at the Dog give me and some other friends
of his, his foy, he being to set sail to-day towards the Streights.
Here we had oysters and good wine. Having this morning met
in the Hall with Mr. Sanchy, we appointed to meet at the play
this afternoon. At noon, at the rising of the House, I met with
Sir W. Pen and Major General Massy,[1] who I find by discourse
to be a very ingenious man, and among other things a great master in the secresys of powder and fireworks, and another knight
to dinner, at the Swan, in the Palace yard, and our meat brought
from the Legg; and after dinner Sir W. Pen and I to the Theatre,
and there saw "The Country Captain," a dull play, and that being done, I left him with his Torys[2] and went to the Opera, and
saw the last act of "The Bondman," and there found Mr. Sanchy
and Mrs. Mary Archer, sister to the fair Betty, whom I did admire at Cambridge, and thence took them to the Fleece in Covent
Garden, there to bid good night to Sir W. Pen who staid for me;
but Mr. Sanchy could not by any argument get his lady to trust
herself with him into the tavern, which he was much troubled
at, and so we returned immediately into the city by coach, and
at the Mitre in Cheapside there 'light and drank, and then set
her at her uncle's in the Old Jewry. And so he and I back again
thither, and drank till past 12 at night, till I had drank something too much. He all the while telling me his intention to get
a girl who is worth £1,000, and many times we had her sister
Betty's health, whose memory I love. At last parted, and I well
home, only had got cold and was hoarse and so to bed.

[27th]. This morning our maid Dorothy and my wife parted,
which though she be a wench for her tongue not to be borne with,

[1] Major-General Edward Massey (or Massie), son of John Massie, was captain of one of the foot companies of the Irish Expedition, and had Oliver
Cromwell as his ensign (see Peacock's "Army Lists in 1642," p. 65). He was
Governor of Gloucester in its obstinate defence against the royal forces, 1643;
dismissed by the self-denying ordinance when he entered Charles II.'s service.
He was taken prisoner at the battle of Worcester, September 3rd, 1651, but
escaped abroad.

[2] This is a strange use of the word Tory, and an early one also. The word
originally meant bogtrotters or wild Irish, and as Penn was Governor of
Kildare these may have been some of his Irish followers. The term was not
used politically until about 1679.

yet I was loth to part with her, but I took my leave kindly of her and went out to Savill's, the painter, and there sat the first time for my face with him; thence to dinner with my Lady; and so after an hour or two's talk in divinity with my Lady, Captain Ferrers and Mr. Moore and I to the Theatre, and there saw "Hamlett" very well done, and so I home, and found that my wife had been with my aunt Wight and Ferrers to wait on my Lady to-day this afternoon, and there danced and were very merry, and my Lady very fond as she is always of my wife. So to bed.

[28th]. At home all the morning; at noon Will brought me from Whitehall, whither I had sent him, some letters from my Lord Sandwich, from Tangier;[1] where he continues still, and hath done some execution upon the Turks, and retaken an Englishman from them,[2] of one Mr. Parker's, a merchant in Marke-lane. In the afternoon Mr. Pett and I met at the office; there being none more there than we two I saw there was not the reverence due to us observed, and so I took occasion to break up and took Mr. Gawdon along with me, and he and I (though it rained) were resolved to go, he to my Lord Treasurer's and I to the Chancellor's with a letter from my Lord to-day. So to a tavern at the end of Mark Lane, and there we staid till with much ado we got a coach, and so to my Lord Treasurer's and lost our labours, then to the Chancellor's, and there met with Mr. Dugdale,[3] and with him and one Mr. Simons, I think that belongs to my Lord Hatton,[4] and Mr. Kipps and others, to the Fountain tavern, and there staid till twelve at night drinking and singing, Mr. Simons and one Mr. Agar singing very well. Then Mr. Gawdon being almost drunk had the wit to be gone, and so I took leave too, and it being

---

[1] Lord Sandwich's Journal has been printed by Kennett. See note to February 20th, 1661-62.—B.

[2] The Ironmongers' Company possess in trust an enormous sum, left by Thomas Betton, for the redemption of Christian slaves in Barbary. Since Lord Exmouth's expedition, no claims have arisen upon the fund, which is now administered for other purposes, under the direction of the Court of Chancery. —B.

[3] John Dugdale, Windsor Herald.

[4] Christopher, first Lord Hatton. Died 1670.

a fine moonshine night he and I footed it all the way home, but though he was drunk he went such a pace as I did admire how he was able to go. When I came home I found our new maid Sarah[1] come, who is a tall and a well favoured wench, and one that I think will please us. So to bed.

[29th]. I lay long in bed, till Sir Williams both sent me word that we were to wait upon the Duke of York to-day; and that they would have me to meet them at Westminster Hall, at noon: so I rose and went thither; and there I understand that they are gone to Mr. Coventry's lodgings, in the Old Palace Yard, to dinner (the first time I knew he had any); and there I met them two and Sir G. Carteret, and had a very fine dinner, and good welcome, and discourse; and so, by water, after dinner to White Hall to the Duke, who met us in his closet; and there he did discourse to us the business of Holmes, and did desire of us to know what hath been the common practice about making of forrayne ships to strike sail to us, which they did all do as much as they could; but I could say nothing to it, which I was sorry for. So indeed I was forced to study a lie, and so after we were gone from the Duke, I told Mr. Coventry that I had heard Mr. Selden often say, that he could prove that in Henry the 7th's time, he did give commission to his captains to make the King of Denmark's ships to strike to him in the Baltique.[2] From thence Sir W. Pen and I to the Theatre, but it was so full that we could hardly get any room, so he went up to one of the boxes, and I into the 18d. places, and

---

[1] Sarah did not stay long with Mrs. Pepys, who was continually falling out with her. She left to enter Sir William Penn's service.

[2] The tables were in vain attempted to be turned in May, 1670, when Arthur Capel, the first Earl of Essex, sent as Ambassador Extraordinary to Denmark in a ship of war, was thrice fired upon with shot by Major-General Holke, who commanded the Castle of Cronenburg, which Essex had neglected or refused to salute. Charles did not submit tamely to this insult. Essex was ordered to obtain the fullest reparation, and he did so promptly. On the 19th of the same month, Sir John Trevor, Secretary of State, acknowledged the good success which Lord Essex had had "about the flagg. His Majesty received your letter with great satisfaction, which came seasonably to be declared here before the French Court. The satisfaction you have obtained is absolute, and a full renounce to all that pretence on their part."—B.

there saw "Love at first sight,"[1] a play of Mr. Killigrew's, and the first time that it hath been acted since before the troubles, and great expectation there was, but I found the play to be a poor thing, and so I perceive every body else do. So home, calling at Paul's Churchyard for a "Mare Clausum,"[2] having it in my mind to write a little matter, what I can gather, about the business of striking sayle, and present it to the Duke, which I now think will be a good way to make myself known. So home and to bed.

[30th]. In the morning to the Temple, Mr. Philips and Dr. Williams about my several law matters, and so to the Wardrobe to dinner, and after dinner stole away, my Lady not dining out of her chamber, and so home and then to the office all the afternoon, and that being done Sir W. Batten and I and Captain Cock got a bottle of sack into the office, and there we sat late and drank and talked, and so home and to bed. I am this day in very good health, only got a little cold. The Parliament has sat a pretty while. The old condemned judges of the late King have been brought before the Parliament, and like to be hanged. I am deep in Chancery against Tom Trice, God give a good issue; and myself under great trouble for my late great expending of money vainly, which God stop for the future. This is the last day for the old State's coyne[3] to pass in common payments, but they say it is to pass in publique payments to the King three months still.

---

[1] Here, as in so many other instances, Pepys gives the second title only of the play. The correct title is, "The Princesse, or Love at First Sight, a Tragi-Comedy: the scene, Naples and Sicily. Written in Naples by Thomas Killigrew." It was published at London, 1663.

[2] Selden's work is in the Pepysian Library, "Joannis Seldeni Mare Clausum. Londini, 1635," folio.

[3] In a speech of Lord Lucas in the House of Lords, the 22nd February, 1670-1 (which speech was burnt by the common hangman), he thus adverted to that coin: "It is evident that there is a scarcity of money; for all the parliament's money called *breeches* (a fit stamp for the coin of the Rump) is wholly vanished—the king's proclamation and the Dutch have swept it all away, and of his now majesty's coin there appears but very little; so that in effect we have none left for common use, but a little old lean coined money of the late three former princes. And what supply is preparing for it, my lords? I hear of none, unless it be of copper farthings, and this is the metal that is to vindicate, according to the inscription on it, *the dominion of the four seas*."—Quoted in Penn's "Memorials of Sir Wm. Penn," ii. 264.

[December 1st] (Lord's Day). In the morning at church and heard Mr. Mills. At home dined and with me by appointment Mr. Sanchy, who should have brought his mistress, Mrs. Mary Archer, of Cambridge, but she could not come, but we had a good dinner for him. And so in the afternoon my wife went to church, and he and I stayed at home and drank and talked, and he stayed with me till night and supped with me, when I expected to have seen Jack Cole and Lem. Wagstaffe, but they did not come. We this day cut a brave collar of brawn from Winchcombe which proves very good, and also opened the glass of girkins which Captain Cocke did give my wife the other day, which are rare things. So at night to bed. There hath lately been great clapping up of some old statesmen, such as Ireton, Moyer,[1] and others, and they say, upon a great plot, but I believe no such thing; but it is but justice that they should be served as they served the poor Cavaliers; and I believe it will oftentimes be so as long as I live, whether there be cause or no. This evening my brother Tom was with me, and I did talk again to him about Mr. Townsend's daughter, and I do intend to put the business in hand. I pray God give a good end to it.

[2nd]. To Savill the painter's, but he not being well I could do nothing there, and so I returned home, and in my way met Mr. Moore and took him with me home, where we staid and talked all the morning, and he dined with me, and after dinner went away to the Privy Seal, this being our first day this month. By and by called on by Mr. Sanchy and his mistress, and with them by coach to the Opera, to see "The Mad Lover,"[2] but not much pleased with the play. That done home all to my house, where they staid and supped and were merry, and at last late bid good night and so we to bed.

[3rd]. To the Paynter's and sat and had more of my picture done; but it do not please me, for I fear it will not be like me. At noon from thence to the Wardrobe, where dinner not being

---

[1] Samuel Moyer, one of the Council of State, 1653.—B.

[2] A tragi-comedy by Beaumont and Fletcher, published in the edition of their plays, 1647.

ready Mr. Moore and I to the Temple about my little business at Mr. Turner's, and so back again, and dinner being half done I went in to my Lady, where my Lady Wright was at dinner with her, and all our talk about the great happiness that my Lady Wright says there is in being in the fashion and in variety of fashions, in scorn of others that are not so, as citizens' wives and country gentlewomen, which though it did displease me enough, yet I said nothing to it. Thence by water to the office through bridge, being carried by him in oars that the other day rowed in a scull faster than my oars to the Towre, and I did give him 6*d*. At the office all afternoon, and at night home to read in "Mare Clausum" till bedtime, and so to bed, but had a very bad night by dreams of my wife's riding with me and her horse throwing her and breaking her leg, and then I dreamed that I . . . [was] in such pain that I waked with it, and had a great deal of pain there a very great while till I fell asleep again, and such apprehension I had of it that when I rose and trussed up myself thinking that it had been no dream. Till in the daytime I found myself very well at ease, and remembered that I did dream so, and that Mr. Creed was with me, and that I did complain to him of it, and he said he had the same pain in his left that I had in my right . . . which pleased me much to remember.

[4th]. To Whitehall with both Sir Williams, thence by water, where I saw a man lie dead upon Westminster Stairs that had been drowned yesterday. To the Temple, and thence to Mr. Phillips and got my copy of Sturtlow lands. So back to the 3 Tuns at Charing Cross, and there met the two Sir Williams and Col. Treswell and Mr. Falconer, and dined there at Sir W. Pen's cost, and after dinner by water to Cheapside to the painter's, and there found my wife, and having sat a little she and I by coach to the Opera and Theatre, but coming too late to both, and myself being a little out of tune we returned, and I settled to read in "Mare Clausum" till bedtime, and so to bed.

[5th]. This morning I went early to the Paynter's and there sat for my picture the fourth time, but it do not yet please me, which do much trouble me. Thence to the Treasury Office, where I

found Sir W. Batten come before me, and there we sat to pay off the St. George. By and by came Sir W. Pen, and he and I staid while Sir W. Batten went home to dinner, and then he came again, and Sir W. Pen and I went and dined at my house, and had two mince pies sent thither by our order from the messenger Slater, that had dressed some victuals for us, and so we were very merry, and after dinner rode out in his coach, he to Whitehall,

and my wife and I to the Opera, and saw "Hamlett" well performed. Thence to the Temple and Mrs. Turner's (who continues still very ill), and so home and to bed.

[6th]. Lay long in bed, and then to Westminster Hall and there walked, and then with Mr. Spicer, Hawly, Washington, and little Mr. Ashwell (my old friends at the Exchequer) to the Dog, and gave them two or three quarts of wine, and so away to White Hall, where, at Sir G. Carteret's, Sir Williams both and I dined very pleasantly; and after dinner, by appointment, came the

Governors of the East India Company, to sign and seal the contract between us[1] (in the King's name) and them. And that done, we all went to the King's closet, and there spoke with the King and the Duke of York, who promise to be very careful of the India trade to the utmost. So back to Sir G. Carteret's and ended our business, and so away homewards, but Sir W. Batten offering to go to the 3 Tuns at Charing Cross, where the pretty maid the daughter of the house is, I was saying that, that tickled Sir W. Pen, he seemed to take these words very captiously and angrily, which I saw, and seemed indifferent to go home in his coach with them, and so took leave to go to the Council Chamber to speak with my Lord Privy Seal, which I did, but they did stay for me, which I was pleased at, but no words passed between him and me in all our way home. So home and to bed.

[7th]. This morning comes Captain Ferrers and the German, Emanuel Luffe, who goes as one of my Lord's footmen, though he deserves a much better preferment, to take their leave of me, and here I got the German to play upon my theorbo, which he did both below and in my wife's chamber, who was in bed. He plays bravely. I find by him that my lute is a most excellent lute. I did give them a mince pie and a collar of brawn and some wine for their breakfast, and were very merry, and sent for Mr. Adamson's neighbour to drink Mr. Shepley's health. At last we all parted, but within a quarter of an hour after they were gone, and my wife and I were talking about buying of a fine scallop which is brought her this morning by a woman to be sold, which is to cost her 45s., in comes the German back again, all in a goare of blood, which I wondered at, and tells me that he is afeard that the Captain is killed by the waterman at Towre Stayres; so I presently went thither, and found that upon some rude pressing of the watermen to ply the Captain, he struck one of them with his cane, which they would not take, but struck him again, and then the German drew his sword and ran at one of them, but they were

---

[1] Charles II.'s charter to the Company, confirming and extending the former charter, is dated April 3rd, 1661. Bombay, just acquired as part of Queen Katherine's dowry, was made over to the Company by Letters Patent dated March 27th, 1669.

both soundly beaten.[1] The Captain is, however, got to the hoy that carries him and the pages to the Downs, and I went into the ale-house at the Stayres and got them to deliver the Captain's feathers, which one from the Captain was come to demand, and went home again, and there found my wife dressing of the German's head, and so did [give] him a cravett for his neck, and a crown in his purse, and sent him away again. Then came Mr. Moore, and he and I to Westminster and to Worcester House to see Mr. Montagu before he goes away (this night), but could not see him, nor do I think he has a mind to see us for fear of our demanding of money of him for anything. So back to Whitehall, and eat a bit of meat at Wilkinson's, and then to the Privy Seal, and sealed there the first time this month; and, among other things that passed, there was a patent for Roger Palmer (Madam Palmer's husband) to be Earl of Castlemaine and Baron of Limbricke in Ireland; but the honour is tied up to the males got of the body of this wife, the Lady Barbary: the reason whereof every body knows. That done, by water to the office, when I found Sir W. Pen had been alone all the night and was just rose, and so I to him, and with him I found Captain Holmes, who had wrote his case, and gives me a copy, as he hath many among his friends, and presented the same to the King and Council. Which I shall make use of in my attempt of writing something concerning the business of striking sail, which I am now about.[2] But he do cry out against Sir John Minnes, as the veriest knave and rogue and coward in the world, which I was glad to hear, because he has given out bad words concerning my Lord, though I am sorry it is so. Here Captain Cox

---

[1] See a similar outrage, committed by Captain Ferrers, September 12th, 1662. Swords were usually worn by footmen. See May 4th, 1662, *post.*—B.

[2] Sir John Burroughs had already written a treatise on "The Soveraignty of the British Seas proved by Records, History, and the Municipall Lawes of this Kingdome. Written in the year 1633 by that Learned Knight, Sir John Boroughs, Keeper of the Records in the Tower of London. London, 1651," copies of which, both in Latin and English, are common, and one of which is in the Pepysian Library. William Ryley, the herald, Deputy Keeper of the Records, had also written on the subject, and had made extracts from the records. Ryley's collections appear to have belonged to James II., and were probably made for him at this time. The Duke of Newcastle afterwards possessed them, and they are now in the British Museum.

then came in, and he and I staid a good while and so good night. Home and wrote by the post to my father, and so to bed.

[8th] (Lord's day). In bed all the morning thinking to take physique, but it being a frost my wife would not have me. So to dinner at the Wardrobe, and after a great deal of good discourse with my Lady after dinner, and among other things of the great christening yesterday at Mr. Rumbell's, and courtiers and pomp that was there, which I wonder at, I went away up and down into all the churches almost between that place and my house, and so home. And then came my brother Tom, and staid and talked with me, and I hope he will do very well and get money. So to supper and to bed. This morning as I was in bed, one brings me T. Trice's answer to my bill in chancery from Mr. Smallwood, which I am glad to see, though I am afraid it will do me hurt.

[9th]. To Whitehall, and thence to the Rhenish wine-house, where I met Mons. Eschar and there took leave of him, he being to go this night to the Downs towards Portugall, and so spent all the morning. At noon to dinner to the Wardrobe; where my Lady Wright was, who did talk much upon the worth and the desert of gallantry; and that there was none fit to be courtiers, but such as have been abroad and know fashions. Which I endeavoured to oppose; and was troubled to hear her talk so, though she be a very wise and discreet lady in other things. From thence Mr. Moore and I to the Temple about my law business with my cozen Turner, and there we read over T. Trice's answer to my bill and advised thereupon what to do in his absence, he being to go out of town to-morrow. Thence he and I to Mr. Walpole, my attorney, whom I never saw before, and we all to an alehouse hard by, and there we talked of our business, and he put me into great hopes, but he is but a young man, and so I do not depend so much upon his encouragement. So by coach home, and to supper, and to bed, having staid up till 12 at night writing letters to my Lord Sandwich and all my friends with him at sea, to send to-morrow by Mons. Eschar, who goes to-morrow post to the Downs to go along with the fleet to Portugall.

[10th]. To Whitehall, and there finding Mons. Eschar to be gone,

I sent my letters by a porter to the posthouse in Southwark to be sent by despatch to the Downs. So to dinner to my Lord Crew's by coach, and in my way had a stop of above an hour and a half, which is a great trouble this Parliament time, but it cannot be helped. However I got thither before my Lord come from the House, and so dined with him, and dinner done, home to the office, and there sat late and so home.

[11th]. My brother Tom and then Mr. Moore came to me this morning, and staid a while with me, and then I went out, and in my way met with Mr. Howell the Turner, who invited me to dine this day at Mr. Rawlinson's with some friends of his, officers of the Towre, at a venison pasty, which I promised him, and so I went to the Old Bayly, and there staid and drank with him, who told me the whole story how Pegg Kite has married herself to a weaver, an ugly fellow, to her undoing, of which I am glad that I have nothing to do in it. From thence home and put on my velvet coat, and so to the Mitre to dinner according to my promise this morning, but going up into the room I found at least 12 or more persons, and knew not the face of any of them, so I went down again, and though I met Mr. Yong the upholster yet I would not be persuaded to stay, but went away and walked to the Exchequer, and up and down, and was very hungry, and from thence home, when I understand Mr. Howell was come for me to go thither, but I am glad I was not at home, and my wife was gone out by coach to Clerkenwell to see Mrs. Margaret Pen, who is at school there. So I went to see Sir W. Pen, who for this two or three days has not been well, and he and I after some talk took a coach and went to Moorfields, and there walked, though it was very cold, an hour or two, and went into an alehouse, and there I drank some ale and eat some bread and cheese, but he would not eat a bit, and so being very merry we went home again. He to his lodgings and I by promise to Sir W. Batten's, where he and my lady have gone out of town, and so Mrs. Martha was at home alone, and Mrs. Moore and there I supped upon some good things left of yesterday's dinner there, where dined a great deal of company — Sir R. Browne and others — and by and by comes in Captain Cox who promised to be here with me, but he staid

206

very late, and had been drinking somewhere and was very drunk, and so very capricious, which I was troubled to see in a man that I took for a very wise and wary man. So I home and left him there, and so to bed.

[12th]. We lay long in bed, then up and made me ready, and by and by come Will Bowyer and Mr. Gregory, my old Exchequer friend, to see me, and I took them to the Dolphin and there did give them a good morning draft, and so parted, and invited them and all my old Exchequer acquaintance to come and dine with me there on Wednesday next. From thence to the Wardrobe and dined with my Lady, where her brother, Mr. John Crew, dined also, and a strange gentlewoman dined at the table as a servant of my Lady's; but I knew her not, and so I am afeard that poor Madamoiselle[1] was gone, but I since understand that she is come as housekeeper to my Lady, and is a married woman. From thence to Westminster to my Lord's house to meet my Lord Privy Seal, who appointed to seal there this afternoon, but by and by word is brought that he is come to Whitehall, and so we are fain to go thither to him, and there we staid to seal till it was so late that though I got leave to go away before he had done, yet the office was done before I could get thither, and so to Sir W. Pen's, and there sat and talked and drank with him, and so home.

[13th]. At home all the morning, being by the cold weather, which for these two days has been frost, in some pain in my bladder. Dined at home and then with my wife to the Paynter's, and there she sat the first time to be drawn, while I all the while stood looking on a pretty lady's picture, whose face did please me extremely. At last, he having done, I found that the dead colour of my wife is good, above what I expected, which pleased me exceedingly. So home and to the office about some special business, where Sir Williams both were, and from thence with them to the Steelyard, where my Lady Batten and others came to us, and there we drank and had musique and Captain Cox's company, and he paid all, and so late back again home by coach, and to bed.

---

[1] This may be Mademoiselle Le Blanc, mentioned on November 15th, 1661.

[14th]. All the morning at home lying in bed with my wife till 11 o'clock. Such a habit we have got this winter of lying long abed. Dined at home, and in the afternoon to the office. There sat late, and so home and to bed.

[15th] (Lord's day). To church in the morning, where our young Reader begun the first day to read. Sir W. Pen dined with me and we were merry. Again to church and so home, and all alone read till bedtime, and so to prayers and to bed. I have been troubled this day about a difference between my wife and her maid Nell, who is a simple slut, and I am afeard we shall find her a cross-grained wench. I am now full of study about writing something about our making of strangers strike to us at sea; and so am altogether reading Selden and Grotius, and such other authors to that purpose.

[16th]. Up by five o'clock this morning by candlelight (which I have not done for many a day), being called upon by one Mr. Bollen by appointment, who has business to be done with my Lord Privy Seal this morning, and so by coach, calling Mr. Moore at the Wardrobe, to Chelsy, and there did get my Lord to seal it. And so back again to Westminster Hall, and thence to my Lord Sandwich's lodging, where I met my wife (who had been to see Mrs. Hunt who was brought to bed the other day of a boy), and got a joint of meat thither from the Cook's, and she and I and Sarah dined together, and after dinner to the Opera, where there was a new play ("Cutter of Coleman Street"),[1] made in the year 1658, with reflections much upon the late times; and it being the first time, the pay was doubled, and so to save money, my wife and I went up into the gallery, and there sat and saw very well; and a very good play it is. It seems of Cowly's making. From thence by coach home, and to bed.

[17th]. Up and to the Paynter's to see how he went forward in our picture. So back again to dinner at home, and then was sent for to the Privy Seal, whither I was forced to go and stay so long

---

[1] Cutter, an old word for a rough swaggerer: hence the title of Cowley's play. It was originally called "The Guardian," when acted before Prince Charles at Trinity College, Cambridge, on March 12th, 1641.

and late that I was much vexed. At last we got all done, and then made haste to the office, where they were sat, and there we sat late, and so home to supper and to Selden, "Mare Clausum," and so to bed.

[18th]. At the office upon business extraordinary all the morning, then to my Lady Sandwich's to dinner, whither my wife, who had been at the painter's, came to me, and there dined, and there I left her, and to the Temple my brother and I to see Mrs. Turner, who begins to be better, and so back to my Lady's, where much made of, and so home to my study till bed-time, and so to bed.

[19th]. This morning my wife dressed herself fine to go to the christening of Mrs. Hunt's child, and so she and I in the way in the morning went to the Paynter's, and there she sat till noon, and I all the while looking over great variety of good prints which he had, and by and by comes my boy to tell us that Mrs. Hunt has been at our house to tell us that the christening is not till Saturday next. So after the Paynter had done I did like the picture pretty well, and my wife and I went by coach home, but in the way I took occasion to fall out with my wife very highly about her ribbands being ill matched and of two colours, and to very high words, so that, like a passionate fool, I did call her whore, for which I was afterwards sorry. But I set her down at home, and went myself by appointment to the Dolphin, where Sir W. Warren did give us all a good dinner, and that being done, to the office, and there sat late, and so home.

[20th]. Lay long in bed, and then up, and so to the Wardrobe to dinner, and from thence out with Mr. Moore towards my house, and in our way met with Mr. Swan (my old acquaintance), and we to a tavern, where we had enough of his old simple religious talk, and he is still a coxcomb in these things as he ever was, and tells me he is setting out a book called "The unlawfull use of lawfull things"; but a very simple fellow he is, and so I leave him. So we drank and at last parted, and Mr. Moore and I into Cornhill, it being dark night, and in the street and on the Exchange discoursed about Dominion of the Sea, wherein I am lately so much

concerned, and so I home and sat late up reading of Mr. Selden, and so to bed.

[21st]. To White Hall to the Privy Seal, where my Lord Privy Seal did tell us he could seal no more this month, for that he goes thirty miles out of town to keep his Christmas. At which I was glad, but only afeard lest any thing of the King's should force us to go after him to get a seal in the country. Thence to Westminster Hall (having by the way drank with Mrs. Sarah and Mrs. Betty at my Lord's lodgings), and thence taken by some Exchequer men to the Dogg, where, being St. Thomas's day, by custom they have a general meeting at dinner. There I was and all very merry, and there I spoke to Mr. Falconberge to look whether he could out of Domesday Book, give me any thing concerning the sea, and the dominion thereof; which he says he will look after. Thence taking leave to my brother's, and there by appointment met with Prior of Brampton who had money to pay me, but desiring some advice he stays till Monday. So by coach home to the office, where I was vexed to see Sir Williams both seem to think so much that I should be a little out of the way, saying that without their Register they were not a Committee, which I took in some dudgeon, and see clearly that I must keep myself at a little distance with them and not crouch, or else I shall never keep myself up even with them. So home and wrote letters by the post. This evening my wife come home from christening Mrs. Hunt's son, his name John, and a merchant in Mark Lane came along with her, that was her partner. So after my business was done, and read something in Mr. Selden, I went to bed.

[22nd]. To church in the morning, where the Reader made a boyish young sermon. Home to dinner, and there I took occasion, from the blacknesse of the meat as it came out of the pot, to fall out with my wife and my maid for their sluttery, and so left the table, and went up to read in Mr. Selden till church time, and then my wife and I to church, and there in the pew, with the rest of the company, was Captain Holmes, in his gold-laced suit, at which I was troubled because of the old business which he attempted upon my wife. So with my mind troubled I sat still, but

by and by I took occasion from the rain now holding up (it raining when we came into the church) to put my wife in mind of going to the christening (which she was invited to) of N. Osborne's child, which she did, and so went out of the pew, and my mind was eased. So home after sermon and there came by appointment Dr. T. Pepys, Will. Joyce, and my brother Tom, and supped with me, and very merry they were, and I seemed to be, but I was not pleased at all with their company. So they being gone we went to bed.

[23rd]. Early up and by coach (before daylight) to the Wardrobe, and took up Mr. Moore, and he and I to Chelsy to my Lord Privy Seal, and there sealed some things, he being to go out of town for all Christmas to-morrow. So back again to Westminster, and from thence by water to the Treasury Office, where I found Sir W. Pen paying off the Sophia and Griffen, and there I staid with him till noon, and having sent for some collar of beef and a mince pie, we eat and drank, and so I left him there and to my brother's by appointment to meet Prior, but he came not, so I went and saw Mrs. Turner who continues weak, and by and by word was brought me that Prior's man was come to Tom's, and so I went and told out £128 which I am to receive of him, but Prior not coming I went away and left the money by his desire with my brother all night, and they to come to me to-morrow morning. So I took coach, and 'lighting at my bookseller's[1] in Paul's Churchyard, I met with Mr. Crumlum[2] and the second master of Paul's School, and thence I took them to the Starr, and there we sat and talked, and I had great pleasure in their company, and very glad I was of meeting him so accidentally, I having omitted too long to go to see him. Here in discourse of books I did offer to give the school what books he would choose of £5. So we parted, and I home, and to Mr. Selden, and then to bed.

[24th]. Home all the morning and dined at home, and in the afternoon to the office. So home.

---

[1] Joseph Kirton (see *ante*, February 12th, 1659-60 note).

[2] Samuel Cromleholme or Crumlum, High-master (see *ante*, January 24th, 1659-60 note).

[25th]. In the morning to church, where at the door of our pew I was fain to stay, because that the sexton had not opened the door. A good sermon of Mr. Mills. Dined at home all alone, and taking occasion from some fault in the meat to complain of my maid's sluttery, my wife and I fell out, and I up to my chamber in a discontent. After dinner my wife comes up to me and all friends again, and she and I to walk upon the leads, and there Sir W. Pen called us, and we went to his house and supped with him, but before supper Captain Cock came to us half drunk, and began to talk, but Sir W. Pen knowing his humour and that there was no end of his talking, drinks four great glasses of wine to him, one after another, healths to the king, and by that means made him drunk, and so he went away, and so we sat down to supper, and were merry, and so after supper home and to bed.

[26th].This morning Sir W. Pen and I to the Treasury office, and there we paid off the Amity (Captain Stokes's ship that was at Guinny) and another ship, and so home, and after dinner Sir William came to me, and he and his son and daughter, and I and my wife, by coach to Moorfields to walk; but it was most foul weather, and so we went into an alehouse and there eat some cakes and ale, and a washeall-bowle[1] woman and girl came to us and sung to us. And after all was done I called my boy (Wayneman) to us to eat some cake that was left, and the woman of the house told us that he had called for two cakes and a pot of ale for himself, at which I was angry, and am resolved to correct him for it. So home, and Sir W. Pen and his son and daughter to supper to me to a good turkey, and were merry at cards, and so to bed.

[27th]. In the morning to my Bookseller's to bespeak a Stephens's Thesaurus, for which I offer £4, to give to Paul's School, and from thence to Paul's Church; and there I heard Dr. Gunning preach a good sermon upon the day (being St. John's day), and did hear him tell a story, which he did persuade us to believe to be true, that St. John and the Virgin Mary did appear to Gregory,

---

[1]   "The wenches with their wassall bowls
        About the streets are singing."—Wither's *Christmas Carol.*

The old custom of carrying the wassail bowl from door to door, with songs and merriment, in Christmas week, is still observed in some of our rural districts.—B.

a Bishopp, at his prayer to be confirmed in the faith, which I did
wonder to hear from him. Here I met with Mr. Crumlum (and
told him of my endeavour to get Stephens's Thesaurus for the
school), and so home, and after dinner comes Mr. Faulconberge
to see me, and at his desire I sent over for his kinsman Mr.
Knightly, the merchant, and so he came over and sat and drank

with us, and at his request I went over with him, and there I sat
till the evening, and till both Mr. Knightly and Mr. Faulconberge
(for whom I sent my boy to get a coach to carry him to Westminster) were both drunk, and so home, but better wine I never
drank in all my life. So home, and finding my wife gone to Sir
W. Pen's, I went thither, and there I sat and played at cards and
supped, and so home and to bed.

[28th]. At home all the morning; and in the afternoon all of us
at the office, upon a letter from the Duke for the making up of a

speedy estimate of all the debts of the Navy, which is put into good forwardness. I home and Sir W. Pen to my house, who with his children staid playing cards late, and so to bed.

[29th] (Lord's day). Long in bed with my wife, and though I had determined to go to dine with my wife at my Lady's (chiefly to put off dining with Sir W. Pen to-day because Holmes dined there), yet I could not get a coach time enough to go thither, and so I dined at home, and my brother Tom with me, and then a coach came and I carried my wife to Westminster, and she went to see Mrs. Hunt, and I to the Abbey, and there meeting with Mr. Hooper, he took me in among the quire, and there I sang with them their service, and so that being done, I walked up and down till night for that Mr. Coventry was not come to Whitehall since dinner again. At last I went thither and he was come, and I spoke with him about some business of the office, and so took leave of him, and sent for my wife and the coach, and so to the Wardrobe and supped, and staid very long talking with my Lady, who seems to doat every day more and more upon us. So home and to prayers, and to bed.

[30th]. At the office about this estimate and so with my wife and Sir W. Pen to see our pictures, which do not much displease us, and so back again, and I staid at the Mitre, whither I had invited all my old acquaintance of the Exchequer to a good chine of beef, which with three barrels of oysters and three pullets, and plenty of wine and mirth, was our dinner, and there was about twelve of us, among others Mr. Bowyer, the old man, and Mr. Faulconberge, Shadwell, Taylor, Spicer, Woodruffe (who by reason of some friend that dined with him came to us after dinner), Servington, &c., and here I made them a foolish promise to give them one this day twelvemonth, and so for ever while I live, but I do not intend it. Here I staid as long as I could keep them, and so home to Sir W. Pen, who with his children and my wife has been at a play to-day and saw "D'Ambois,"[1] which I never saw. Here we staid late at supper and playing at cards, and so home and to bed.

---

[1] "Bussy D'Ambois," a tragedy by George Chapman, first published in 1607.

[31st]. My wife and I this morning to the Paynter's, and there she sat the last time, and I stood by and did tell him some little things to do, that now her picture I think will please me very well; and after her, her little black dogg sat in her lap, and was drawn, which made us very merry; so home to dinner, and so to the office; and there late finishing our estimate of the debts of the Navy to this day; and it come to near £374,000. So home, and after supper, and my barber had trimmed me, I sat down to end my journell for this year, and my condition at this time, by God's blessing, is thus: my health (only upon catching cold, which brings great pain in my back . . . as it used to be when I had the stone) is very good, and so my wife's in all respects: my servants, W. Hewer, Sarah, Nell, and Wayneman: my house at the Navy Office. I suppose myself to be worth about £500 clear in the world, and my goods of my house my own, and what is coming to me from Brampton, when my father dies, which God defer. But, by my uncle's death, the whole care and trouble of all, and settling of all lies upon me, which is very great, because of law-suits, especially that with T. Trice, about the interest of £200, which will, I hope, be ended soon. My chiefest thought is now to get a good wife for Tom, there being one offered by the Joyces, a cozen of theirs, worth £200 in ready money. I am also upon writing a little treatise to present to the Duke, about our privilege in the seas, as to other nations striking their flags to us. But my greatest trouble is, that I have for this last half year been a very great spendthrift in all manner of respects, that I am afeard to cast up my accounts, though I hope I am worth what I say above. But I will cast them up very shortly. I have newly taken a solemn oath about abstaining from plays and wine, which I am resolved to keep according to the letter of the oath which I keep by me. The fleet hath been ready to sail for Portugall, but hath lacked wind this fortnight, and by that means my Lord is forced to keep at sea all this winter, till he brings home the Queen, which is the expectation of all now, and the greatest matter of publique talk.